DESIGNS
AND
MEMORABILIA

IDENTIFICATION AND PRICE GUIDE

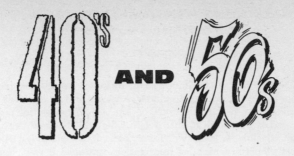

40's AND 50's

DESIGNS
AND
MEMORABILIA

IDENTIFICATION AND PRICE GUIDE
1st Edition

ANNE GILBERT

Photographs by Liz Cunningham

The CONFIDENT COLLECTOR™

AVON BOOKS ◆ NEW YORK

Important Notice: All of the information, including valuations, in this book has been compiled from the most reliable sources, and every effort has been made to eliminate errors and questionable data. Nevertheless, the possibility of error always exists in a work of such scope. The publisher and the author will not be held responsible for losses which may occur in the purchase, sale, or other transaction of property because of information contained herein. Readers who feel they have discovered errors are invited to *write* the author in care of Avon Books so that the errors may be corrected in subsequent editions.

THE CONFIDENT COLLECTOR: 40s AND 50s DESIGNS AND MEMORA-BILIA IDENTIFICATION AND PRICE GUIDE (1st edition) is an original publication of Avon Books. This edition has never before appeared in book form.

AVON BOOKS
A division of
The Hearst Corporation
1350 Avenue of the Americas
New York, New York 10019

Copyright © 1993 by Anne Gilbert
Cover photo by Tom Nikosey
Interior design by Suzanne H. Holt
The Confident Collector and its logo are trademarked properties of Avon Books.
Published by arrangement with the author
Library of Congress Catalog Card Number: 94-3861
ISBN: 0-380-77088-1

Library of Congress Cataloging in Publication Data:
Gilbert, Anne, 1927–
    The confident collector : 40s and 50s designs and memorabilia / Anne Gilbert.
        p. cm.
    1. Design—History—20th century—Themes, motives—Catalogs.
2. Design—Collectors and collecting—Catalogs.   I. Title.
NK1390.G55   1994   94-3861
745′.09′044075—dc20   CIP

First Avon Books Trade Printing: June 1994

AVON TRADEMARK REG. U.S. PAT OFF. AND IN OTHER COUNTRIES, MARCA REGISTRADA, HECHO EN U.S.A.

Printed in the U.S.A.

OPM   10 9 8 7 6 5 4 3 2 1

▦ CONTENTS

▓ Acknowledgments

First, my thanks to the many talented people who traveled back in time to the 1940s and 1950s, furnishing bits of their creative history—from photos and press clippings to personal reminiscences. All were creative forces during those decades, and all continue to influence design in the 1990s. They include Alfred Browning Parker, architect; Michael and Frances Higgins, glass designers and craftsmen; Jack Lenor Larsen, textile designer; Ben Rose, textile and wallpaper designer; Jack Denst, textile and wallpaper designer; Vladimir Kagan, furniture and decorative arts designer; and Wendell Castle, furniture designer.

Appreciation to David Hanks, Curatorial Consultant and author, who, as always, spearheaded a new collecting category by curating the all-important "Design 1935–1965 What Modern Was" exhibit at Le Musee Des Arts Decoratifs De Montreal, in Canada. Thanks also to Luc d'Iberville Moreau, Director, Le Musee des Arts Decoratifs de Montreal, who, with David Hanks, contributed the foreword to this book.

- My thanks to Jerryll Habegger, designer and author, for his input on silver flatware designs and prices.
- To Jody Kingrey, who introduced the modern look to the marketplace, and the works of many new designers and companies.
- Special thanks to David Pinson, dealer extraordinaire, whose expertise and personal contacts made my task of gathering facts and figures easier.
- To auction press department aides Anne Trodella of Skinner's and Magda Grigorian of Sotheby's, Pamela Tapp of Butterfield and Butterfield, Roberta Maneker of Christie's,

and Helene Petrovic, Christie's East expert on modern decorative art.

- To Leonard Riforgiato, whose enthusiasm for Heywood-Wakefield furniture has caused a reevaluation and appreciation of this mass-produced furniture that typified the mainstream look of Modern.
- To Harvey Hesse, dealer and collector, who showed me exciting new ways to mix and match with aluminum.
- To Gillian Hine for facts on Czechoslovakian glass.
- To Linda Gershon, who provided the West Coast connections.
- To Dorothy Harris, former editorial director of The Confident Collector (Avon Books), and Karen Shapiro, her assistant, who sparked my interest in this tough undertaking.
- To computer whiz and artist Kevin Kichar, who continues to teach me the wonders of computers.
- And especially to my husband, George, who, as always, was patient above and beyond.

▓ AUCTION HOUSE AND DEALER ACKNOWLEDGMENTS . . .

My deep appreciation to the auction houses and dealers who provided catalogs and prices. Chief among them were Butterfield and Butterfield, Christie's, DuMouchelle Art Galleries, Freeman/Fine Arts, Leslie Hindman Auctioneers, Ripleys' Antique Gallery, Skinner Inc., Sotheby's Inc., John Toomey Gallery, and Don Treadway Galleries.

- Special thanks to toy appraisers and columnists Carol and Jerry Dinalli for contributing invaluable comments and photos.
- My thanks go to George Theofiles, poster dealer, for sharing his thoughts, prices, and photos.

Further auction house and dealer acknowledgments are listed in the Resources at the back of this book.

▨ FOREWORD

We are delighted at the publication of a book on collecting 1940s and 1950s design. The Montreal Museum of Decorative Arts began collecting works from this period in 1978; at that time collectors and museums devoted little attention to the period and there were few serious dealers to meet growing interest in the works. After all, significant designs of the 1950s were not yet a generation removed from their date of origin. Some people looked at their parents' furniture and interiors of that era with disdain, and a Charles Eames molded plastic chair—a masterpiece of the twentieth century—might easily have been thrown out.

The French recognized Art Deco, which had become famous with the 1925 Paris exhibition, as an area for collecting after 1965, as the United States and Britain did a few years later. A forty-year time lag was narrowed even further with the growing enthusiasm for the fifties. The discrete gap in collecting past periods has become progressively smaller.

As with any discovery of a collectible period, there was a concurrence of events in which museums, such as the Montreal Museum of Decorative Arts, played an important part. In addition to museum collecting and exhibition programs, other influences include the publication of books on individual designers or particular aspects of the period in general. The rise of dealers and auction houses specializing in the period also plays an important role. Post-1935 design is included in the Art Nouveau/Art Deco sales in most international auction houses.

Among the pioneer dealers were Fifty/50, in New York City, and Yves Gastou, in Paris. Avant-garde collectors of this period include Barbara Jacobson, who acquired American and European objects of the 1950s in the early 1980s. While certain collectors looked back at the period, others merely maintained interiors with furniture they had acquired when they themselves were younger.

The collecting of 1940s and 1950s objects is possible for a wider public because the industrial designs of the period were inexpensive. The Montreal Museum of Decorative Arts collected low-cost industrial products as an important aspect of design. For example, the museum acquired a Tupperware pitcher in 1987 as a donation. Such objects might be found in a flea market for under five dollars. The intriguing prospect of finding 40s and 50s design in shops or flea markets at affordable prices is only one part of the appeal. At last we have arrived at a collecting period with something for everyone!

Luc d'Iberville Moreau
*Director, The Montreal Museum of
Decorative Arts*
David A. Hanks
Consulting Curator

New York City,
November 1992

Because I believe that a price guide should offer more than skeleton descriptions and prices, you may find this book has a different but enriched format. A price guide should do more than list prices. It should inform and educate the reader about what brought about these design changes and the important designers and craftsmen responsible for these changes.

On the other hand, it is up to the collector to get acquainted with the names and styles introduced in this guide.

In writing this price guide I have been particularly fortunate in being able to speak to many of the influentials who lived and worked in the 1940s and 1950s (many of whom are still creating at the cutting edge). I feel a new dimension is added to this work to hear in their own words what it was like to be a young designer introducing a radical new approach to furniture, textiles, or glass. I only regret I couldn't have begun this book a decade ago, when I would have had access to many others' personal accounts.

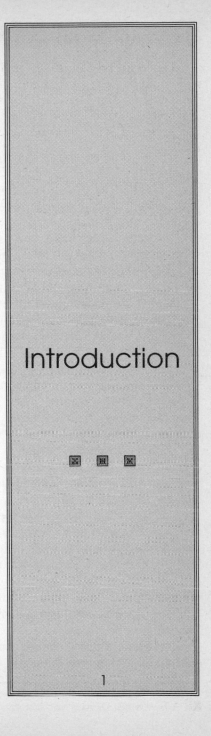

Introduction

▨ STATE OF THE MARKET

Since I began this project, an interest in Modern works continues to grow. Several years ago there were no shows devoted strictly to 1940s and 1950s and no auctions specializing in even quality items from those years. A few of the major auction galleries however, included pieces in their twentieth-century auctions.

One of the few shows that included 1940s and 1950s pieces along with other early twentieth-century designs is the Sanford Smith MODERNISM show, now in its eighth year. As Smith commented after a recent show, "Modernism has become an event that goes onto every curator's calendar each year, and every year there are more new finds." He also pointed out that "The original intent of MODERNISM was not only to exhibit and sell works but also to instruct and inform visitors about the period; a goal that seems to have been achieved."

A new show commanding attention is the "Miami Modernism" Show, which debuted January 6, 1994.

It is a whole different auction scene these days. As of this writing, Sotheby's New York gallery devoted a major portion of its June 10, 1993 auction to the collection of The Fifty/50 New York-based gallery with 1940s and 1950s items (along with Art Deco and 1960s items). The gallery owners, the late Mark Isaacson and Mark MacDonald, pioneered this collection when they opened their gallery in 1981.

Barbara Deisroth, Sotheby's expert in charge of the Fifty/50 auction, was very pleased with the results, and rightly so: "It was our first auction devoted to this type of twentieth-century design. Interest in furniture, especially from the 1950s, was very strong, with vigorous competition for rare pieces by Charles and Ray Eames, Isamu Noguchi, and George Nelson. There was strong interest from private collectors, dealers, and institutions. Overall, the sale exceeded our expectations." Proving that the rarer items can fetch far over estimate was an Isamu Noguchi prototype laminated-wood and metal "fin" stool that more than doubled its already-high estimate of $5,000, by bringing in $12,650.

The same week Christie's East held a sale that included not only 40s and 50s, but 60s and 70s objects as well. Their expert,

Helene Petrovic, was also enthusiastic about the results: "Both dealers and collectors were very active bidders," she said. "There is certainly a developing market for 60s and 70s quality items, and we will continue to explore it in future sales."

Other auction houses on the East Coast have cautiously been including 40s and 50s pieces in their Arts and Crafts and Art Deco auctions for the past several years.

At Skinner's October 1992 auction of Modern works, a Fornasetti screen and a Venini vase, both Italian objects from the 1950s, fared very well. "This makes for an interesting addition to antique auctions—both are modern and represent a whole new area of collecting which has a strong following both in New England and in the world," commented Skinner's Modern glass expert, Louise Luther. Garrett Sheehan, Skinner's furniture and decorative arts expert, was not as enthusiastic. "What works against us are the 60s' and 70s' knockoffs. They lend uncertainty to the market." However, on the positive side he noted that "currently the strength of the market is with the war-horses of design and their recognizable forms." He pointed out that condition is all-important in pricing. "For the buyer willing to do research, however, this is the perfect time to buy." More and more museums are buying pieces from these decades.

In November 1992, David Rago, who is known primarily for his Arts and Crafts auctions, had great success with Modern works. The top price of the sale was a "marshmallow" sofa designed by George Nelson. Found in a New Orleans thrift shop, with its original fabric, it sold for its low estimate of $8,000, not including the 10 percent dealer premium. But, at the November 15, 1992, Toomey-Treadway auction in Oak Park, Illinois, an identical marshmallow sofa sold for $11,000. In analyzing the price difference of the two sales there are several factors to consider. The first being that Toomey-Treadway, which has gained a following among collectors and dealers for Modern, attracted buyers who were there specifically looking for Modern pieces. There is also greater dealer interest in the Midwest than on the East Coast. At the November Rago show, pottery by Gertrud and Otto Natzler and the Scheiers (Mary and Edwin) sold for slightly over estimate. The best pieces sold well; small, common pieces such as bowls and tumblers went unsold.

On the West Coast, Butterfield and Butterfield Auction Galleries in San Francisco were among the first to test the waters with specialized sales. In a fall 1992 auction they noted that "in the area of twentieth-century design the 1950s and 1960s continued to develop a strong following. A noteworthy offering in this category was George Nakashima's walnut trestle table and set of four conoid chairs from New Pennsylvania that sold above estimate to a local collector for $9,350. A Hans Wegner ash dining suite, dated c. 1949, brought $2,750." Something for collectors to consider is that at that same auction, a Charles Eames laminated rosewood swivel lounge chair and ottoman, manufactured by Herman Miller in 1983, sold for $1,760. It seems that even late issues are doing well.

At the May 2, 1993, Toomey-Treadway auction, in Oak Park, Illinois, furniture with original fabric from name designers sold extremely well.

In most instances objects included in these sales were designer furnishings and studio pottery and jewelry. A few mass-produced pieces such as Haywood-Wakefield case pieces were also included and sold well.

While this book lists a variety of memorabilia, the emphasis is on Modern design, as reflected by the many quality pieces still available at reasonable prices.

The more unusual pieces by a quality designer are apt to be priced higher than others. Pieces that were once commercial failures, because their designs were too advanced for popular taste, are now those sought by serious collectors. One example is children's furniture designed by Charles Eames. A single chair can have a retail price of $5,000. Another Eames piece, though more common than children's furniture, is his two- or three-stack storage unit. These were made of perforated metal and dimpled wood to mix-and-match and they didn't initially appeal to consumers. Currently a complete unit can sell from $5,000 to over $10,000. The biomorphic chess set designed by Isamu Noguchi in the 1950s, now a rarity, once sold for a whopping $38,000 at auction. It wasn't popular when originally introduced.

Dealers who specialize in 40s and 50s design point out that prices have been increasing 10 to 20 percent every two years, depending on quality, rarity, and designer. However, it's simply not possible to predict how prices will change in the coming years.

A decade ago individuals who collected designs from the 40s and 50s were usually art dealers, artists, and architects; now that has changed to include collectors on every economic level. When one of the collectors of this time period is David Hanks, author and museum curator and once consulting curator for the Montreal Museum exhibit "What Modern Was," you know Modern is on the move. As a major influence in the rediscovery of unfamiliar designers of this period, he says that "most museum curators don't even know their names." His own collection of designs from those decades includes everything from textiles and wall coverings to furniture and glass. He suggests that collectors should look beyond a piece's original use when collecting. "Lengths of wallpaper and fabric should be considered as art and displayed like a picture."

▦ WHERE PRICES COME FROM

Most of the prices listed in this book are a combination of realized auction prices and dealer and flea market prices. They cover sales on the West Coast, East Coast, Midwest (Chicago, Indianapolis, Detroit), and in the Southeast (Florida). They represent prices of sales from 1991 to the summer of 1993. The listed auction prices don't include buyer premiums. Where items have only come to auction once—say, in 1991—that price is used. Otherwise, listed prices have been made as up-to-date as possible. Since many pieces such as the Eames plywood lounge chair, LCW, have come to auction and are available in shops regularly, I have noted the high end. Higher prices usually reflect pieces from early production runs in good condition. The same applies to Italian glass, ceramics, and other categories. Some dealers preferred to furnish price ranges, and are so noted.

As more dealers begin to include or specialize in designs of the 40s and 50s, collectors will become more aware of them. As the "baby boomers" (adults born after World War II who are now beginning to discover the fascination of collecting) start spending, prices will be affected. The best pieces will eventually disappear from the marketplace. Needless to say, some dealers are anxious to remain a step ahead of general collectors. A couple of years ago one pair who used to deal in Americana switched their emphasis to Art Deco jewelry; more recently they are including 40s and 50s pieces.

Dealer David Pinson was among the avant-garde who began buying and selling in his Chicago shop, Boomerang, in the early eighties.

Florida collector and dealer Yvon Belisle began collecting Modern objects as a hobby ten years ago. "I started with Art Deco," he said. "Then I became fascinated with the color and unusual shapes of glass and decorative objects that caught my eye." An early purchase was a red Charles Eames fiberglass chair. "I do my hunting in thrift shops from Miami to Palm Beach. One of my recent finds was a Charles Eames storage unit that had been painted black. The price was thirty dollars. A similar one, restored, had sold not too long ago at auction for several thousand dollars. Needless to say, I am restoring my discovery. It is an important piece because it represents the first example of modular storage units designed with industrial materials. It is made of steel, birch-faced plywood, and plastic." Belisle sees major problems ahead for beginning collectors who aren't knowledgeable. "Reproductions are being made. Companies like Palazzetti in New York buy up the design copyrights and make new, old pieces. The same, of course, is true of Venini glass. There are many reproductions of the glass figures."

In a developing market such as this, prices are determined by what is trendy. In the glass field, Venini and other Italian makers, such as Murano, seem to be leading the pack. Why have these makers been recognized and not Scandinavian manufacturers or others? One reason is name recognition. For the moment Italian glass is the most widely recognized possibly because large quantities were made and much of it is now coming to auction. Scandinavian designs, on the other hand, were made in smaller quantities and don't come to market as often. However, the finest examples by known artists will always bring top dollar, regardless of where they were made.

Louise Luther, Skinner Gallerie's twentieth-century glass expert, had a lot to say about Venini pieces and their prices: "The clown frenzy has let up because people now realize they were made for export . . . and not studio-designed work. In fact, many were whimseys for the tourists or throwaways filled with liquor. The sleepers these days are Scandinavian glass. Collectors are just becoming aware of them. Prices are still on the low side for some really important names." Luther also pointed out that the reason some pieces, often by top designers, don't do well is because so many were made. Such was the case at the May 22, 1993, Skinner auction where a Finnish "jack-in-pulpit" form crystal vase, a variation of an original design by Tapio Wirkkala, sold far under its estimate.

The traveling Montreal Museum exhibit has certainly stimulated interest. The exhibition was the result of ten years of collecting by Liliane and the late David M. Stewart, and includes many private and public collections. The museum collection is housed in the Chateau Dufresne, and was first shown to the public on June 14, 1979. It reflects the changing looks of Modernism. Objects include examples of prewar, postwar, and 60s designs.

If many of the prices in this book seem on the low side it is because the pieces haven't come to auction often enough to be recognized as worthy of collectors' dollars. These pieces haven't set any auction records or generated publicity hoopla.

Much is said about regional price differences in other areas of collecting. It's true that golden oak furniture sells better in the Midwest, and Victorian Renaissance revival furniture is a winner in the Deep South, but not in New York. However, at the fall 1992 Triple Pier Show in New York, dealers of Italian art glass remarked that pieces were fetching higher prices in Chicago. One reason is that Italian glass and other Modern objects are getting big play at auction at Toomey-Treadway Galleries in Oak Park, Illinois. Geography does play a part in interest for these pieces, since many innovators in textiles, glass, and furniture had their beginnings in Chicago. They left their mark on the interiors of still-existing office buildings and private homes. Among them were Ben Rose, Jack Denst, Angelo Testa, and Michael and Frances Higgins.

▓ RESEARCH CAN BE FUN AND IMPORTANT

You are probably saying, "If only I could see how actual rooms were furnished in the 1940s and 1950s." Perhaps you would like to know what to collect to furnish rooms in the styles of these decades. What better place to begin your research than in decorating magazines and books published during those decades? Good sources for these publications are secondhand book and magazine stores. Ask dealers who may also carry magazines. Estate sales and thrift shops are other possibilities. When you take out-of-area trips, check stores in those locations. I found a source for the entire 50s decade of *House Beautiful* magazines at a bookstore in Glendale, California (see Sources). The November 1953 issue was exciting, introducing the "Pace Setter House for 1953: Here Modern Living Comes of Age." Among other things, their ads told me this was the beginning of the do-it-yourself era.

However, it was the 1954 Pace Setter House, designed by Alfred Browning Parker (who discusses his role as an architect and designer in this book), that was considered a milestone in modern architecture and interior design. The house, of textured coral stone (hauled and laid by Parker), glass, and salvaged scrap steel columns and concrete, was the ultimate do-it-yourself project. Then as now, architect Parker designed built-in furniture and lighting. Built-ins were a radical new concept at the time and previously associated only with custom-built homes, such as those designed by architect Frank Lloyd Wright.

▨ How Magazines Brought the Modern Look to Every Home

The shelter magazines we look to every month to tell us what is new in color, design, and decorating . . . as well as products . . . didn't play an important role in the life of the average family until after World War II. True, *House and Garden* and *House Beautiful* had been around for many years, but their importance changed as returning GIs were able to buy housing inexpensively on GI home loans. GIs and their brides took advantage of a chance to own their own homes, and housing was mass-produced for the first time around the country. Places like Levittown and Park Forest became the new "suburbia." These magazines took on the responsibility of advising people how to furnish them. Decorators contributed ideas, bringing the "decorator look" to Middle America. What appeared in the magazine *Architectural Digest* was modified and digested for the newly important suburban market. While traditional and antique reproductions were still around, it was the bright, new look of "Modern" that sold magazine subscriptions. If subscribers couldn't afford the most expensive pieces, they found ways to achieve the same look. The do-it-yourself era was born.

What began as expensive designer pieces filtered down to mass-produced objects with a few design changes along the way.

▦ WHAT THE ADS SAID IN 1953

"Design and build your own wrought iron furniture. Simply fasten wrought iron hairpin legs with a screwdriver to plywood flush doors. Can also be attached to create sofas, coffee tables, etc. $6.95 to $14.95."

These and other sets of "modern" legs, when added to doors, and foam rubber were the answer for budget-conscious former GIs and their brides. These materials are still a good idea today if you want to create "the look." The ads were geared to the smaller rooms of new tract houses, as were the furnishings.

A lighting manufacturer of the time advertised: "Lightolier—for the new way of living. Scaled to fit your smaller rooms."

If you ever wondered when TV tray tables entered the scene, 1953 was the year. Are they collectible? They could be, if the laminated tops show Modern designs. Many, unless they are designer pieces, are throwaways.

Remember when old radios and TVs were junked for newer models? Now, as you'll see in this price guide, some 50s radios are fetching high prices. I don't mean just any old radio, but those that are examples of Modern design. Again, design and material are all important.

Right along with Marilyn Monroe, "blond" was beautiful when it came to furniture finishes. Mahogany and other dark woods became bleached blondes, mostly in medium-priced furniture lines such as Stewartstown and Heywood-Wakefield.

Lloyd Manufacturing Company was one of many to offer chrome dining groups. As the ads said, they were "upholstered in wonderful, washable plastic." Scaled down, of course, "to fit smaller dining areas."

Upholstery also met the requirements for the lighter, scaled-down furnishings as foam rubber cushions replaced traditional springs and other fillings. It was used even in the top-of-the-line pieces, as it is today.

Textures were important. Grasscloth covered walls and sometimes ceilings. A popular do-it-yourself craft was a revival of embroidery to add texture to the new mass-produced fabrics. It was a way to cheaply customize inexpensive sheer draperies and bed and table linens.

▓ IDENTIFYING THE NEW MATERIALS

PLASTIC

Plastic can be humble and utilitarian or beautifully elegant. Its impact depends on a particular piece's purpose and design. While it became part of everyday life in the 1930s, it was not until 1945, with the introduction of a new plastic dinnerware known as Melamine, that designers began to give this material serious consideration. In 1949 Russel Wright was asked to design a line of Melamine dinnerware for American Cyanamid. It was marketed to the Bickford restaurant chain in New York under the name of Meladur. In 1953, Wright designed the first plasticware for consumer use. It was named "Residential" and used the new organic form and exciting colors that could be mixed and matched. Manufactured by the Northern Industrial Chemical Company, it received the Museum of Modern Art's Good Design Award for both 1953 and 1954. Other companies followed the lead, using their own designs. One of the most popular was designed by Irving Harper of George Nelson and Associates. It got its inspiration from Japanese lacquerware.

Plastic began to take many forms that led it from the kitchen to the living room and the playroom. As acrylic resin, it offered transparency and transmitted light. As a thermoplastic it can be heat-formed into many shapes. Under the trade name Lucite it became a status material for top designers by the late 40s. Many wealthy members of the avant-garde commissioned special pieces and sets of Lucite furniture, among them the late cosmetic queen Helena Rubenstein. Lucite achieved peak elegance with the use of engraved decorations and the Modern look with embedded colored plastic designs and special lighting effects.

Plastic laminates, such as Formica, became the epitome of Modern by the 1950s, with organic motifs on kitchen and bathroom counters.

Side Table, one of a pair, designed by Lorin Jackson of "Glassic" Lucite, c. 1940. Wood, and glass; 26¾ inches high x 14 inches deep x 20 inches wide; $1,650/pair. *Courtesy of Christie's, New York.*

▒ PLASTICS WERE USED CREATIVELY

Plastics were used in the 50s by architects to give the illusion of natural light in the form of translucent plastic sheets used as skylights. Adding to the effect, real foliage was laminated between the translucent plastic sheets. For do-it-yourselfers, decorated plastic sheets were available in hardware stores.

Plastics were increasingly used at the dinner table and in the kitchen, whether for food storage or food service. New designs filtered down to the average American, who for the first time was able to afford one of the many tract development houses. These new home owners were faced with the question of how to furnish in the new designs. Rooms in tract houses were smaller and usually there were no formal dining rooms. Furnishing had to meet these new requirements and the needs of the first generation looking for a casual life-style.

Not only was the mass-produced furniture scaled down in size, but it became multifunctional and "modular." Nobody wanted to polish silver, so stainless steel became the new standard material for flatware. If someone spilled food or drink on a living room or kitchen table, not to worry. The tops were people-resistant plastic, wood grained or patterned.

For the budget-minded, the hardware store was the equivalent of having a decorator in your pocket. Furniture and walls were no longer simply painted. There were new color stains that let the wood shine through, and most wondrous of all, a product that could be bought by the roll to change a piece of plywood shelving into a marbleized tabletop or give it any of a myriad of designs. "Wall-tex" was the first in a long line of peel-and-stick items. Many popular faux finishes were created by shellacking and sanding the surface till a hard glaze appeared. Like the new veneers, they were water resistant.

Is everything collectible? As any purist will tell you, the collectible items reflect the motifs and materials of the 40s and 50s. This goes for fashion, small appliances, and even playthings.

Part of the fun of collecting the Modern look is that there are treasures waiting to be discovered. It's a good time to buy at reasonable estate sale prices. Many people who were young adults in the 40s and 50s are now senior citizens, unloading their possessions and modifying their life-styles.

There are also reproductions, cheap copies, faked signatures, and restorations—just as there are in the antiques world. Beware of craft pieces or do-it-yourself items that are overpriced. It was, after all, the beginning of the do-it-yourself age. On the other hand, perhaps these are examples of the folk art of the future. As always, buy only the best examples.

It's generally accepted that in the world of antiques and collectibles things aren't always what they seem. This is especially true with Modern designs. They seem to have a language all their own, a language the serious collector needs to learn, with words like *parabolic, biomorphic,* and *attenuated.* For starters, mail away for various auction catalogs, where descriptions of objects are also illustrated with photos.

You can pay as much at a flea market for a mass-produced plastic lamp, so ugly your dog would bite it, as for a small handcrafted ceramic bowl by a studio potter.

Modern design work is not picked over, as antiques are. If you are willing to review the material available and focus on designer, manufacturer, and product names, only lack of display space can stop you from assembling a quality collection.

▩ EARLY INFLUENTIALS

Some of the most important names of the Art Deco era carried over into the early Modern movement. Among them is Walter Dorwin Teague, one of America's first industrial designers. His work in the 1930s and early 1940s is detailed elsewhere. However, in midcentury his influence continued with designs for everything from pens to beer cans and cameras. Another designer, Raymond Loewy, worked in many mediums from the 1920s until his death in the 1980s. Others, such as Gilbert Rohde, Russel Wright, and Donald Desky, are well covered in the many books on Art Deco.

▩ INFLUENCES IN THE MARKETPLACE

The Herman Miller Company of Zeeland, Michigan, began the introduction of Modernism to the mass of 1940s–1950s Americans looking to furnish homes and offices. They brought not only the early designs of Charles Eames to the mass market, but other design innovators such as George Nelson and Isamu Noguchi. It was here that such avant-garde creations as the Eames "potato chip" chair and the Nelson "coconut chair" first saw the light of day.

Baldwin-Kingrey of Chicago, Illinois, co-partner Jody Kingrey began a totally new concept in retailing in 1947 with Harry and Kitty Baldwin Weese.

I had had some experience in Minnesota in interior design before World War II. After coming to Chicago, where I began working as a decorator for Watson and Boaler, I became interested in the new modern furniture that was being produced by the Herman Miller Company. I convinced Watson and Boaler to give me space on the third floor to display their pieces. At that time I met young designers, such as Ben Rose, Angelo Testa, and Jack Denst, who were just beginning to print wallpapers and fabrics, and Elsa Regensteiner and Julia McVickers, who brought in some of their early weavings. When we opened Baldwin-Kingrey we were the first to combine the new modern furniture—Scandinavian and American—with glassware, china, stainless steel flatware, jewelry, fabrics, and wallpaper. I remember when the representative for Arsberg china brought samples wrapped in newspapers. It was inexpensive at the time and became very popular. We also sold Arabia china and Finnish glassware and pottery. Since we bought direct, we kept the prices low. We were able to offer, for the first time, Alvar Aalto, Arne Jacobsen, and Borge Morgensen furniture; the Kofud Larsen lounge chair; and pieces from Eero Saarinen, Florence Knoll, and the Hans Wegner classic furniture at affordable prices. We sold Tupperware in the simple crucible shape and pastel colors, when it first came out in the fifties. The same bowls are in the Museum of Modern

Art, and we displayed it right along with the
Venini glass from Murano, Bertoia jewelry,
Natzler pottery, Heitzke porcelain, and Ward
Bennett sculpture and jewelry.

▦ Museum Shows Revved Up Interest

"The Cranbrook Vision" opened in 1983 at the Metropolitan
Museum, followed by the 1986 "Machine Age" show, organized
by the Brooklyn Museum. "Design since 1945" at the Philadelphia Museum, "High Style" at the Whitney Museum, and "Blue-
prints for Modern Living" at the Museum of Contemporary Art
in Los Angeles all took place in 1989 and 1990.

▦ The Many Forms of Modern

STREAMLINING

The use of tapered curves and the emphasis on sleek, rectangular forms was first introduced in Europe in the late 1920s.
As Streamlining, it caught the fancy of American designers, who
began using it by the mid thirties in designs for trains and automobiles. The fronts of these vehicles featured sweeping curves
and color combinations to make them appear longer. A look at
vintage auto design into the late forties shows the heavy, curved
fenders and the use of ornamental bands to give a "streamlined"
effect.

The architects of the day used curved corners and bookcases
inside apartment buildings with curving exteriors. The streamlined look found its way to Hollywood, and the set designs for
rooms and their furnishings can be studied in movies from the
late 1930s. It is mentioned here since it was a design influence
lasting into the 1940s and because many industrial designers,
such as Walter Dorwin Teague, Harry Bertoia, and Russel
Wright, found it a bridge to postwar Modern design. Characteristic of this look are wraparound details, cone shapes, rectangular curves, and curved ends.

BIOMORPHIC MODERN

Like Streamlining, Biomorphism was first used in Europe
several decades before it became a part of the Modern design

movement. Artist Jean Arp began with doodles on paper of blobs and designs that resembled living organisms, such as amoebae. He eventually developed these into flat, two-dimensional designs, or sculptures. Abstract, undulating, sometimes with rounded holes, they were echoed in the mobiles shaped by Alexander Calder and the paintings of Joan Miró and Salvador Dali.

Biormorphism was adapted by designers in the mid 1930s. Such furniture designers as Alvar Aalto and Frederick Kiesler, along with architects, made cocktail tables, tables, and chairs in amoeboid shapes. Not until the 1940s were small decorative objects made in these forms.

Biormorphism reached its peak of popularity and mass production in the postwar period. Items were referred to as "kidney-shaped," "boomerang," "free-form," "organic," and "amoeboid."

THE TULIP LOOK

Yet another example of the use of exaggerated forms of the 50s was the tulip shape. It was used in designs from Eero Saarinen's "Tulip" chairs (1956) to Orrefors' hand-blown "Tulip" glass goblets to Christian Dior's "Tulip" suit.

▥ DESIGN SUBJECTS

Since the end of the 40s ushered in the atomic-nuclear age, some design motifs reflected American interest in science and molecular structures. Wallpapers, drapes, and upholstery fabric surfaces were covered with flying saucers, amoebae, molecules, and satellites. Even the new Formica countertops were patterned in scientific-inspired designs, as were linoleum floors.

The "organic" influence, much of which filtered to American designers from Scandinavia, combined irregular forms with flora and foliage. Earth tones were mixed with bold colors. The whole was often brought together with black lines, sometimes straight, at other times shaped into calligraphic swirls.

While patterns of the 40s used large-scale forms, by the 1950s smaller designs became popular.

MAGAZINE ADS FROM 1950S OFFER CLUES TO PRICES, NEW DESIGNS

Magazines like *House Beautiful* and *House and Garden* from the 1950s featured examples of the new designs and how to decorate with them and advertising that gave prices and materials. It may come as a surprise that many of the items from butterfly chairs to TV trays, were first offered to the mass market in these ads. The few that I have listed should prove helpful to collectors.

SOME *HOUSE BEAUTIFUL* ADS
FROM NOVEMBER 1953

LIGHTOLIER "For the new way of living." Scaled to fit smaller rooms.

BROCK "Sets the New Pattern for informal dining." California dinnerware. Lawndale, California. "The marvels of stainless steel." This facette pattern, imported from Sweden, was made by Genese. Six-piece place setting was $8.

LLOYD "Modern dining furniture. Formica tabletops are heat, scratch, stain-resistant." Chrome, plastic.

PLAS-TEX WARE Thunderbird 2½ quart pitcher, $1.95. "Simple Modern styling." Los Angeles, California.

Butterfly Chair. Originally made in the United States from the 1950s on; many copies have been made over the years. *Courtesy of the author.*

THE BUTTERFLY CHAIR "Like classic original," $14.95.

WOOD FINISHES "Blond-new-super-pale wood finish."

"DESIGN AND BUILD YOUR OWN WROUGHT IRON FURNITURE . . . simply fasten hairpin legs with screwdriver to plywood flush doors (attach to sofa, coffee table, desk, etc.," $6.95 to $14.95.

"THE ERA OF TRAY TABLES . . . TV TRAY TABLES."

THE PACE SETTER HOUSE, 1953 "Here Modern Living Comes of Age. See how this house solves human problems while it achieves a quiet beauty."

THE NEW KIND OF LIVING ROOM "We expect it to be all things to all people at all times, yet always be beautiful. The new house for the new life . . . the frame for the cultural revolution now occurring, where everything co-operates for the flowering of your personality.

"In this new phase, wisdom will use industry as the servant of a better life."

HARDWARE AND LIGHTING FIXTURES—"THE JEWELRY OF THE MODERN HOUSE." Brass fixtures, perforated with stars to twinkle with light, designed by Paavo Tynell.

TEXTILES Place mats using Mariska Karasz's embroidery.

CREATIVE TABLE SETTINGS Sterling flatware blends Early American design with modernity. Forks, spoons have tongued backs. "Hannah Hull" pattern. Tuttle Silver Co., Inc., North Attleboro, Massachusetts.

CHINA Franciscan Fine China plates. "Encanto Nuevo" pattern. Gladding, McBean & Co., Los Angeles, California.

GLASSES Hemlock-green "Flair" glasses designed by Russel Wright. Imperial Glass Co., Bellair, Ohio.

PLACE MATS Polyplastex United, Inc., New York.

ON THE LOWER END Quaker Fantasy cloths: "spots sponge off quickly." Plastic tableclothes.

NEW CARPET FABRICS Woven of Saran.

DINING SETS "Chip, peel and rust resistant. Textured plastic upholstery." Daystrom wood-grain tabletops of Daystromite.

Parker, one of the icons of modern architecture, whose career began in 1946, believes, as did Frank Lloyd Wright, in designing furnishings for his structures. Parker has won many honors and awards, and his 1954 Pace Setter House was featured in House Beautiful magazine. Frank Lloyd Wright wrote the captions for the photos. Parker's work, influenced by his postgraduate study at the Royal Academy of Stockholm, Sweden, and further study in Mexico, combined the Scandinavian design concept of form with the textures and stonework of ancient architecture. His Pace Setter House typified the philosophy of the fifties' organic architecture, as did the furnishings he designed for it. Built for his own family, it took advantage of the natural beauty of its southern Florida site, bringing the outdoors inside. It was an important influence on architecture and interior design. Unfortunately, many of Parker's early homes have fallen victim to wrecking balls, and the furniture and lighting he designed has disappeared along with them. Collectors would be wise to seek out his remaining work. He favored rosewood, along with native stone, onyx, and marble. Since many items were built-ins, salvage yards and auctions are places to seek out this work.

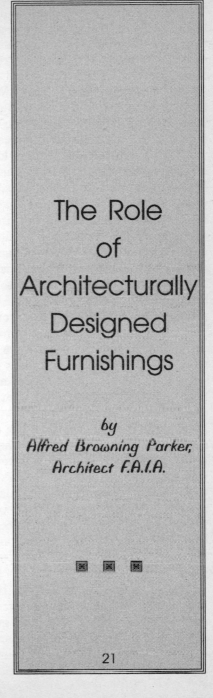

The Role
of
Architecturally
Designed
Furnishings

by
Alfred Browning Parker,
Architect F.A.I.A.

21

The role of the architect in designing interior furnishings has been miniscule. Those who have attempted to integrate architecture with furnishings sometimes achieved significant results. Much inspiration for such efforts came from early twentieth-century architectural pioneers. Charles Rennie Mackintosh, the Greene brothers, Frank Lloyd Wright, and Alvar Aalto began their practices with the avowed goal of unifying their buildings by designing custom furnishings as well. They continued this laudable aim throughout their careers.

These architectural leaders knew that the cumulative effect of their work resulted from the building itself, its siting, its landscaping, and its furnishings. Architecture is beautiful, purposeful space. To enclose this space and furnish it so that beauty and utility become one is the proper goal of both the architect and the owner. This total unified concept requires knowledge and discipline. The architect can and should lead the team in making the many furnishing decisions required by any project.

Visualization is the ability to create mental images of these dimensional spaces and forms. This is referred to as spatial imagination. The greater the architect's power in this visualization, the greater the quality of his buildings. The most efficient utilization of space is not always the most complete. Frequently we discover buildings or rooms where space at first glance is wasted or thrown away. However, by the very emotional effects that space can create, what is apparently excess actually has a specific purpose.

This is the true realm of the creative architect, and furnishings are part of that realm. To assign these prerogatives to others is a sure way to fail. Architecture has to be a total, unified concept.

Interior "decoration" is a misnomer. I prefer "the fittings of a room." These fittings fall into two broad categories—basic furnishings and accessories. The accepted design process is to work from the general to the particular, so the basic furnishings must be considered by the architect in the preliminary stage of his work.

For example, an architect's beginning studies should locate all seating, tables, music sources, and storage for the living room. Tables, chairs, and storage should be established in the dining room. Working surfaces and all equipment need to be located in the kitchen and laundry. Beds, chests, and seating should be sketched in for the bedrooms.

Making early decisions on such furnishings, whether built-in or freestanding, even before the working drawings are made, is one way to test the validity of the proposed plans. If such matters are left unresolved until the building is completed, all kinds of unfortunate mistakes may be discovered—too late to be rectified.

There are unique advantages to basic built-in furnishings. A harmonious relationship can then be established with the building. Materials of the furnishings may echo materials of the structure. Such furnishings become a direct part of the architecture, thus creating greater unity. A table cantilevered from the wall and built of the same wood as the wall will unmistakably belong to the building.

The art of understatement becomes invaluable in achieving an integrity of both building and furnishings. It seems likely that the greatest architectural achievements of the future will be those in which the main furnishings will be built-in appurtenances of the buildings themselves.

To furnish a space usefully and handsomely requires knowledge and discipline—knowledge of what to do and the discipline to do it. When you enter a truly beautiful interior, you are less intrigued by individual objects and more engaged by the total result. Colors, textures, finishes, shapes, and sizes are some of the elements that create beautiful furnishings.

Accessories are equally important to a proper basic arrangement, although they have a secondary position in the sequence of planning. They involve all of the things we need and use for our education, convenience, comfort, and nourishment. Some architects have gone to considerable lengths to design accessory items for their interiors. Mackintosh, for example, designed the following items for a Scottish tearoom: exterior signage, doors, windows, hardware, rugs, lighting, fixtures, tables, table linen, chairs, draperies, fabrics, crystal, china, silver, the menus, and more.

The arrangement of accessories is an art in itself. Architect John Hill, a disciple of Frank Lloyd Wright, is a master of arranging not only the usual items but also living plants, dried grasses, rocks, fruits, berries, and blooms. In these areas a good sense of color is imperative.

A safe guide is to keep in mind what situations will work for the user. There is no single solution, only endless alternatives. When an architect has accomplished an efficient and useful layout, he will then make it beautiful. Use and beauty must of their very nature co-exist, and it does not follow that they can exist separately in architecture. When a thing does not work, it cannot possess beauty; and if it is not beautiful, it cannot work.

Use and beauty may be compared to partners, one dependent upon the other, each giving, each receiving. The Yin and Yang principle of the Orient symbolizes the relationships between male and female but it also may serve as a diagram of utility and aesthetics. The most creative architects recognize the fact that furnishings should never dominate. Rather, they should afford a useful and handsome background for the life patterns that flow around them. Rooms are completed by the individuals who use them.

Whether you decide to collect pieces within a category, like ceramic vases, or fit entire rooms in the Modern look of the 40s or 50s, collecting begins with recognizing the colors, lines, designs, and materials that are characteristic of these times. In the case of furniture, for example, ask yourself whether the upholstery is original. If it has been replaced, is the replacement of the period and consistent with the quality of the piece? In other words, a piece of upholstery should be as good as the object it covers.

You can collect "kitschy" or "classy," there's plenty of both waiting for you. Fill your shelves with California pottery and cover your windows with barkcloth drapes. These and other remnants of the postwar decades are making their way to the growing number of shows specializing in twentieth-century collectibles. Surprisingly, the kitsch is quite costly, one of the problems when a collectible or antique becomes trendy. Just keep in mind that if it was ugly when it was originally made, time hasn't made it beautiful—even if it has become popular.

As with any area of collecting, you have to ask yourself if you can live with your collections. Is the design of the piece

How to Begin Collecting

you're considering typical of the Modern look? Does the material it is made of represent new scientific developments such as plastics, nylons, and acrylics? Even if the design and materials are unappealing, should this be overlooked because they were innovations of the time? Even a humble plastic pitcher can be worthwhile if it depicts one of the modern forms. The trick is avoiding a collection that looks like flea market rejects.

Names are important. Familiarize yourself with the names of influential designers, craftsmen, and companies. At the top of the list in furniture design are Charles and Ray Eames, Isamu Noguchi, Harry Bertoia, and George Nelson, for starters. Companies who mass-produced new designs of this era included Herman Miller of Zeeland, Michigan; Knoll Associates; and the Heritage-Henredon Furniture Company (who mass-produced Frank Lloyd Wright furniture designs).

Names in Modern design cover the international spectrum, with the Scandinavian representatives in the lead, followed by the Italian and the French. Arne Jacobsen, Henning Koppel, Gio Ponti, and Fulvio Bianconi may not be familiar to you yet, but you'll find examples of their work and the current prices for their work throughout this book. Their work is already represented in many museum collections.

All of the above names represent the high end of collectibles. Yet, surprisingly enough, most are affordable even for a beginning collector.

Sometimes the memorabilia can cost almost as much as the name designer items. For example, there are driftwood lamps selling for several hundred dollars at mall shows. When something is trendy it automatically costs more than it should. Consider Catalin table model radios and Japanese robot toys. Prices ranging from several hundred dollars to over a thousand, in the case of the toys, are the norm. Plastic lamps, planters, and clocks that once ended up at flea markets or in the trash have been upgraded to the mall shows and speciality shows such as "Baby Boombazaar." Whether they have lasting merit or even historical or design significance doesn't seem to matter. They are part of the Modern age and, for the moment, they are mostly affordable.

◼ WELCOME TO THE ATOMIC WORLD

In the early 50s, the realization that we were living in the age of atomic energy, with all of its good and bad ramifications, spawned a variety of forgettable movies and songs, along with the memorable Bikini bathing suit. From the collector's standpoint there were T-shirts with such blackly comic messages as "That's All Folks." Other collectors are attracted to fallout shelter signs, books, and old movie videos. Prices depend on where you find the items, since the market isn't exactly established.

Condition is all when you have a manufactured item. Now is the time to buy pieces in perfect condition—while there is a quantity available at reasonable prices.

If a mass-manufactured piece is in a museum collection, it is included there on the basis of its good design. One example is a Tupperware bowl that shows the lines of Modern design.

Tupperware Bowl, manufactured by Tupper Corporation, Farnumsville, MA, 1945. Translucent green polyethylene; 2⅞ inches high x 5½ inches in diameter. *Courtesy of the Museum of Modern Art Collection, gift of the manufacturer, New York, NY.*

How do you evaluate a Tupperware bowl? Obviously not every one is worthy of display in a museum. Professional appraisers advise that while the prototype for the modern museum-quality bowl could have a value of $1,000, others are worth only a few dollars. It is up to the dealer, appraiser, or collector to be familiar with the early Modern design pieces and their model numbers.

Elin Lake Ewald, president of the New York chapter of the American Society of Appraisers (1992–93), advises collectors to "find an area that hasn't yet been exploited. Be aware of what museums are showing, before the general public does, and buy out of areas where there are dealers specializing in forties and fifties."

An interest in collecting mid-century Modern objects, that began in 1980, started David Pinson on a new career. One year later he opened Boomerang, one of the first Chicago galleries devoted to furniture and decorative arts of the 1940s and 1950s. This led to a position as an assistant curator in modern decorative arts at the Art Institute of Chicago. He became affiliated with the John Toomey Gallery in Oak Park, Illinois, in 1990, where he continues to supervise auctions of Modern and 60s furnishings and art.

As with all periods of design, the 1950s had its share of significant design contributions. Many of these have resurged as historically important examples, sought after by museums, serious collectors, and newcomers attracted by the unique sculptural forms as well as affordable prices.

Although many of these pieces are already recognized as important, prices remain relatively low compared to those of comparable significance in other markets. There are many variables that affect the value of these pieces, including whether a piece is still in production, and if so, what changes, if any, have been made in the manufacturing.

The classic Eames rose-

Evaluating Collectible Furniture

by
David Pinson,
Dealer and Specialist

wood lounge chair and ottoman, for example, are no longer available in rosewood. Early examples are down filled. Later production, as well as current models, are padded with foam and Dacron. The manufacturer's label is also helpful in determining the age of such pieces as they have changed significantly over the years.

The classic glass-top coffee table designed by Isamu Noguchi was first introduced by Herman Miller in 1944, manufactured through 1972, then reintroduced in 1984. However, the plate glass tops of the earliest examples have a unique, pale-green colored edge. Mid-production examples have a deep blue-green edge. Later or current production models have a much darker, almost gray, edge. There were also a variety of finishes available in the early years, the most desirable of which now is natural birch. Current examples also have a different pin that locks the two-part adjustable base.

Prices are affected not only by availability, production numbers, and finishes but also by condition. A refinished piece can often be acquired for much less than the same piece in pristine, original condition. Rare examples in excellent, original condition have consistently proven to be good investments and should continue to escalate in value.

It is also important to realize that not all furniture from this period represents significant design contributions. Less than 5 percent of the furniture produced in the 1950s was designed by recognized architects or designers.

In the 40s and 50s, unlike other periods in furniture design, the U.S. led the design world. Technology and new materials developed during the war created a new palette for some of the most brilliant minds in design history, the most important of which was Charles Eames. There are many Eames designs still in production or being reproduced by companies such as Palazzetti and Vitra. Early Eames designs are permanently out of production and experimental pieces are considered the most important by far.

Even these pieces, however, vary slightly in use of materials and design. These variations also can affect the value of a piece. The Eames E.S.U. storage system, one of the more important designs, went through many manufacturing changes, even though it was in production for only a short time. Originally the angled-iron frame continued from the top of the piece to the bottom. The frame was replaced by a more stable tubular chrome leg configuration that attached to the bottom of the lower shelf. The earlier version also was equipped with a thin, molded-plywood dimple door. These too were replaced, with fiberglass doors. Another element used in early E.S.U. production was a panel of perforated metal. The most desirable piece would be one possessing all of the above early production elements.

LCW, Molded Plywood Lounge Chair by Charles Eames, Evans/Herman Miller, early piece. Original birch finish, gold label; 27 inches high x 22 inches deep x 22 inches wide; $650. *Courtesy of Troadway Gallery, Ohio.*

The classic molded-plywood L.C.W. lounge chair is another good example of a piece that was produced in a number of variations. The chair was originally designed with metal legs, which were changed to wooden legs during the war, rather than discontinue production. The chairs were available in a variety of finishes, many of which are considered quite rare. The pony or skunkskin, in original condition, is the most desirable.

These chairs were also available in red or black analine dyes for a short period. Sometimes they show up in odd combinations (usually custom-ordered), which definitely adds to their desirability.

Because designs of the 40s and 50s constitute a relatively

new market, these odd examples are sometimes overlooked, but they should not be underestimated. Now is the time that rare and important examples are turning up, and they may not show up again—at least not at the same price level.

▣ OVERLOOKED ITEMS WORTH COLLECTING

WOODEN OBJECTS

Rarely do handcrafted wooden objects come to auction or to the booths of dealers specializing in mid-century Modern items. They turn up mostly in consignment and thrift shops. Even though I haven't been able to list prices, I feel many are important and overlooked examples of modern design and something for collectors to consider. In the 1950s, it was Danish designers who began using the beauty of wood to create utilitarian objects and furniture in the new modern forms. From turned wood bowls to pepper mills, they changed the way we entertained and the look of our dining tables. You probably take the ritual of tossing salad in a handsome wood bowl for granted . . . along with the pepper mill. But it wasn't until Dansk International Designs began production in 1954 that the salad bowl came to the table (along with many other products from glassware to stainless steel flatware).

The designers were Danish, but it was Ted Nierenberg, an American, who founded Dansk. He saw and acted on the need for objects befitting the laid-back life-style of the postwar decade. Among the designers working for Dansk was Jens Quistgaard. His ice bucket is considered a classic, and it's well worth hunting down.

Well-known Danish furniture designer Finn Juhl also tried his hand at woodworking. From solid blocks of teak he fashioned bowls that dramatized the grain of the wood. The bowls and other examples of Danish woodwork had a finish of rubbed oil rather than varnish, so items could be constantly used without refinishing. This same concept made Scandinavian oil finish furniture so popular; it could be refurbished rather than refinished.

Dansk Designs signatures are branded on the bottom of pieces.

WOOD TOYS

By the late 50s Scandinavian wooden toys were introduced to the American market. Sparse of line, and often brightly painted, they were in keeping with the Modern look. Doubtless because they were sturdily made, many have survived rough-and-tumble times. Everything from pull toy trains to blocks were made, and they are worth looking for. They were expensive in their day. Prices aren't included in this book, simply because there is no established market for them, but the category is a real sleeper for collectors.

Harvey Hesse, a transplanted Texan, opened his own company in New York, where he produced unique Christmas decorations that sold to stores around the country. In the 1970s he became interested in collecting hammered aluminum made in the 30s, and became one of the first professional dealers in the field.

Long ago, as the newly formed earth cooled, aluminum combined with other elements to form rare gemstones. It combined with oxygen to produce rubies, sapphires, Oriental amethyst, and even emeralds. Aluminum and silica together form garnets; phosphate and aluminum form turquoise; aluminum, sodium, silica, and oxygen produce jade.

Aluminum wasn't found in pure form until 1825. A Danish scientist isolated the element in powder form. In 1854, a French discovery led to a workable form of the metal. The price consequently dropped from $550 per pound to $15 to $20 per pound but it was still too expensive to use outside of the jewelry trade.

In 1850, Napoleon II had a service of all-aluminum flatware that was used only for his most important guests.

In the 1880s a process for cheaply manufacturing alumi-

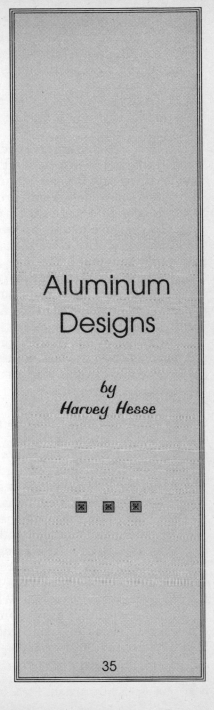

Aluminum Designs

by
Harvey Hesse

35

num resulted in a drop in the price to $4 to $5 per pound. By the 1890s the process was refined and the price reached fifty cents per pound. The age of aluminum had come.

Great advances in the automobile, train, and construction industries helped to fire interest in the use of this material. Artists of the day's Arts and Crafts movement were quick to realize the potential of this new product and began working in this new medium at once.

In 1923 Alcoa commissioned a prolific artist and sculptor, Wendell August, of Grove City, Pennsylvania, to open new horizons for them with the use of aluminum. With genius and speed he fulfilled the challenge and produced a new art form with intaglio designs that were used as "negatives" for finished products. Heavy-gauge aluminum was placed on these designs and then hammered with a ballpeen hammer. The result was hand-hammered aluminum. The once flat surface had depth and detail, creating a sculptured image. These designs were artistic and required very little care. Unlike things made from copper and silver they didn't tarnish. Aluminum found a new role in hundreds of American homes.

Aluminum, the preferred wedding gift of the 30s and 40s, was closeted from the 50s to the 80s, but it has become an exciting collectible in the 90s, combining beauty with utilitarian functions.

Prices vary widely, as is the case with most new collecting categories. Regionally, collectors may find higher prices for aluminum in California, northern midwestern states, and the upper East Coast region. There are slower price increases in New England, Florida, Georgia, and North and South Carolina, where interest in these pieces is growing. The best bargains can be found in the Rocky Mountains, Washington State, Texas, and the lower Midwest. Regardless of what you pay, be careful to look for good quality, design, and condition. You can still afford to be discriminating in this category.

Aluminum office furniture from the 40s can add the original modern look to your office. Look for pieces in secondhand office furniture shops and galleries. What you want is the patinated aluminum-and-leather desk chairs with the curving early modern design. These are real finds at $15 to $25. Expensive knockoffs abound for over $300.

ARTHUR ARMOUR

Like Wendell August, Arthur Armour lived in Grove City, Pennsylvania. His work, like that of August, was done in great detail using very heavy aluminum. He reproduced fine, old prints in stylized relief. All of his designs are of superior quality. Some fine examples were finished in anodized gold. Unfortunately, they rarely come to market in mint condition, but such pieces are well worth the search.

WENDELL AUGUST

Mentioned above in his connection with Alcoa, he could be considered the father of the decorative aluminum industry. The Wendell August Forge, which began as a blacksmith shop, is still in existence, making forged metal articles (including aluminum) entirely by hand. Many of the objects originally designed by August are reproduced by the Forge today.

Left: Folding Tray Table. Wendell August wheat pattern; $440.
Right: Arthur Armour World Map pattern magazine rack, carbon highlighted; $210. *Both courtesy of Steven Butler Collection.*

BUENILUM

In the late 40s and 50s Buenilum designs clearly represented modernism. The look was sleek, clean, and "silver" finished with rod handles finished in acorn finials. It was the look of Royal Danish. Trays with Formica-type bottoms were alcohol-proof for functional use. They patented a combination of aluminum and other additives for special use. These designs can be seen in the Smithsonian Institution in Washington, D.C.

CANTERBURY ARTS

Their designs usually featured ferns, seeds, and leaves, incorporating the artist's name. Canterbury pieces are always good quality, and are hard to find.

CELLINI

Chicago-based Cellini was known for pure gold and silver designs. The shop often duplicated designs in aluminum with the same loving care. This maker is one of my personal favorites, and examples of its work are very difficult to find. The simple designs make it hard to distinguish from the work of imitators.

The pieces of hammered aluminum made after 1934 have a variety of marks, among them Cellini-Craft, handmade Argental. Because of the growing Scandinavian influence in design, and the silvery finish, the name *Argental,* a Scandinavian word for silver, was used. Sometimes the pieces were also marked M. W. for Max Wille, an East Coast distributor.

RODNEY KENT

His designs are quite collectible for ribbon and openwork handles, and wonderful raised tulips. He created a variety of service pieces, including boudoir sets.

PALMER-SMITH

This Grove City, Pennsylvania, manufacturer produced quality works equal to those of August and Armour. Most works were simple with a "carved-in-line" design. He is best known for his linens.

RUSSEL WRIGHT

Unique in his approach, Russel Wright designed simple and pure pieces that were spun to leave fine lines on the surface. Handles were usually made of rattan, then finished and attached with aluminum; some were wrapped with raffia. Due to the fragile nature of these ultramodern beauties, not many have survived. Treasure your finds as they are among the most valuable in the aluminum category.

▣ OTHER TECHNIQUES AND FORMS

A wide range of designs that are not as fine as the handmade originals were produced in pressed aluminum. Most are of lesser value. Exceptions are those made in England by Soma. Soma manufactures the charming Blue Willow design in many styles, including full tea sets.

Aluminum furniture is available in many periods and styles. Pieces are usually fluid and clean-lined with rivet connectors or bolted together. Wendell August, Everlast, and Russel Wright all created numerous lamp designs. Wright used cypress, pine, or pecan wood in twisted rope designs or carved in modern shapes with aluminum findings. Desks, tables (some with glass tops), and chairs of all kinds are available to collectors. Even wastebaskets have become works of art, especially those featuring Wendell August designs.

Because of the fragile nature of jewelry pieces, many haven't survived the years. Others were simply tossed away as objects of no value by younger generations, who didn't recognize the value of the techniques or the materials involved in their creation. Belt buckles, clip-on shoe ornaments, belts, and pins were among the most popular pieces.

Many unsigned pieces were the work of home craftsmen. Making small aluminum objects was a popular hobby in the early 40s. Aluminum's lighter weight made it an ideal material for the home hobbyists who used tools at hand. Coasters, clip-on pins, small trays, and dishes were most frequently made. Some can be quite well done. Craftsmanship is all-important.

Tip: You may find unsigned pieces, or even signed objects, that resemble those of well-known makers such as the Wendell

Picture, one of a pair. Hand-hammered aluminum; 12 x 15 inches each; $120/pair. *Courtesy of Harvey Hesse Collection.*

August Forge. Many craftsmen worked at the important forges, perfected their techniques, then went on to start their own businesses; they often copied popular patterns and used them in their own pieces.

PRICES

Bowls

Covered Bowl, manufactured by Buenilum. With liner, acorn finial; 7½ inches round; $125.

Covered Bowl, manufactured by Continental Silver. Chrysanthemum design with liner; 11½ inches × 9 inches; $45.

Footed Bowl, designed by Rodney Kent. Tulip-design interior; 10 inches in diameter; 3 inches high; $40.

Bowl, manufactured by Palmer-Smith. Stylized leaf intaglio; 8½ inches in diameter; $30.

Dishes

Chafing Dish, designed by Rodney Kent. With alcohol burner; 8 inches × 9 inches; $45.

Charger, manufactured by Kensington Brass. Zodiac applied center decoration; 18 inches in diameter; $125.

Trays

Broiler Tray, manufactured by Forman Family. Clip-on Bakelite legs; 11 inches × 17½ inches × 3 inches; $100.

Rectangular Tray, designed by Wendell August. Overall bittersweet; divided into five compartments; 15½ inches × 20 inches; $125.

Round Tray, designed by Wendell August. Forest lilies; pie crust edge; 18 inches in diameter; $90.

Round Tray, manufactured by Canterbury Arts. Handled; fern and flower motif; signed "J. Hattick"; 13 inches in diameter; $55.

Round Tray, manufactured by Cromwell. Handled; fruits and flowers center; 15 inches in diameter; $60.

Round Tray, manufactured by Stede. Turned-up lip; dogwood branch motif; 10 inches in diameter; $35.

Serving Tray, manufactured by Cellini. Round, 4-inch center dish with four oval serving wells around border; 18 inches in diameter; $140.

Tray, manufactured by Palmer-Smith. Kidney-shaped with water lilies; 22 inches × 12 inches; $225.

Miscellaneous

Basket with Handles, designed by Arthur Armour. Orange blossom motif; 10 inches × 7 inches; $70.

Candle Holders (pair), manufactured by Everlast. Double S curve; 6½ inches high; $45.

Double Candle Holder. 10½ inches × 2 inches (base); 6½ inches high; $45.

Desk Set, manufactured by Kensington. Includes blotter roller, blotter holder; with brass cover and plume/ribbon applied decoration; $275/set.

Ice Bucket, manufactured by Keystone. Handled; Pyrex liner; gadroon border; 8 inches × 5½ inches; $50.

Aluminum Satellite Punch Set, designed by Russel Wright. Sphere-shaped covered bowl; eight cups and ladle with brushed finish and wood ball handles; impressed "Russel Wright"; bowl 10 inches in diameter; cup 3¼ inches in diameter; 2 inches high; $990/set.

Aluminum intaglio design on flat sheet, framed; caricature by Al Hirshfeld; 18 x 12 inches; $550. *Courtesy of Phillip and Charlotte Rosenberg Collection.*

Salad Serving Set, designed by Bruce Fox. Includes spatula, fork, and lettuce server; asparagus design; 13 inches × 4 inches; $125/set.

Aluminum, Glass, and Bakelite Table, c. 1940. American; circular glass top above a tapering standard set with amber and black Bakelite rings, above a lower circular base with three angular feet; 26 inches high; 21¾ inches in diameter; $920.

Other Metal Designs

Chromed-Metal Vase, designed by Russel Wright, c. 1955. Simple flaring cylindrical vessel with domed foot; unsigned; 10⅛ inches high; $1,150.

Back: Everlast Vase, 9 inches, $325; *Center:* Farberware Serving Tray, blackberry pattern with 22 karat white gold Limoges plate, 16½ inches, $55; *Front:* Everlast Dish, leaf dish, 6½ inches, $6.

This chapter includes sections on designers who worked for major pottery companies, the small pottery companies themselves, and those who were strictly studio potters. Collectors of ceramics from this period can be selective since many pieces made by the pottery companies are at the low end of the market pricewise, though they are not always available as sets. The designers and companies listed below typify organic modernism. Their brightly colored pieces are easy to spot. Don't wait too long to go hunting. Remember what happened to Fiesta Ware.

Leading designer Russel Wright (1904–1976) worked in a variety of media, including ceramics. Over the past couple of years his name has become widely known to collectors, mainly for his glazed earthenware of the American Modern line produced by Steubenville Pottery, founded in Steubenville, Ohio, in 1879. Its initial products were ironstone and whiteware, but it is best remembered for its production of Russel Wright's designs. The American Modern line was successfully manufactured until 1957. It is hard to believe that Wright had a hard time finding a pottery to produce his design, since it proved to be the best-selling dinnerware ever made.

Ceramics

Wright originally designed the line in 1937, incorporating fluid forms well in advance of other potters. His color selection and glazes were new, and for the first time different colors were meant to be mixed and matched. So, though it was designed in the 30s, the line is appropriately included in this book as an influence on the later designs of the 40s and 50s.

The problems associated with collecting Wright's dinnerware are emblematic of problems for collectors of any mass-produced item. In the late 1980s collectors were hot on the trail of American Modern ceramic pieces. Prices were on the upswing. These pieces exemplified the look of Modernism. A new range of colors was introduced from 1950 to 1955. Shiny glazes and the unique Modern forms made them popular then and now, but currently only hard-to-find pieces are holding their own.

Many pieces were flawed during production. Some had unevenly applied glazes. Some colors—such as white, seafoam, and chartreuse—have crackled glazes. Another common flaw is the appearance of small bumps. Like most other varieties of earthenware, it also chips easily.

Beware of copies that do exist. Authentic pieces are marked with "Russel Wright" and "Mfg by Steubenville, USA." Pieces from matching pairs are marked on just one piece of the pair.

Serving pieces are the most expensive, since fewer were made. Condition, as ever, is important. Look for rare colors such as bean brown, glacier blue, canteloupe, and white. Common colors—such as chartreuse, granite gray, curry, and coral—are accountably less expensive.

Wright also designed a line of dinnerware, produced by Iroquois China, called Casual China. It was similar in design to his Steubenville pieces but featured the novelty of being able to go from oven to table.

Eva Zeisel holds a position of similar prominence in ceramic design of the 40s and 50s. She designed the Museum Service manufactured in porcelain by Castleton China in 1946 for the Museum of Modern Art in New York City. Its production was a testament to the museum's interest in organic design. Perhaps her best known designs are from the Town and Country line produced by Red Wing in 1946, using biomorphic, often whimsical, shapes for dinnerware. In addition, Zeisel designed Tomorrow's Classic earthenware in 1956 for Hall China. She designed a second earthenware service for the company in 1956 called The Century.

▣ AMERICAN CERAMIC DESIGNS ▣

EVA POLANYI STRICKER ZEISEL (1906–)

Through her many years as a ceramics designer she has been one of the most influential designers of the Modern movement. Her style, based on her early training as a traditional potter in Hungary, shifted to the International Style when she began work in Germany in the late 1920s. She worked in various cities in the Soviet Republic until the Stalinist purges, when she returned to Hungary, only to be forced to flee from the Nazis.

Arriving in New York in 1938, she eventually was commissioned to design a dinner service for Castleton China, sponsored by the Museum of Modern Art. When it was finally produced after the war, Museum dinnerware was introduced to the public as "the first Modernist porcelain dinnerware in the United States." Zeisel's Town and Country dinnerware and Tomorrow's Classic dinnerware, made by Hall China, were very popular and sold well. Over the years she has designed for many china manufacturers both here in the United States and abroad, including Rosenthal (West Germany), Noritake (Japan), and Mancioli (Itlay). She also turned her talents to designing an experimental aluminum-steel chair and biomorphic Plexiglas serving pieces. She is still actively designing and received the Brooklyn Museum/Modernism "Design Award for Lifetime Achievement" in 1992.

HAEGER POTTERIES

One of America's oldest potteries, Haeger was founded in 1871 by David Haeger in Dundee, Illinois. Today, Haeger continues under the fourth generation of the Haeger family ownership. In the 1950s their colors and designs reflected the modern look. Chartreuse, for instance, was a popular color. Some pieces, such as a footed cake plate, used the Italian look of multicolor enamel squares. Prices are for the most part modest.

Salt-and-pepper Shakers
(pair), designed by Eva Zeisel,
manufactured by Red Wing
Potter, c. 1945-1946. Town-
and-country pattern
dinnerware, offered in five
different color combinations,
organic biomorphic style;
$50/pair. *Courtesy of Kim and
Al Eiber Collection.*

Figurine. Ceramic lamb
plant vase, HAEGER USA
incised mark; $25. *Courtesy
of Antiques & Collections.*

Pitcher, c. 1950s. Cream-
colored with black Modern
design, marked HAEGER POTTER
USA, thrift-shop find; $8.
Courtesy of the author.

PRICES

Vase, Haeger pottery. Swirled blues, greens; marked "Royal Haeger"; 15 inches high; $45.

Small tazza, Haeger Potteries. Multi-color; 6 inches high; $10.

RED WING POTTERIES, INC.

Founded in 1878 in Red Wing, Minnesota, the company originally made utilitarian objects. Over the years its name changed more than once, but in 1936 it changed to Red Wing Potteries, Inc., and the company began specializing in dinnerware. In 1945 the company hired industrial designer Eva Zeisel to create a line of informal dinnerware. Her Town and Country service, produced in 1947, introduced the increasingly popular organic, biomorphic forms into Red Wing's products. The color range was soft blue and chartreuse, dark brown, gunmetal black, sand, and peach. It could be mixed and matched like Russel Wright's American Modern pottery.

PRICES

Modern Art Pottery Pieces (two). Red Wing ridged chartreuse, olive green, and blue; biomorphic oval form with extended neck; Rowan half-round yellow center bowl; impressed "Rowan Vermont"; 18½ inches high and 4¾ inches high × 8¾ inches in diameter respectively; $300/set.

ROOKWOOD POTTERY

There is much reference material available on the history of the Rookwood pottery. It was founded in 1880 and over the years prices have risen for the finest examples by its top artists. However, by 1941 Rookwood had stopped turning out quality pieces and new, noteworthy designs. By 1949 the pottery no longer had a staff of artists. In 1956 Rookwood was purchased by James Smith, but his attempts to market the Modern-style pieces failed by 1959. When these pieces come to market, prices are on the low side.

Ashtrays (two). White hi-glaze ashtray; 1959; modern boomerang shape; impressed "Rookwood, Cinti., O." Green hi-glaze ashtray; 1955; modern design, #7111; 7 inches wide and 9 inches square, respectively; both mint condition; $60/set.

Ceramic Lamp, c. 1950s. Three stacked cubes with bull's-eye design in mauve; 6 inches × 6 inches at base, 32 inches high; mint condition; $180.

Figural Shell, c. 1950s. Ceramic, marked VAN BRIGGLE, 8½ inches in diameter; $90. *Courtesy of Antiques & Collections.*

RUSSEL WRIGHT (1904–1976)

One of the best known of American designers in the Modern style, Wright began his career in the 1930s. He began as a set and costume designer, but his marriage in 1927 marked his transition to decorative art design. His wife, a sculpture student, encouraged him to broaden the scope of his work.

Among his first efforts were a line of spun-aluminum household items that included tea sets. His next designs were radios for the Wurlitzer Company and the familiar metal accessories for Chase Brass and Copper Company.

Much has already been written about his other designs of the 1930s—from furniture to his famous dinnerware pattern, American Modern, of 1937—to his post–World War II Casual China, designed for the Iroquois China Company in both pottery and melamine plastic. His American Modern dinnerware was in production until 1957. He designed glassware, table linens, and stainless steel flatware to go with it.

Fiesta carafe, after 1943. Bright orange glaze; bulbous shape with cork stopper; impressed "Fiesta, made in USA"; 10 inches high; mint condition; $110.

Bauer Pottery (four pieces). Pair of candlesticks, vase, and folded bowl, each with slipped yellow glaze; 11 inches high, 9 inches high, and 5 inches high, respectively; some bubbling and skips; $605/set.

Candlesticks, Vase, and Bowl (four pieces), designed by Russel Wright for Bauer Pottery. Slipped yellow glaze; $605/set. *Courtesy of Skinner, Inc., Boston/Bolton, MA*

Vases (pair), designed by Russel Wright for Bauer Pottery, c. 1940s. Terra cotta matte glaze, impressed marks; 8⅜ inches high and 10¾ inches high; $796/pair. *Courtesy of Skinner, Inc., Boston/Bolton, MA.*

▨ AMERICAN STUDIO POTTERS ▨

The art pottery movement began in the United States in Cincinnati, Ohio, in 1871 and continued to expand and evolve through the Art Deco period to encompass the Modern movement. It is well documented in *Art Pottery of the United States* by Paul Evans (1974, Everybody's Press; Hanover, Pennsylvania). He describes it as "not identified by particular styles or techniques, specific operation or span of years, but rather by the philosophy or attitude of the individuals involved in its execution." Whereas industrial or production pieces required many different people for each step, the studio potters worked either by themselves or with a partner, as was the case for Gertrud and Otto Natzler, as well as Mary and Edwin Scheier.

In the early 1950s, many potters showed a strong Scandinavian influence. Later, Abstract Expressionism and various philosophical movements, such as Zen, popular in the 1950s, influenced many of the potters, notably Peter Voulkos.

For other potters, such as Hawaiian-born Toshiko Takaezu, British potter Bernard Leach was a strong influence. Leach used many Oriental approaches to glazes, form, and design. Like others influenced by him, Takaezu later studied at Cranbrook, and then with Harvey Littleton at the University of Wisconsin from 1945 to 1955. Her mid-twentieth-century work shows the influence of Zen and Abstract Expressionism.

Because of the distinctive nature of California pottery and its importance to American decorative arts of the 40s and 50s, a separate section has been devoted to California potters and their designs.

Collectors should consider that there were hundreds of studio potters working after World War II and into the late fifties. Many pieces will be signed by unfamiliar names. Some may be "sleepers." Others may never be considered of great value.

NORMAN ARSENAULT (1912–1984)

Born in North Grafton, Massachusetts, Arsenault studied at Worcester Museum of Fine Arts School; Ecole Des Artes Decoratifs, Paris; Alfred University, New York; and with Hamada and Kojo in Japan. In 1939 he established the Department of Ceramics in the School of the Museum of Fine Arts, Boston. Retiring in 1972 to Wells, Maine, he continued his work with pottery until his death. He spent years working to perfect what he would call his Tourmaline glaze, of which there are only a few known examples.

Bowls

Earthenware Bowls (four), designed by Norman Arsenault. Sgraffito and applied designs; glazed in shades of brown, maroon, and blue; incised signature; largest bowl 5½ inches high × 8 inches in diameter; $330/set.

Earthenware Bowl. Raku glaze in shades of brown with stylized floral design on interior in black-incised signature and cipher; 6¼ inches high × 20 inches in diameter; $358.

Bottle, by Norman Arsenault. Tourmaline glaze, earthenware, mottled green-blue glaze on flowing ribbed form, incised signature; 9 inches high; $220. *Courtesy of Skinner, Inc., Boston/Bolton, MA.*

Earthenware Charger and Vases (three pieces), by Norman Arsenault. Glaze decoration in shades of brown, olive, and gray, incised signature; 14½ inches in diameter; $200. *Courtesy of Toomey-Treadway Galleries, Oak Park, IL.*

Dishes/Plates

Earthenware Plates (set of six), designed by Norman Arsenault. Square with flared sides; gloss brick glaze with blue stylized floral decoration; incised signature; 8¾ inches wide; $275/set.

Miscellaneous

Earthenware Charger and Two Vases, designed by Norman Arsenault. Glaze decoration in shades of brown, olive, and gray; incised signature; charger 14½ inches in diameter; $247/set.

GERTRUD NATZLER (1908–1971)
OTTO NATZLER (1908–   )

Considered the most creative of the mid-twentieth-century studio potters, the Natzlers left Vienna in 1938 for the United States. They opened a studio in California, where their small pots showed the influence of the simple forms of glazed stoneware made in China during the Sung Dynasty. The hallmark of their work is the textural quality used in many of their glazes. Always experimenting, they developed unique glazes, including their well-known color, bright applegreen, used from 1960 on.

PRICES

Bowls

Glazed Earthenware Bowl, c. 1950. Signed; 8 inches in diameter; $2,000.

Glazed Earthenware Bowl, mid-twentieth century. Circular bowl with sharply tapering sides and ribbed interior; in streaked and mottled olive green, gray-blue, and brown glaze; "NATZLER" in black, 8 inches in diameter; $460.

Glazed Earthenware Bowl, mid-twentieth century. Oval bowl with two upturned sides; glazed in a rough beige glaze over tan ground; "NATZLER" in blue; 13¾ inches long; $1,380.

Bowl, designed by the Natzlers. Footed form with flaring sides, blue high-glaze with variations of medium blue to darker blue, original paper label, #846; 3½ inches high x 8 inches wide; $900. *Courtesy of Toomey-Treadway Galleries, Oak Park, IL.*

Volcanic Ceramic Bowl, c. 1950. Wide-mouthed vessel with white lava-textured glaze; signed "NATZLER"; 9¼ inches in diameter; $172.

Earthenware Bowls (four). Uranium-yellow/green glaze bowl; bowl with bent rim, rust/brown centering yellow "hare's fur" glaze; bowl with powder blue glaze; bowl glazed black under sand/tan; three signed "AVG."; 4⅛ inches in diameter; $467/set.

Dishes/Plates

Dish, mid-twentieth century. Shallow round form; brown rim; blue shading to lavender-beige in center; horizontal ink mark; 6 inches in diameter; $330.

Plate, c. 1955. Blue crystalline glazed earthenware together with bronze stand; signed and numbered; 11¼ inches in diameter; $2,000.

Urns/Vases/Vessels

Volcanic Ceramic Urn, c. 1955. Gourd-form ovoid vessel with lava-textured surface; in warm earth tones of brown, green, and ocher; signed "NATZLER"; 11⅛ inches high; $575.

Vase, c. 1950. Glazed earthenware; signed; 7½ inches high; $2,000.

Miscellaneous

Earthenware Pieces (four). Charger with tiger-eye orange and central maroon crystalline glaze, repaired crack, 13⅝ inches in diameter; bowl with volcanic blue glaze; bowl with textural "Pompean" green, brown, and yellow; bowl with "Pompean" red and brown textural glaze; all signed "Natzler"; $1,210/set.

MARY SCHEIER (1910–)
EDWIN SCHEIER (1910–)

In the 1950s it was the work of the Scheiers that most significantly influenced the look of American studio pottery. Their work can be recognized by designs incised into the clay or through the glaze, using Sgraffito. These designs were sometimes abstract forms clearly influenced by Joan Miró. Other times they used biblical themes in primitive and linear graphic style. They worked in Oaxaca, Mexico.

Bowls

Bowl, c. 1941. Wide mouth on tapering cylindrical form; relief decorated with repeating figures, flowers, and the sun; in brown bisque with glossy brown interior glaze; 7 inches high × 8¾ inches in diameter; $2,500.

Footed Bowl, c. 1950. Matte yellow glaze; inscribed "Scheier"; 2¼ inches high × 6¼ inches in diameter; $100.

Footed Bowl. Repeating Sgraffito leaf decoration; oatmeal glaze with glossy brown rim and mottled interior; inscribed "Scheier"; 3¾ inches high × 6 inches in diameter; $220.

Glazed Ceramic Bowl, c. 1950. Wide-mouthed vessel with creamy and brown glazed interior; the exterior in chocolate brown with continuous intaglio abstract figural drawing; signed "Scheier"; 8½ inches in diameter; $920.

Glazed Ceramic Bowl, c. 1950. Footed side-mouthed vessel with exterior stoneware surface in pale beige decorated with continuous amusing facile line drawings of faces; the interior glazed in pale brown; signed "Scheier"; 5⅜ inches in diameter; $2,587.

Dishes/Plates

Sgraffito-decorated Charger, c. 1955. Chocolate-brown slip over rose-beige ground; decorated with stylized head figures; incised "Scheier"; rim hairline; 16¾ inches in diameter; $550.

Charger, c. 1948. Abstract figural line decoration in soft matte mauves, black, and white; hi-glaze border and side; very unusual example; 1 inch high × 10 inches in diameter; mint condition; $375.

Dish, c. 1950. Elephant-gray background with three abstract faces decorated in Sgraffito; dark gray lip; 1 inch high × 8 inches in diameter; $220.

Dishes (two). Sgraffito portraits under blue and beige glaze, the second caramel with blue interior ring and tan; inscribed "Scheier"; rim chip; 7½ inches in diameter; $220/set.

Green Glaze Open Dish. 9¾ inches in diameter; $750.

Glazed Ceramic Platter, c. 1950. Circular slightly dished

form with uranium glaze and abstract line drawing on upper surface of plate; underside light mocha color glaze; underside signed "Scheier"; 11 inches in diameter; $172/set.

Lamps

Lamp Base, c. mid-twentieth century. Large ovoid form; Sgraffito decorated with man, woman, and child; blue glaze ground; inscribed "Scheier"; 16 inches high; $1,100.

Urns/Vases/Vessels

Vases (two). Footed ovoid form with glossy caramel mottled glaze; and footed ovoid form with glossy brown and blue dust glaze; both inscribed "Scheier"; 6⅞ inches high and 8 inches high, respectively; $150/set.

Glazed Ceramic Vessel, c. 1950. Flaring ovoid vessel with gently ribbed surface; glazed in brown and cream and decorated in bas-relief and intaglio with supine bodies and open-mouthed fish; signed "Scheier"; 11¾ inches high; $460.

Miscellaneous

Four Pieces. Large cylindrical vase raised on circular foot with volcanic glaze band, Sgraffito-decorated green glaze ground, rim damage; bowl raised on circular foot, Sgraffito decorated with a band of human stick figures with fish bodies, medium blue glaze; ovoid-shape vase, Sgraffito decorated with band of fish; plate with incised and glaze-painted abstract decoration in white and green glazes on navy blue ground; all signed by maker; 17 inches high, 4¼ inches high, 6¼ inches high, 10⅞ inches high, respectively; $1,700/set.

Five-Piece Drink Set, mid-twentieth century. Pitcher Sgraffito decorated with cows; mugs decorated with cows, horses, and landscape in highlighted glaze against cream ground; inscribed "Scheier"; 9¼ inches high and 5½ inches high, respectively; $325/set.

Glazed Ceramic Twenty-two-Piece Partial Tea Set, c. 1950. Comprising a teapot, covered sugar bowl, creamer, nine teacups, and ten saucers; glazed in pale yellow and Indian red; each piece signed "Scheier"; teapot 7⅝ inches high; $1,380/set.

Peter Voulkos (1924–)

One of America's most influential studio potters in the 1950s and 1960s, Voulkos began his education in his native Montana, at Montana State University. While majoring in painting, a required course in ceramics changed his career direction. In 1952 he received his master of fine arts degree at the California College of Arts and Crafts, in sculpture. His work was influenced early on by Abstract Expressionism. Often his large ceramic sculptures could be as much as eight feet high. He continuously experimented with new techniques—slashing surfaces, allowing slips and glazes to flow freely. Often his pieces are vertically stacked. Other times he used the plate as a base form, enlarging it and turning it into a ceramic sculpture.

PRICES

Urns/Vases/Vessels

Covered Jar, c. 1955. Stoneware with paper resist decoration; signed; 9 inches high; $2,500.

Vase. Wax resist glazed stoneware; signed; $3,000.

▨ VARIOUS AMERICAN STUDIO CERAMICS ▨

PRICES

Bowls

Ceramic Bowl, designed by F. Carlton Ball and Aaron Bohrod, c. 1955. Bulbous ovoid vessel with dry oxidized stoneware exterior decorated with Miro-style abstract shapes; in coffee and white shades; the interior glazed in pale pink; signed "F. C. Ball" and "A. Bohrod"; firing crack on interior; 8¾ inches high; $460.

Ceramic Bowl, designed by Marguerite Wildenhain, c. 1940s. Shallow bowl in heavily textured hi-glaze brown-and-white exterior with deep blue interior; concentric circular decoration; 10 inches wide × 3 inches high; mint condition; $240.

Glazed Ceramic Bowl, designed by Gerald Williams, c. 1955. Wide-mouthed vessel with gray glazed interior; exterior with oxidized copper color glaze decorated with a continuous line of intaglio-carved abstract figural images, signed "Williams"; 16¼ inches in diameter; $2,070.

Shallow Ceramic Bowl, designed by Eugene Deutsch, c. 1947. Heavily textured brown-and-blue exterior; deep blue interior with unglazed matte crescent lip; 7 inches in diameter; $45.

Ceramic Bowl, designed by Eugene Deutsch, c. 1942. Heavily textured matte exterior with hi-glaze blue interior; very early signature (before change in spelling of name); 11 inches wide × 5 inches high; excellent condition; $260.

Studio Ceramic Bowl in the form of stylized bird, designed by Eugene Deutch, c. 1954. Heavily textured body; exterior brown glaze; interior darker brown with green feathered decoration; 17 inches wide × 5 inches deep x 6 inches high; mint condition; $70.

Large Ceramic Bowl, designed by Gordon Martz, c. 1950. Internally textured and decorated with colorful spirals and spheres; 24 inches × 21 inches x 9 inches; mint condition; $425.

Dishes/Plates

Ceramic Charger, designed by Nancy Wickham, c. 1950. Unusual coil and line decoration in matte brown and beige glaze; 1 inch high × 11 inches in diameter; mint condition; $240.

Charger, designed by Wayland Gregory, c. 1950s. Hand-thrown studio piece; brown stoneware body with hi-glaze; hand-decorated abstract decoration; 18 inches in diameter; minor chip; $250.

Dishes (three), designed by Lotti, Scheier school. Deep dish with mustard glaze; redware-style dish with interior swirl white glaze abstraction; and deep dish with sea-green glaze; inscribed "Lotti"; 7 inches, 9¾ inches, and 7¾ inches, respectively. $140/set.

Urns/Vases/Vessels

Stoneware Vase, designed by Marguerite Wildenhain, c. 1950. Square-shouldered bottle with flaring neck; textured about the sides and glazed in mint green and white; impressed mark; inscribed "Pond/Farm"; 6½ inches high; $240.

Vase, designed by Raymond Koechlin, c. 1952. Beautiful

pink-and-gray volcanic glaze; impressed circular mark; 7 inches wide × 10 inches high; mint condition; $210.

Vase, designed by Polia Pillin, c. 1948. Bottle form in heavily textured red-and-black lava glaze; signed "Pillin"; 15 inches high × 5 inches in diameter, mint condition; $550.

Vase, designed by Maija Grotell. Bulbous body with small top; cream-and-gray matte with pink highlights and brown spots; initials "M. G." on bottom; 7 inches high, mint condition; $1,800.

Glazed Pottery Vessel, designed by Rose Cabat. Flattened globular vessel with very narrow protruding mouth with a matte turquoise blue around the top streaking over a glossy cobalt blue running unevenly over the brown matte ground around the base down to the small ring foot; incised "CABAT"; 4 inches high; $275.

"Feelie" Vase, marked CABAT. Brilliant blue, soft drop-over dark brown glaze; 3 inches high; $260. *Courtesy of Toomey-Treadway Galleries, Oak Park, IL.*

Bud Vase, designed by Harold Riegger, California. Thick blue-green matte glaze over a bright blue matte; black signature; " '58" date; 7 inches high; mint condition; $225.

Colorful Vessel, designed by Jim Leedy. Signed; dated " '54"; glazed hand-built earthenware; 14⅛ inches high; $4,000.

Vase, mid-twentieth century. Flared rim on narrow neck swelling to ovoid form; ribbed texture; green glossy glaze with patches of speckled blue and light green glaze; inscribed "Robinson"; 12 inches high; $75.

Miscellaneous

Six Pieces of Studio Pottery from Syracuse, New York, c. 1955. Covered jar, incised design under brown-and-gray glaze, signed "RML 58," 13⅜ inches high; covered jar designed by Henry Gerhardt, glazed in brown, 9⅛ inches high; goblet designed by Henry Gerhardt, blue glaze with green mottling, 8⅝ inches high; spherical vase designed by Henry Gerhardt, blue glaze, 9⅞ inches high; covered jar designed by Henry Gerhardt, glazed in browns, mustard, and white, 9⅞ inches high; covered jar designed by Henry Gerhardt, glazed in browns, mustard, and white, 11 inches high; $523/set.

Six Pottery Pieces, designed by Paul Bellardo, Boston, c. 1955. Lamp base with carved rings at neck and scallop pattern, white glaze, inscribed, 17¾ inches high; bowl with ridged interior glazed rust and black, exterior rust and green-black, inscribed, 4⅜ inches high × 9⁷⁄₁₆ inches in diameter; bowl with outer cutwork design, blue glaze, inscribed, 4¼ inches high × 7½ inches in diameter; lamp base with speckled blue and purple on white, inscribed, 15⁹⁄₁₆ inches high; lamp base with carved ribbing, glazed in brown, moss green, and cream, inscribed, 17¼ inches high; lamp base with incised leaf design and repeating linear pattern, glazed in white with brown, inscribed, 11 inches high; $523/set.

Three Pieces of Studio Pottery, American. Vase designed by Scarlatti, Sgraffitoed and glazed design in black and white, 9½ inches high; molded and carved face vase glazed in white, black, salmon, and green, unsigned, 8¹¹⁄₁₆ inches high; slab pottery vase raised on two legs with irregular brown-and-white glaze, unsigned, 11⅛ inches high; $138/set.

Two Pieces of American Studio Pottery. Punch bowl designed by James Wozniak of Fort Worth, Texas, c. 1955, incised linear and abstract geometric design glazed in white with pale green in terior glaze, inscribed and paper label, 6⅞ inches high × 12 inches in diameter; tazza designed by Richard Lafean, interior red-and-gray splash glaze, pedestal glazed white with red traces, signed, 13⅞ inches high × 13⅞ inches in diameter; $248/set.

Ceramic Tile Portrait, designed by Harris G. Strong. Abstract portrait in shades of green and blue high-fired hand-painted ceramic tiles; Modernist work; label on reverse; 12 inches wide × 36 inches high; excellent condition; $475.

▨ CALIFORNIA STUDIO POTTERS ▨

LAURA ANDRESON (1902–   )

A pioneer in California ceramics, she studied and taught at UCLA, experimenting with new techniques. Her pieces show the influences of her trips to Scandinavia and other parts of the world. She is associated with many well-known potters such as Gertrud and Otto Natzler and Vivika and Otto Heino, and her works have been included in many exhibitions, with pieces now in many private and public collections.

PRICES

Glazed Stoneware Bowl, c. 1940. Gray-glazed; low circular bowl pierced with two bands of circular disks within incised unglazed concentric rings; incised "Laura Andreson" (date obscured); $1,045.

PAUL A. SOLDNER (1921–)

Paul Soldner was an important contributor to the 1950s ceramics revolution in California. He began annual one-man exhibits in 1956 at the Lang Gallery, at Scripps College in Southern California. He also taught at Scripps until his recent retirement to Aspen, Colorado. His work endlessly reinvented itself with new approaches to the medium of ceramics.

Vase, by Laura Andreson. Terra cotta, inscribed LAURA ANDRESON 1940, TO POLLY, in script; 6⅛ inches high; $330. *Courtesy of Butterfield and Butterfield Auctioneers, CA.*

Covered Vase, by Paul Soldner. Pottery, signed, slight damage. *Courtesy of Toomey-Treadway Galleries, Oak Park, IL.*

PRICES

Covered Jar, c. 1950. Bulbous form with abstract decoration in blues, grays, browns and taupe; 12 inches in diameter × 17 inches; $350.

BEATRICE WOOD (1893-)

A native of San Francisco, California, and a graduate of the University of Southern California, she studied with Glen Lukens, Gertrud and Otto Natzler, and others. Her work is a part of museum collections from the Metropolitan Museum of Art in New York to the Victoria Albert Museum in London.

PRICES

Earthenware Birds (two), second half of the twentieth century. Each stylized figure of a duck with wings spread, long neck extended and mouth open with tongue protruding, each with tan irregularly textured matte and iridescent glaze along the back, wings, and head; one with mottled iridescent blue and tan neck, the underside in green-tinged iridescent mottled blue; the other with iridescent pale green and tan neck, the underside with shades of green mottled iridescence; each signed "BEATO"; 7¼ inches × 8⅛ inches; $3,300.

Vase. Footed vessel in iridescent adobe red glaze with white and green drips; signed "BEATO"; 6 inches in diameter × 6 inches high; mint condition; $700.

⧈ VARIOUS CALIFORNIA POTTERS ⧈ AND POTTERIES

Until recently pottery made in Southern California has been a flea market staple. It has also been most closely associated with the colorful mass-produced dinnerware made first in the Depression years by Bauer Pottery in Los Angeles. With their introduction of vivid, opaque-colored, glazed pottery in the "ring" design, they opened their doors and consumers' eyes to a totally new approach to entertaining and dining. It was part of the beginning of what we now refer to as the "California Lifestyle." Casual dining and dinner parties were centered around another new phenomenon, the patio. What Bauer started quickly spread, and other California potteries sprang up by the late forties. Even during World War II, when imports were in short supply, some Southern California companies began developing dinnerware and decorative pieces. Many cottage industry potteries created decorative items during the same period.

Though colorful and inexpensive by the early fifties, they couldn't compete with the Japanese and Italian ceramic products newly on the market again. By the early 1960s only a few California potteries remained.

With today's renewed interest in 40s and 50s designs, many Californian pottery pieces have made their way to quality antique shows, shops, and auctions. Not every piece is worth collecting. Now is a time for collectors to be selective. Not everything is marked with a stamp, and original paper labels have disappeared. Names may be unfamiliar.

Begin your search by examining pieces that appeal to you. If you like the form, colors, and design, never mind who made it. Hedi Schoop, Brayton Laguna, Sascha Brastoff, and Bauer pieces may not be readily identifiable. They and other California potters are being seriously reevaluated today. On the down side, many examples are recognized by savvy collectors as strictly kitsch, made for tourist giftware shops. Prices for most pieces are on the low side; generally, you won't pay more than $300, even for a high-quality piece.

Keep in mind that some potteries made both high- and low-end lines. Don't pay top dollar just for a name when the piece may not be of top quality produced by that pottery. Unusual colors and glazes always bring higher prices. Remember that both hand-thrown pieces and pieces made from molds can make wonderful additions to your collection.

Many companies changed their signatures over the years, and familiarizing yourself with these changes is a good way to date some of the pieces. Examples of some signatures can be found in *The Collector's Encyclopedia of California Pottery* by Jack Chipman (see Bibliography).

Coffee Service, Catalina Ware, Gladding, McBean and Company, California, c. 1942. Cream-colored coffeepot with lid on cylindrical neck on bulbous body; wooden handle attached with metal collar at base of neck and six cylindrical mugs with loop handles; one each in colors of cream, turquoise, blue, green, yellow, and orange glaze; impressed "Catalina"; coffeepot 8 inches high; mugs 2¾ inches high; $60.

SASCHA BRASTOFF (1918–)

Brastoff, though included in any listing of California potters, was born in Cleveland, Ohio. After studying for two years at Western Reserve Art School in Cleveland, he moved to New York City. There he worked at the Sculpture Center, where two of his terra-cotta figurines won awards. After a stint in the U.S. Army Air Force's entertainment services during World War II, he became interested in theater. In 1945 he moved to Los Angeles and worked as a costume designer for 20th Century Fox. It was Winthrop Rockefeller who started him on his way in ceramics, after seeing examples of his terra-cotta sculpture.

Rockefeller financed Sascha Brastoff's small West Los Angeles plant in 1948, and he began making earthenware. It was his use of unusual color combinations, especially with metallic colors, that would eventually come to be his trademark. Rockefeller's plan was to have him produce a quality line of American dinnerware. In 1954 production of his first fine china dinnerware line began. Nine more lines followed. He also made earthenware table settings using a marbleized pattern of platinum or gold against different color backgrounds. After retiring from his successful ceramic business in 1963, he turned his attention to custom jewelry.

Brastoff's decorative pieces were never inexpensive. Prices for his early work continue to climb at auction. Most pieces were signed "Sasha Brastoff," though the earliest were signed "Sascha." Others included a rooster above his signature.

Vase. Dark-brown textured matte ground with bright orange enameled decorations in abstract style; signed "Sascha B" with R in a circle, and numbered; 20 inches high; mint condition; $200.

Ceramic Charger, c. 1950. Platinum glaze with whimsical figure in relief; marked front and back; 17 inches in diameter; $210.

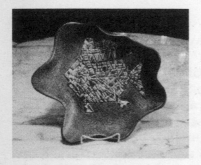

Ceramic Tray, by Sascha Brastoff, 1953. Signed with rooster and SASHA BRASTOFF on back, signed in front with block letter SASHA B; $35. *Courtesy of Decor Moderne.*

HEDI SCHOOP (1906–)

Like so many artists of her generation, Swiss-born Hedi Schoop and her husband fled from the Nazis in 1933 to the United States. With a varied background in the arts acquired in Vienna and Berlin, she began a new career in Hollywood making fashionable clothing for plaster of paris dolls in 1938. This led to the making of the ceramic giftware figurines for which she is best known. Her business was so successful that she soon employed other artists and added ashtrays, candle holders, animal figurines, and decorative plates to her line of products.

Her figurines could also be used as flower holders. The female subjects ranged from mermaids to fashionable debutantes. For years they were standard flea market fare, priced at just a few dollars. Another generation has rediscovered Schoop, along with other California potters, and today her pieces can be found at mall shows with prices beginning at $30. Some of her more unusual pieces have been sold at auction for more than $400.

Unfortunately there are many spin-offs mostly made in the 40s. Authentic pieces have several distinguishing marks. Among them are both stamped and incised versions of her signature. Sometimes the words "California" and "Hollywood, Cal." were added. When her plant was destroyed by fire in 1958 she didn't rebuild.

PRICES

Ceramic Sculpture Lamp. 14 inches high; $350.
Free-form Ashtray. "Swimming pool"; $28.

▓ BRITISH CERAMICS ▓

Due to the ravaging effects of World War II on every aspect of life in the United Kingdom, it wasn't till the early 1950s that the British ceramics industry and studio potters became involved in the Modern movement. Several artisans stand out. The most famous of all was Bernard Leach (1887–1979), who revived the tradition of hand-thrown pottery. He was the first British potter to combine philosophical and spiritual aspects into his creation of Japanese-influenced ceramics. Over his long career he created over 100,000 pieces. After World War II he was an important influence on Western ceramics. As a lecturer and traveler he personally influenced many young potters of the time. However, within the context of Modern design, he is considered a conservative.

Distinctly modern in her work, Lucie Rie was born in Vienna but moved to London in 1938. She greatly influenced the postwar generation. Sgraffito rims and monochrome glazes are characteristic of many of her bowls. As did many other studio potters, Rie also designed tableware.

Among the studio potters influenced by Rie was Hans Coper, who acted as her assistant in 1946. Coper's vessels were inspired by ancient Chinese bronzes. He achieved the texture of ancient patina by scraping the finished surfaces.

Two other important studio potters, Irwin Hoyland and Waistel Cooper, both adopted Ries's incised and Sgraffito techniques. Cooper's work also shows the influence of Coper.

American-born sculptor Mitzi Cunliffe changed the look of

commercial wares when she was hired to design new shapes for the Pilkington Tile and Pottery in Lancashire in the early 50s. The resulting bowls were in keeping with the Modern asymmetrical and free-form shapes popular at the time in the United States.

Staffordshire potters were slow to produce Modern tableware. However, that changed when Roy Midwinter, influenced by Eva Zeisel and Russel Wright designs, introduced his own version of Modern to his family firm of W. R. Midwinter. The first pattern was notably abstract and named Primavera. It and others that followed were successes for the firm. Soon other Staffordshire potteries, including Ridgway Potteries and Burgess and Leigh added Modern tableware designs to their lines.

Others outside of Staffordshire began using Modern designs. Among them was Poole Pottery. Its best-known line was called Twintone.

PRICES

Bottle Form Vase, designed by Hans Coper, c. 1956. $23,700.

Stoneware Vase, designed by Lucie Rie, c. 1960. White; $11,000.

▣ ITALIAN CERAMICS ▣

PRICES

Bowls

Bowl, designed by Guido Gambone, c. 1950s. Studio ceramic vessel with pushed-in thumbprints; abstract decoration in heavy salt-glazed blues, aquas, and eggplant; off-white background; signed "Gambone, Italy" with donkey; 3 inches high × 7 inches in diameter; mint condition; $500.

Bowl, designed by Guido Gambone, c. 1950. Free-form with colorful geometric decoration; red and blue; 9 inches wide × 9 inches deep; excellent condition; $180.

Bowl, designed by Guido Gambone, c. 1955. Simple wide-mouth vessel; base glazed in pale pink mottled with white; highly decorated with abstract geometric shapes in pale yellow outlined and dotted with brown; signed "GAMBONE/ITALY" with artist's mark; 12½ inches in diameter; $690.

Dishes/Plates

Charger, designed by Marcello Fantoni. Brown matte textured background with hi-glaze stylized jousters and horses in sgraffito; 11 inches square; mint condition; $325.

Ceramic Plate, designed by Piero Fornasetti, 1956. Decorated with implements; outlined in black against a white ground with gilded surround marked "Fornasetti Milano/6/Pasateria/1956/made in Italy"; 10 inches in diameter; $200.

Plate, designed by Fornasetti, Italy, late 1950s. Porcelain, musical series; $50.
Courtesy of Al and Kim Eiber Collection.

Archimboldesca Ceramic Plates (series of twelve), made in Milan, Italy. Each plate hand-decorated with polychrome vegetables creating unique faces; numbered 1–12; stamped mark; minor staining; 9½ inches in diameter; $1,320/set.

Ceramic Dish, designed by Guido Gambone. Free-form dish; off-white background; red, teal, and eggplant geometric decoration; 9 inches wide × 9 inches deep × 2 inches high; mint condition; $175.

Dish, designed by Guido Gambone. Flared triangular form; stylized gazelle decoration; brown and white background; image green and white; 5 inches wide × 6 inches deep × 2 inches high; mint condition; $80.

Lamps

Ceramic Lamp Base, designed by Marcello Fantoni. Four oval indentations, two with depiction of two men partially clothed in bright harlequin costumes; background spotty yellow; signed 8 inches wide × 15 inches high; mint condition; $750.

Ceramic Lamp Base, designed by Marcello Fantoni. Uneven shape with numerous indentations and pinch marks; raised decoration of sea horse, eels, and horse in blues, reds, yellows, and greens on a white ground; signed "Fantoni, Chantal"; 18 inches high; mint condition; $600.

Ceramic Lamp Base, designed by Guido Gambone, c. 1950s. Vibrant blue-and-teal figures and animals on white ground; crackled salt glaze; 19 inches high x 11 inches in diameter; mint condition; $1,000.

Glazed Ceramic Lamp Base, designed by Guido Gambone, c. 1950. Bulbous vessel decorated with stylized native warriors on either side in cobalt and turquoise-blue against a white crackled ground; signed in oxide "GAMBONE/ITALY" with trademark; 18½ inches high; $920.

Lamp Base, designed by Guido Gambone, Florence, c. 1950s. Mottled mauve and off-white Modern design; stylized mark "Gambone" pottery; 14½ inches high; $165.

Urns/Vases/Vessels

Vase, designed by Marcello Fantoni. Flattened shape with small opening; thick brown, yellow, and orange matte glaze; signed "Fantoni Italy for Raymor"; 9 inches wide × 10 inches high; mint condition; $275.

Vase, designed by Marcello Fantoni. Suspended yellow matte glaze on white background over orange, yellow, and brown matte, very colorful; 7 inches high; mint condition; $600.

Unique Ceramic Vase, designed by Marcello Fantoni, 1957. Flattened irregular vessel with boat-shaped neck in rough textured slip coated with coarse grog; decorated with stylized figures; signed "FANTONI/1957"; 45¼ inches high; $6,325.

Ceramic Vase, designed by Guido Gambone, c. 1950s. Freeform vessel with Cubist decoration in soft pastel turquoise, yellow, and green on off-white background; 7 inches wide × 12 inches high; mint condition; $650.

Vase, designed by Guido Gambone. Tall cylindrical flattened form with tapered neck; deep brown background with incised and painted white band of decoration around shoulder; signed "Gambone, Italy"; 20 inches high; mint condition; $300.

Ceramic Vase, designed by Guido Gambone. Modern design with irregular indentations and ribs; blue, red, and green raised decoration of fish and eel on yellow to white to red ground; signed; 7 inches high; mint condition; $250.

Glazed Ceramic Ewer, designed by Guido Gambone, c. 1950. Irregular hand-built bulbous vessel with geometric design in copper green under a thick matte white glaze; signed in oxide "GAMBONE/ITALY" with factory mark; 18⅝ inches high; $1,495.

Ceramic Vase, designed by Guido Gambone, c. 1955. Bulbous ovoid vessel with slender neck and slightly flaring lip; decorated with geometric shapes; in hot orange, pale yellow, marine blue, ocher, mint green, and black glaze; signed "GAMBONE/ITALY" with artist's mark; 13½ inches high; $2,012.

Ceramic Vase, designed by Fausto Melotti, c. 1955. Ovoid vessel with side canoe-form neck; pale pink glaze heightened with blue-gray hues; artist's mark on base; 11⅛ inches high; $920.

Figural Vase. Heavily textured glaze in off-white and blues with three circular cutouts creating three separate Picasso-style faces; label says "Made in Italy"; 8 inches high × 10 inches in diameter; mint condition; $170.

Seguso Vetri Vases (two), attributed to Flavio Poli. Heavy-walled ovoid vessels with split and pulled rim design; each of green glass cased to cobalt blue; unsigned; 9½ inches high and 9 inches high, respectively; $247/set.

Ceramic Vase. Enameling and applied leather; dark-brown stitched leather covering; Picasso-like figure of knight decorated with blue, red, and green enameling; 12 inches high; very good condition; $290.

Ceramic Vase. Medium-brown leather covering; Modern design with woman and goose in black, green, blue, red, pink, and yellow on ceramic face; 13 inches high; mint condition; $270.

Oversized Pepper Shaker, late 1950s. Pottery, multi colors, marked ITALY; 8 inches high; $70. *Courtesy of the author.*

San Polo Ceramic Vase. Individually decorated multicolored free-form shapes creating form; signed "O. Rosa Rito Indiand"; 15 inches wide x 10 inches high; mint condition; $900.

Miscellaneous

Ceramic Boxes (three-piece lot), designed by Guido Gambone, c. 1950s. Three uniquely different designs in the style of Paul Klee and Mondrian; all signed; 2 inches high x 4 inches in diameter; mint condition; $400–550.

Three Italian Pottery Items, designed by Guido Gambone. Horizontally striped white-brown-green bowl, 3¾ inches high; whimsical orange bottle with fish decor, 5 inches high; shallow bowl with mottled glaze and abstract green-and-white elements, 9¼ inches in diameter; each signed "Gambone Italy" with animal figure; $550.

Italian Pottery Box. Thick hi-gloss glaze in black; design of white horse with black and gray highlights; marked "W. C. & G. Italy #3206"; 2 inches high x 6 inches; mint condition; $35.

◼ SCANDINAVIAN CERAMICS ◼

ARABIA OY

Founded in Finland in 1873 as a subsidiary of the Swedish Rorstrand pottery, Arabia Oy became the country's most important pottery. By 1916 Finnish geometric designs had come into their own and the subsidiary was purchased by three Finnish businessmen. The firm again changed hands in 1924 and was German-owned until 1927, when it again became Finnish-owned. The company gained recognition in 1945 with the arrival of Kaj Franck as chief designer. By 1952 modern designs were used for dinnerware and artware. Some of the top artware names from that era are Kylikki Saimenhaara, known for distinctive glazes, and Taisto Kaasinen, known for his sculptural forms.

PRICES

Bowls

Decorated Bowl, designed by Bjorn Wiinblad, Denmark, 1953. Interior depicting a whimsical portrait in colors of turquoise, pink, and black on speckled white ground; signed; 3½ inches high × 14 inches in diameter; $250.

Urns/Vases/Vessels

Vase, manufactured by Gustavsberg Argenta Stoneware. Turquoise-green glaze with inlaid silver spray of flowers and ferns; marked and numbered "978 IS"; 5¾ inches high; $138.

Vase, manufactured by Gustavsberg Argenta Stoneware. Round cylinder with mottled turquoise glaze inlaid with silver horizontal stripes; 13 inches high; $660.

Ceramic Vases (two), designed by Rostrand, c. 1955. Bulbous form with tapered neck and everted lip, sage and mint-green glaze; elongated ovoid form with powder and sky-blue glaze speckled with brown; each signed "R/Sweden/HS", 9¾ inches high and 9⅞ inches high, respectively; $575/set.

Ceramic Vessels (two), designed by Rostrand, c. 1955. Bulbous vessel with narrow neck, gray and brown speckled glaze; narrow cylindrical vessel with broad flaring lip, mottled gray-and-blue glaze; each signed "R/Sweden/HS"; 7¾ inches high and 10 inches high, respectively; $1,150/set.

Glazed Porcelain Vases (two), designed by Friberg, c. 1950. Elongated bulbous bottle with flaring cylindrical neck, striated blue-and-gray glaze, inscribed "Friberg" with monogram; squat bottle form with narrow neck in mottled blue-and purple glaze, inscribed "Friberg" with monogram; 11⅜ inches high and 4⅞ inches high, respectively; $1,380/set.

Ceramic Vessels (three), designed by Saxbo, c. 1955. Bulbous form with narrow neck, pale yellow glaze; bulbous onion form, glazed in shades of brown; wide-mouthed vessel tapering at base, gray-brown glaze, the rim with mid-blue glaze; each signed "SAXBO/DENMARK"; numbered and with manufacturer's mark; 7 inches high, 6 inches high, and 5⅛ inches high, respectively; $805/set.

Bisque Pitcher, designer and ceramist Stig Lindenberg, manufactured by Gustavsberg Pottery, 1935–1940. Open pod shape; impressed mark; 5 inches high; $225.

Ceramic Vase, designed by Stig Lindenberg, Gustavsberg, Sweden. White glaze with blue and dark gray, hand-painted Scandinavian designs of ocean life, signed SWEDEN monogrammed; 6 inches high; $250. *Courtesy of Toomey-Treadway Galleries, Oak Park, IL.*

Miscellaneous

Glazed Ceramic Centerpiece, designed by Wilhelm Kage, c. 1950. Cast as a bottle and a bowl with intersecting flattened planes; matte white crackle glaze; unsigned; 12¾ inches high; $2,760.

Glazed Ceramic Plaque, designed by Karl Stalhane, c. 1950. Rectangular plaque with rounded corners; depicts stylized figures in the act of making pottery; glazed in shades of blue, green, and black; signed in glaze; 18 inches x 16¼ inches; $287.

Ceramic Wall Plaque, Finland, mid-twentieth century. Rectangular form depicting a school of fish in glossy glaze of deep purple and green on matte blue ground; marked with logo "Arabia, Made in Finland"; 14¼ inches long x 8 inches wide; $200.

Two Pottery Figures, Bjorn Wiinblad Studio. Pair of whimsical Danish ladies wearing long gowns with applied ceramic ruffles and broad-brimmed hats; blue-and-gray tin-glaze; fully signed and dated "1957–58"; one minor glaze chip on bow; 9½ inches high; $550/set.

Bowls

"Owl" Ceramic Bowl. Imprinted "Edition Picasso/Madoura" on reverse; 6 inches in diameter; $450.

Dishes/Plates

"Little Face No. 12 (A.R. 460)" Terre de Faience Plate, 1963. Partially glazed; painted in blue, yellow, black, and tan; numbered "93/150"; inscribed "No. 12, Edition Picasso" and "Madoura" on the reverse; incised inventory number on the reverse; 10 inches in diameter; good condition; $3,025.

Ceramic Charger, by Pablo Picasso, Jacqueline au Chevalet, c. 1956. Glazed in white, green, and black, numbered 164/200 on the verso, inscribed F.219, bearing the stamps MADOURA PLEIN FEU and EMPREINTE ORIGINALE DE PICASSO; 16¾ inches in diameter; $9,500. *Courtesy of Leslie Hindman Auctioneers.*

"Tete de Chevre" Ceramic Charger. Glazed in multicolors; numbered "35/100" and bearing the stamps "Madoura Plein Feu" and "Empreinte Originale de Picasso"; 16 inches in diameter; $7,500.

"Still Life (A.R. 219)" Terre de Faience Vase, 1953. Partially glazed; painted in green, brown, blue, and black; from the edition of 400; stamped "Edition Picasso" and "Madoura Plein Feu" on the reverse; 12 inches × 14¾ inches; good condition; $2,200.

Urns/Vases/Vessels

"Wood Owl with Spots (A.R. 120)" Terre de Faience Vase, 1953. Glazed; painted in black and brown; from the edition of 300; inscribed "Edition Picasso" and "Madoura" and stamped "Edition Picasso" and "Madoura Plein Feu" on the base; 11 inches × 9 inches; good condition; $1,760.

Square-Headed Terre de Faience Pitcher (A.R. 223), 1953. Partially glazed; painted in black; numbered "36/300" on the base; inscribed "Edition Picasso" and with "Edition Picasso" and "Madoura" pottery stamps on the base; 5½ inches high; good condition; $1,870.

"Bearded Man's Wife (A.R. 193)" Terre de Faience Pitcher. Partially glazed; painted in black, beige, green, and gray; from the edition of 500; inscribed on the base "To Erwin/Paloma Picasso" in metallic gold felt pen; "d'apres Picasso" and "Madoura Plein Feu" stamps on the base; "Made in France" ink stamp on the base; 14½ inches × 9½ inches; good condition; $3,850.

Earthenware Pitcher. 28 centimeters high; $9,000.

Miscellaneous

Earthenware Plaque. 8½ inches x 8½ inches; $2,500.

Tile, designed by Desimone. Abstract figures at a table with a fish; 13½ inches × 13½ inches; $375.

Tile, designed by Desimone. Abstract figure with a pineapple; 13½ inches × 13½ inches; $375.

Ceramic Tiles (set of six), designed by Salvador Dali. Signed; depicting life, death, love, music, war, peace; each 7½ inches × 7½ inches; $495/set.

Ceramic Tiles (set of six), by Salvador Dali, c. 1954. Individually decorated with starfish in motion, merging arrows, musical instruments, sun god, bird in flight, shellfish; 8 inches square; $500. *Courtesy of Skinner, Inc., Boston/Bolton, MA.*

Tiles (set of six), designed by Salvador Dali. Polychrome decorated pottery squares depicting arrows, starfish, eyes and lips, the sun, guitars, peace; impressed "Made in Spain JS"; 7¾ inches square; $770/set.

Ceramic Tiles (four), designed by Salvador Dali, c. 1954. Square; polychrome abstract designs; impressed and stamped marks; 7¾ inches wide; $165/set.

PRICES

Bowls

Bowl, designed by Hamada, Japan, mid-twentieth century. Wide mouth with spout; iron-pigmented organic forms against neutral ground; accompanied by receipt of purchase; 4½ inches high × 8¼ inches in diameter; $450.

Earthenware Bottle, Shoji Hamada, Japan, c. 1955. Shades of brown, highlighted with cobalt blue, unsigned; 7¾ inches high; $770. *Courtesy of Skinner, Inc., Boston/Bolton, MA.*

Dishes/Plates

Austrian Chargers (set of three), designed by Anzengruber, c. 1940s. Wall plates, studio ceramics with abstract underwater scenes, matte black background; hi-glaze; white relief decoration; 15 inches in diameter; mint condition; $1,400/set.

Urns/Vases/Vessels

Cuban Ceramic Vase, attribution. Black and white stripes in geometric design against a light-green ground; painted mark "C.A.C. Habana" and "#592/A"; 12 inches high; mint condition; $95.

Vase, designed by Gilbert Portanier. Black matte terra-cotta front with hi-glaze white and green feathered shield decoration; footed base; back and top hi-glaze chartreuse; signed "Decor E'au main Portanier Edition Vallauris"; 17 inches wide × 4 inches deep × 12 inches high; mint condition; $300.

Miscellaneous

Two Pieces of Art Pottery, mid-twentieth century. Floor vase, pinched form with abstract patchwork in glaze colors of lavender, turquoise, green, and white on brown ground; bowl with painted rib decoration in black on white ground with orange spherical accents, interior glaze in yellow with green rim, painted and incised "gB" and "Hungary," some crazing interior of bowl; 18½ inches high and 5¾ inches high, respectively; $175/set.

Faceted Pottery Bottle, designed by Hamada, Japan, mid-twentieth century. Iron-pigmented brown glaze; 10 inches high; $175.

You could say that American designer George Nelson changed the faces of wall clocks. Maybe they weren't what you'd expect a clock to look like, but they did keep time ... and many still do. They were first designed and produced in 1947 by Howard Miller Clock Company (Zeeland, Michigan), and at that time their lack of a traditional clock face was considered a radical, modern departure. The hands moved against the background of a wall. They didn't require numbers since time could be told by the positions of the hands on the balls, spheres, or whichever twelve representational forms were mounted on the wall. Nelson designed an entire series of these clocks from 1947 to the late 1950s. His Ball and Asterisk wall clocks are thought to have been inspired by Alexander Calder's sculpture of the 1930s and 1940s.

Clocks

Wall Clock, designed by George Nelson, manufactured by Herman Miller Furniture Company. Starburst design, metal and wood; $250. *Courtesy of Decor Moderne.*

Atom Clock, designed by George Nelson, manufactured by Howard Miller. Circular dial with twelve radiating arms terminating in red spheres; signed with manufacturer's decal; 13½ inches in diameter; $250.

Ball Clock, designed by George Nelson, manufactured by Howard Miller, c. 1950s. Original orange-painted birch, steel, brass; plugs directly into wall socket; 3 inches high × 14 inches in diameter; excellent condition; $350.

Desk Clock, designed by George Nelson, manufactured by Howard Miller, c. 1950. Walnut ball form with circular brass base; black clock face has stylized hands and numbers; 7 inches high × 6 inches in diameter; excellent condition; $500.

Wall Clock, designed by George Nelson, manufactured by Howard Miller, c. 1950s. Opaque glass with undulating black filigree appliqué around brass face; black hands and brass dots as hour markers; 18 inches in diameter × 2½ inches deep; very good condition; $475.

Asterisk Wall Clock, designed by George Nelson, manufactured by Howard Miller, c. 1950. Orange zinc-plated steel body with black hands; 10 inches in diameter × 2 inches deep; excellent condition; $350.

Ball Wall Clock, designed by George Nelson, manufactured by Howard Miller, c. 1947. Multicolored painted birch balls with brass arms and painted steel face and hands; 14 inches in diameter × 2½ inches deep; excellent condition; $350.

Giant Sunburst Clock, designed by George Nelson, manufactured by Howard Miller. Black-lacquered tapered spokes and hands with orange-and-gray tips; brass face; very rare; 30 inches in diameter × 3 inches deep; excellent condition; $325.

Sunflower Clock, designed by George Nelson, manufactured by Howard Miller. Dramatic woven molded plywood form in walnut with birch and black metal face; stylized white enamel hands, red second hand, and circular brass numbers; 28 inches in diameter × 2 inches deep; excellent condition; $500.

Chromed and Painted Metal Clock, designed by George Nelson, manufactured by Howard Miller, c. 1955. Composed of twelve chromed metal rods around a black-painted circular clockworks; impressed factory marks and numbers; original paper label; 24 inches in diameter; $690.

Chromed Metal and Glass Alarm Clock, designed by Gilbert Rohde, c. 1955. Clock face with simple black dots denoting numerals; enclosed by a circular wooden frame with a simple rectangular foot supported by a chromed metal side bracket; wood stamped "404 B."; 8⅛ inches long; $3,680.

A practicing designer and lecturer at the Harrington Institute of Interior Design in Chicago, Illinois, Jerryll Habegger has written about Modern flatware as well as Modern furniture, architecture, plastic dinnerware, and the Modern door lever handle. He has been responsible for the interior design concepts of some of Chicago's most important buildings. His work is also featured in important European buildings. He is a professional affiliate of the Institute of Business Designers.

The pleasures found in collecting Modern flatware are based in an understanding of silver and stainless steel as materials. Stainless steel's hard nature makes it a difficult material to work, resulting in simpler designs. The totally three-dimensional Rosebud ornament of traditional silver patterns would be impossible to imprint into this tougher steel. Silver is a more malleable material, thus designs in silver can be more totally three-dimensional, that is to say, with undercuts that are executed by hand, not machine.

Beauty is found in the plain simplicity of Modern flatware. The plain object requires a far greater degree of skill in designing and fabrica-

Flatware

by
Jerryll Habegger

83

ting than the ornate object as ornate complexity hides all manner of defects.

Desirable qualities in Modern flatware include a strong visual expression, a heavier physical weight, and quality workmanship. Modern detailing achieves ornament through the modeling of the basic form. In the manufacturing process, hot stainless steel bars are beaten (forged) into a die by a drop hammer, to change both their form and the thickness of a section. Variations in the material's thickness contribute to a strong expression and a heavier visual weight. On fine-quality pieces, over fifty percent of the operations for manufacturing and the achieving of a fine finish are done by hand.

▓ CHARACTERISTICS OF MODERN FLATWARE

Modern eating habits have resulted in food that is smaller in size and softer in consistency. In turn, knife blades have become smaller, with a greater curve. The shorter tines of the fork fit the smaller food quantities and the smaller eliptically shaped bowl of the spoon passes easily into the mouth. In many flatware patterns, all of the utensils are of the same length and are balanced for good weight distribution in the hand. Another characteristic of modern flatware is the one-piece (non-hollow) handle. It is often given greater width at the center for a better grip. Additionally, the handles on some of the patterns allow for easy stacking.

COMPOSITION OF SILVER AND STAINLESS STEEL FLATWARE

Sterling silver, the most expensive material used in flatware design, is 925 parts silver, 75 parts copper, and is marked "925" or "Sterling." Silver, slightly less expensive, is 800 parts pure silver, 200 parts copper, and is marked "800" or "Silver." Silver plate flatware is 90 grams of silver over alpaca (copper, zinc, and nickel alloy), and is marked "Plated." Stainless steel, the most reasonably priced of these materials, is 74 percent iron, 18 percent chromium, 8 percent nickel, and is marked "18/8" or "18/10."

Always keep the various metal types apart from each other. In the presence of moisture, the stronger metal alloys will corrode the weaker alloys. Corrosion may also occur with exposure to the following solutions: well water with a high iron content; oxalic acid found in rhubarb; and acids found in mustard, vinegar, lemon juice, and salt.

DISCERNING QUALITY PIECES OVER IMITATIONS

If a particular flatware has been fabricated in the country of its origin, it is generally considered to be of higher quality than pieces fabricated elsewhere. The following listing of manufacturers can be used as the basis for developing a quality collection.

Denmark
Dansk
Georg Jensen
Hans Hansen

Finland
Hackman
Kultakeskus

France
Chabanne

Germany
Mono
Pott
Rosenthal
WMF

Great Britain
Mellor
Oneida

Italy
Alessi
ICM
Mepra
Sabattini
Sambonet
Zani + Zani

Norway
Norsk Stalpress

Sweden
Gense

USA
International Silver
Lauffer
Reed + Barton
Retroneau
Towle

Japan
COM
Hull
Sasaki
Yamazaki

▨ POPULAR FLATWARE PATTERNS DESIGNED DURING THE 1940S AND 1950S

STAINLESS STEEL

By the late 1940s, stainless steel was accepted as the appropriate material for Modern flatware. Due to the scarcity of metals during World War II, very few designs were developed and only one pattern stands out as significant. It is the 2720 pattern designed by Paul Voss in 1948 for Pott. This transitional pattern is smaller and more compact than traditional flatware. It is still in production today. The following listings show retail prices for 2720.

Large teaspoon	$16
Dinner fork	$20
Dinner knife	$34
Butter knife	$32
Salad fork	$22
Dessert spoon	$20

Flatware, Pattern 2720, designed by Paul Voss, manufactured by Pott, 1948. Stainless steel, three pieces. *Courtesy of Jerryll Habegger Collection.*

The Highlight pattern, designed in 1952 by Russel Wright, established sculptural ideas as the basis for quality stainless flatware designed after World War II. The knife is pinched at the neck and the organically shaped open handle is contoured to fit the hand. All pieces are signed with the designer's name in script. This place setting is very rare and out of production.

Large teaspoon	$40
Dinner fork	$40
Dinner knife	$50
Butter knife	$50
Salad fork	$40
Dessert spoon	$40

Flatware, Pattern Highlight, designed by Russel Wright, c. 1952. Stainless steel, three pieces. *Courtesy of Jerryll Habegger Collection.*

Design I, 2721 was designed by Don Wallance in 1953 for Lauffer and is today manufactured by Pott. Wallance was the predominant American designer of sculptural flatware in the 1950s. The handles of the fork and spoon are concave, thus easily stacked. The one-piece knife has a very graceful curve.

Deutsche Lufthansa utilized this pattern for its in-flight service during the 1950s. This pattern is still in production.

Large teaspoon	$16
Dinner fork	$20
Dinner knife	$34
Butter knife	$32
Salad fork	$20
Dessert spoon	$18

Flatware, Pattern Design I (2721), designed by Don Wallance for Pott, c. 1950. Stainless steel, three pieces. *Courtesy of Jerryll Habegger Collection.*

The Ponti pattern was designed by Gio Ponti in 1954 for Krupp Italiana. Ponti searched for a design of perfect form; the dimensions of all the handles are of the same length as are the bowls and blades. The pattern is rare and out of production.

Large teaspoon	$20
Dinner fork	$20
Dinner knife	$20
Butter knife	$22
Salad fork	$18
Dessert spoon	$15

 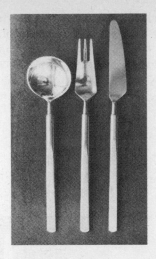

Flatware, Pattern Ponti, designed by Gio Ponti for Krupp Italiana, 1954, Stainless steel, three pieces. *Courtesy of Jerryll Habegger Collection.*

Flatware, Pattern Obelisk, designed by Eric Herlow, manufactured by Universal Steel, c. 1954. Stainless steel, three pieces. *Courtesy of Jerryll Habegger Collection.*

The Obelisk pattern was designed by Eric Herlow in 1954 for Universal Steel. All pieces of this pattern are produced from single pieces of rectangular stainless bar stock. The handles are matte in finish for easier maintenance, whereas the bowls and the blades are highly polished. This pattern is rare and out of production.

Large teaspoon	$15
Dinner fork	$15
Dinner knife	$15
Butter knife	$18
Salad fork	$16
Dessert spoon	$10

The Focus pattern was designed by Folke Arstrom in 1955 for Gense. The shapes are elongated, as seen in the blade of the knife, which flows smoothly into the shape of the tapered handle. Focus Deluxe of 1956 has a black nylon handle. This pattern is rare and out of production.

Large teaspoon	$15
Dinner fork	$15
Dinner knife	$15
Butter knife	$18
Salad fork	$16
Dessert spoon	$10

Flatware, Pattern Focus, designed by Folke Arstrom, manufactured by Gense Manufacturers, c. 1955. Stainless steel, three pieces. *Courtesy of Jerryll Habegger Collection.*

The 7000 pattern was designed around 1955 for Amboss. The pieces are of a wide proportion and are highly sculptural with deep concave voids. The knife handle is a full pistol grip type. This pattern is very rare and is out of production.

Large teaspoon	$20
Dinner fork	$20
Dinner knife	$20
Butter knife	$22
Salad fork	$18
Dessert spoon	$15

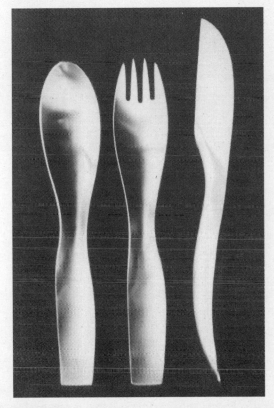

Flatware, Pattern 7000, manufactured by Amboss, c. 1955. Stainless steel, three pieces. *Courtesy of Jerryll Habegger Collection.*

The AJ pattern was designed by Arne Jacobsen in 1957 for Georg Jensen. Jacobsen was a master of the careful articulation of pure naked form. He reduced the knife, fork, and spoon to primary shapes of great abstract simplicity. This pattern is still in production.

Large teaspoon	$13
Dinner fork	$16
Dinner knife	$16
Butter knife	$14
Salad fork	$15
Dessert spoon	$15

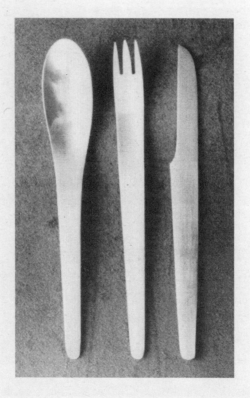

Flatware, Pattern AJ, designed by Arne Jacobsen for Georg Jensen, c. 1957. Stainless steel, three pieces. *Courtesy of Jerryll Habegger Collection.*

The Jet Line pattern was designed by Sigurd Persson in 1959 for KF (Kooperative Forderbund). It is small in scale and utilizes soft shapes. The now-classic knife form is the dominant element of the set. This pattern is rare and out of production.

Large teaspoon	$5
Dinner fork	$5
Dinner knife	$5

Flatware, Pattern Jet Line, designed by Sigurd Persson, manufactured by Kooperative Forderbund, c. 1959. Stainless steel, three pieces. *Courtesy of Jerryll Habegger Collection.*

The Caravel pattern was designed by Henning Koppel in 1957 for Georg Jensen. Caravel is the most convincingly unified set of flatware produced in modern times. The top surfaces of the handle run along the edge of the spoon and fork bowl. Thus the bowls appear as clear vessels. The pieces are heavy with handles of varying thicknesses. This stainless steel pattern is still in production.

Large teaspoon	$24
Dinner fork	$30
Dinner knife	$45
Butter knife	$33
Salad fork	$27
Dessert spoon	$28

Flatware, Caravel Pattern, designed by Henning Koppel for Georg Jensen. Stainless steel, three pieces. *Courtesy of Jerryll Habegger Collection.*

STERLING SILVER

Koppel also produced Georg Jensen's Caravel pattern in sterling silver, but it is no longer in production.

Large teaspoon	$185
Dinner fork	$260
Dinner knife	$240
Butter knife	$245
Salad fork	$260
Dessert spoon	$230

The 86 pattern was designed by Josef Hoffmann in 1954 in sterling silver for Pott. Hoffmann felt that all utensils should be of a uniform length. The organic shapes of the spoon bowl and the knife blade are serene abstractions of plant forms. The tines of the fork undulate to prevent peas from falling off. The contrasting tapered handle has an elliptical sphere at the end. This pattern is still in production.

Large teaspoon	$100
Dinner fork	$190
Dinner knife	$140
Butter knife	$120
Salad fork	$190
Dessert spoon	$150

SILVER PLATE

The TWA pattern of 1950 is typical of quality silver-plated flatware used during the 1950s for airline in-flight service. The pieces are typically smaller in scale and have soft forms. This pattern is out of production.

Large teaspoon	$4
Dinner fork	$4
Dinner knife	$4

Flatware, 86 Pattern, designed by Josef Hoffman, manufactured by Pott, c. 1954. Sterling silver, three pieces. *Courtesy of Jerryll Habegger Collection.*

Flatware, TWA Pattern, manufactured by International Silver, c. 1950s. Silver plate, three pieces. *Courtesy of Jerryll Habegger Collection.*

Writing about both American and international designers can be a confusing process. The problem arises when trying to create a listing with a properly organized sequence. Many designers worked not only in their own studios but for other manufacturers as well. To add to the confusion, they were a creative lot who often designed in other media, from glass to metals. In an effort to make this listing as straightforward as possible, what follows is an alphabetical listing of manufacturers' and designers' names. When a designer created a piece for a particular manufacturer, the piece is listed under the manufacturer's name. If a piece was created independently it is listed under the designer's name.

Because many of these designers, such as Charles Eames and Jens Risom, were so prolific, it has been difficult to condense their backgrounds in the small space allotted. A bibliography in the back of the book offers further information.

This is also true for architect Frank Lloyd Wright, who has been written about extensively. His work included in this book is furniture designed for mass (though relatively small) production.

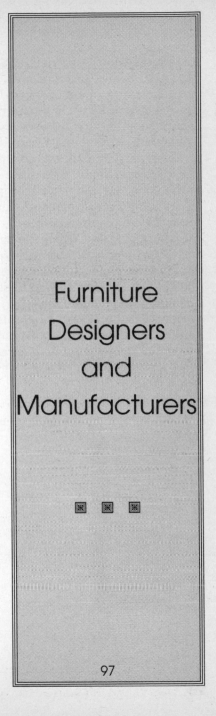

Furniture Designers and Manufacturers

ARIETO (HARRY) BERTOIA (1915-1978)
(SEE ALSO KNOLL ASSOCIATES)

Like many designers who began working in the late 30s, Bertoia selected one medium for his work, metal, and adapted it to furniture, jewelry, hollowware, and art. Born in Italy, he came to America in 1930 and received a scholarship to the Cranbrook Academy of Art. This was an important influence on the direction his work would take, since at the time the school was combining the new industrial designs with the philosophy of the Arts and Crafts movement. While there, Bertoia began teaching metalcraft and producing some of his own designs using the Streamlined style. When the metal shortages of World War II closed the metalcraft department, he was moved to the graphics department. During the 1940s he began creating monoprints, at first in the manner of Kandinsky and Klee; later his work became completely abstract.

In 1943 he moved to California and began working with Charles and Ray Eames. Bertoia, whose primary interest was metal (including its use in furniture design), left the Eameses after a short period to work on his new concept of metal wire furniture.

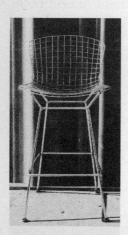

Bar Stool, by Harry Bertoia, manufactured by Knoll Associates, 1952. Chrome; 41¼ inches high x 21¾ inches deep x 21¾ inches wide; $175. *Courtesy of Skank World, Los Angeles, CA.*

It was Knoll Associates, of Pennsylvania, who produced his Diamond chair, in 1953. Bertoia described it, and his other metal wire furniture, as "functional sculpture." The Diamond armchair, model 421–1, is still being made. The original models were made by hand. Early labels were printed in black on paper, were attached to the cushion, and read: "KNOLL/KNOLL ASSOCIATES INC/320 PARK AVE. N.Y." (a stylized K printed in red).

In spite of the success of his furniture designs, Bertoia expressed his disdain in the November 1965 issue of *Interiors:* "Furniture is nothing to me—it was a means of eating."

PRICES

Benches
Slat Bench. Rectangular wooden slat top; upholstered cushion; set on painted welded steel rod base; $375.

Chairs/Lounges/Stools
Armchairs (pair). Vinyl-upholstered back, seat, and arms; set on laminated wooden legs; $40.

Side Chairs (set of four). Molded lacquered fiberglass back; upholstered seat; set on steel legs; $250.

DUNBAR FURNITURE CORPORATION OF INDIANA
Founded in 1919, this furniture company came to prominence when furniture designer Edward J. Wormley joined them in 1931. Early designs were Traditional, until Wormley introduced works influenced by Swedish Modern. By the end of the 1930s the company manufactured both Traditional and Modern pieces. By 1957 the company had introduced its largest line: the 150-piece Janus Collection. While the designs are for the most part conservative, they concentrated on fine craftsmanship and materials. Many of the older Wormley designs are still being made.

Chairs/Lounges/Stools

Upholstered Laminated-Wood and Metal Chaise Longue, designed by Edward Wormley, c. 1948. Curved channel upholstered seat and back raised on laminated wood legs; conjoined by circular rods and an X-form tension cable; metal manufacturer's tag; 6 feet 3 inches long; $5,175.

Sideboards/Buffets

Janus Sideboard and Superstructure, designed by Edward Wormley, 1957. Black faux marble drop-in top over four cabinet doors with inlaid panels and single long drawer below; superstructure made up of four cabinet doors, each mounted with two unique Japanese carved woodblocks, and four short drawers below; manufacturer's pamphlet included; 77½ inches high × 66 inches wide × 20¼ inches deep; $3,025.

Tables/Stands

Coffee Table, designed by Edward Wormley, c. 1950s. Rectangular walnut top with molded plywood; original finish; 71 inches × 19 inches × 13 inches; good condition; $100.

CHARLES EAMES (1907–1978)
RAY KAISER EAMES (1913–1988)
(SEE ALSO EVANS PRODUCTS COMPANY
AND HERMAN MILLER FURNITURE COMPANY)

Both Charles Eames and his wife, Ray, are important to modern American design. Their career work included not only furniture but also architecture, interior design, filmmaking, and exhibition design. Charles Eames first studied architecture at Washington University in Saint Louis, Missouri. He was awarded a fellowship to study architecture and design in 1938 at Cranbrook Academy of Art in Bloomfield Hills, Michigan. His friendship with faculty member Eero Saarinen led to a joint project on modular furniture. Their molded plywood chair won them two first prizes in a competition, sponsored by the Museum of Modern Art, called "Organic Design in Home Furnishings." Ray Kaiser, a sculptor and artist, who assisted in the project, shortly became Eames's wife. They became lifelong collaborators. In 1946, the Eameses exhibited in a major show devoted to their work at the Museum of Modern Art. A series beginning in 1949 introduced their furnishings in molded polyester and, in 1958, aluminum. Their classic lounge chair and ottoman of aluminum, rosewood, and leather was exhibited in the U.S. in 1958. During their long careers they produced some fifty films on a variety of subjects from toys to history.

PRICES

Chairs/Lounges/Stools

Laminated Plywood Prototype Chair Frame, design attributed to Charles Eames and Eero Saarinen, c. 1950. Curvilinear laminated plywood seat frame and base; two separate parts; 35 inches high × 21 inches wide; $220.

Storage Unit, by Charles and Ray Eames for Herman Miller Furniture Company, c. 1949. Zinc-plated steel, birch-faced plywood, plastic coated plywood and lacquered masonite, unmarked; 58⅝ inches x 47 inches x 16¾ inches; $13,200. *Courtesy of Treadway Gallery, OH.*

Molded Plywood Child's Chair, designed c. 1945. T-shaped back with heart-shaped cutout conjoined to a molded seat raised on four tapering legs; $6,900.

Plastic, Wire, and Wood "Eiffel Tower" Rocking Chair, c. 1951. Molded fiberglass reinforced plastic shell seat raised on a metal base supported by wooden rockers; retains original paper label; $460.

Plastic and Wire Classic Armchair, c. 1950–1953. Molded fiberglass reinforced plastic shell seat raised on a metal "Eiffel Tower" base; retains original paper label; $460.

Rocker, c. 1956. Black bikini upholstery on black metal cage seat; wooden rockers; 19 inches wide × 24 inches deep × 29 inches high; excellent condition; $500.

Steel, Wood, and Leather Wire Mesh Side Chairs (pair), designed c. 1951–1953. Each wire mesh shell seat raised on four tapering legs conjoined by X-form wire stretcher; brown leather seat pads; one retains original manufacturer's label; $1,150/set.

Wire and Upholstered "Eiffel Tower" Chair, c. 1952. Wire mesh back and seat supported by "Eiffel Tower" base; upholstered in woven blue fabric; retains original label; $1,150.

Sofas

Rare Eames Wire Sofa (one of four examples known to exist, two of which are in the Vitra Museum, Germany), designed in 1951. Button-tufted three-section cushion supported by a wire frame raised on strutlike supports and four shaped wooden feet; 6 feet 2 inches long; $31,050.

Storage Units

Plywood and Chromed Metal Storage Unit, c. 1952. Rectangular top raised on angled supports above a lower shelf and raised on tubular legs; 20¼ inches high × 24 inches long × 16 inches wide; $1,840.

Tables/Stands

Molded Plywood Child's Table, c. 1945. Molded rectangular top continuing to tapering legs; 16½ inches high × 26½ inches long × 15½ inches wide; $4,600.

Molded Plywood Coffee Table, c. 1946. Dished circular top raised on molded legs; ebonized; 15¼ inches high × 34½ inches in diameter; $460.

Miscellaneous

Molded Plywood Leg Splints (two). Each stamped "S2-1790"; 42 inches long; $805/set.

Molded Plywood Division, Evans Products Company

In November 1942 in West Los Angeles, Charles and Ray Eames and three colleagues established what was then called the Plyformed Wood Company. They began making molded wood splints for the military and worked on developing other molded plywood products. Because of cash flow problems, they sought additional backing from Evans Products Company in 1943. This Detroit-based supplier of wood products and owner of fir wood forests agreed to help finance the Eames venture, and the company was renamed the Molded Plywood Division, a subsidiary of Evans Products Company. The patents for products developed were held by the parent company. In the fall of 1945 models of molded tables, chairs, and a storage system were introduced and then marketed and distributed by Evans Products. The furniture was shown in February 1946 at the Architectural League of New York. In March of the same year it appeared in a major exhibit of the Eameses' work at the Museum of Modern Art. In October 1946 the Herman Miller Company of Zeeland, Michigan, acquired exclusive rights to market and distribute the plywood furniture.

PRICES

Chairs/Lounges/Stools

"DCW's" (set of four), designed by Charles Eames. Laminated, molded plywood dining chairs; ash veneer with exotic swirled wood grain pattern; early Evans label; extremely rare matched set; minor veneer nicks on edges of two chairs; 20 inches wide × 21 inches deep × 29 inches high; very good condition; $2,000/set.

"DCW's" (four separate chairs), designed by Charles Eames. Seat and back in original red aniline dye; legs and spine original black aniline dye; revarnished years ago; early Evans label; 20 inches wide × 21 inches deep × 29 inches high; excellent condition; $400–$950.

Laminated Molded Plywood "LCW" Chair, designed by Charles Eames, c. 1946. Molded seat and back raised on molded legs; retains early paper label; $1,610.

Laminated Molded Plywood "LCW" Chair, designed by Charles Eames, c. 1946. Molded seat and back raised on molded legs; $690.

Laminated Molded Plywood "LCW" Chair, designed by Charles Eames, c. 1946. Molded seat and back raised on molded legs; retains early paper label; $1,610.

Laminated Molded Plywood "LCW" Chair, designed 1946. Molded back and seat raised by molded legs and back support; $2,415.

Molded Laminated Plywood "LCW" Chairs (pair), designed c. 1946. Molded seat and back raised on molded legs; $2,760/set.

"LCW," designed by Charles Eames. Seat and back of molded ash plywood with exotic wood grain; spine and legs original black aniline dye; revarnished years ago; early Evans label; 22 inches wide × 19 inches deep × 26 inches high; excellent condition; $750.

Plywood and Chromed Steel "DCM" Chair, designed by Charles Eames, c. 1947. Molded seat and back supported by a chromed steel frame; original decal label; $1,150.

Tables/Stands

Cocktail Table, c. 1945. Molded plywood dish top with four molded plywood legs; revarnished original birch finish; early Evans label; 15 inches high × 35 inches in diameter; very good condition; $950.

Experimental Dinette Table. Laminated, molded plywood table; influenced, if not executed, by Charles Eames; birch veneer top; chrome-plated paper clip legs; never produced (from collection of an Evans employee who received it as a gift from Charles Eames); 42 inches wide × 28 inches high × 30 inches deep; minor crazing to top; very good condition; $800.

Miscellaneous

Folding Screen, c. 1946. Six panels of laminated molded plywood connected with canvas webbing; original ash finish; 61 inches wide × 68 inches high; minor chip reglued in bottom corner; very good condition; $6,500.

Plywood Traction Leg Splint, designed by Charles and Ray Eames, c. 1941. Following the shape of the foreleg with holes to attach around the leg; branded "S2-1790"; 42½ inches long; $165.

Paul Theodore Frankl (1878–1962)

Though Paul Frankl primarily achieved recognition as a modernist, shortly after coming to America from his native Austria in 1914, his work carried over to the Modern postwar years. His pieces in the 1920s and 1930s were influenced by the New York skyscrapers. His furniture designs of that era are high-priced, selling for thousands of dollars. However, his pieces designed in the 1940s for the Johnson Furniture Company are much more reasonable and sell at auction for high hundreds to over a thousand dollars.

<hr>

Tables/Stands

Cocktail Table, manufactured by Johnson Furniture Company. Organic-shaped top of cork over molded plywood; refinished top; 48 inches wide × 36 inches deep × 14 inches high; very good condition; $900.

Corktop Dining Table, manufactured by Johnson Furniture Company, c. 1940. Rectangular top on mahogany slated base with two leaves; 29 inches high × 42 inches wide × 70 inches deep; $800.

Side Tables (pair), manufactured by Johnson Furniture Company. Rounded triangular cork tops; legs and molded magazine shelf in mahogany finish; refinished tops; 28 inches wide × 23 inches high × 16 inches deep; very good condition; $350/set.

Miscellaneous

Dining Room Set, manufactured by Johnson Furniture Company. Elegant set in rich mahogany with almond lacquered cork tops; dining table with bentwood supports, center pedestal, and three leaves; seven-drawer, two-door buffet with brass X-shaped pulls and recessed platform base; six-drawer two-door china cabinet with brass X-shaped pulls; modular china hutch with cork front and glass shelves; two bentwood armchairs with V-shaped cut-out backs in original lavender-and-celadon silk brocade, optical disk pattern; four matching side chairs with crisscrossed mahogany backs in matching fabric; table 29 inches high × 42 inches deep × 70 inches wide without leaves; buffet 32 inches high × 20 inches deep × 70 inches wide; china cabinet 71 inches high × 23 inches deep × 48 inches wide; armchairs 31 inches high × 27 inches deep × 25 inches wide; side chairs 31 inches high × 21 inches deep × 20 inches wide; excellent condition; $1,800/set.

<hr>

The Herman Miller Company has been known since the 1940s as one of the leading manufacturers of Modern furniture in the United States. Under the direction of design consultant George Nelson (discussed on p. 125 and in the clocks chapter), beginning in 1946 the company concentrated on producing Modern designs from such leading designers as Isamu Noguchi and Charles and Ray Eames.

PRICES

Benches

Platform Bench, designed by George Nelson. Multifunctional bench with slat top in primavera finish with black ebonized base; original finish; 48 inches long × 19 inches deep × 14 inches high; excellent condition; $750.

Platform Bench, designed by George Nelson. Multifunctional bench with slat top in primavera finish with black ebonized base; original finish with label; 56 inches long × 19 inches deep × 14 inches high; excellent condition; $1,100.

Cabinets

Cabinet, designed by George Nelson. Primavera finish with black lacquered door and legs; lacquered wood and aluminum pull; Herman Miller label; back drilled to house turntable; 24 inches wide × 18 inches deep × 29 inches high; very good condition; $500.

Four-Drawer Cabinet, designed by George Nelson. Primavera finish; black ebonized legs; turned chrome-plated steel pulls; 34 inches wide × 18 inches deep × 30 inches high; very good condition; $600.

Four-Drawer Cabinet, designed by George Nelson. Primavera finish; sculptural molded chrome-plated handles; black lacquered wood legs; 34 inches wide × 19 inches deep × 29 inches high; excellent condition; $600.

Thin Edge Cabinet, designed by George Nelson. Reminiscent of the miniature jewelry chest with its elegant slender lines, tapered steel legs, and black golf-tee-shaped pulls; 34 inches wide × 19 inches deep × 33 inches high; excellent condition; $750.

Three-Drawer Cabinet, designed by George Nelson. Primavera finish; sculptural molded chrome-plated handles; black lacquered wood legs; 34 inches wide × 19 inches deep × 29 inches high; excellent condition; $600.

Chairs/Lounges/Stools

Red "DCW," designed by Charles Eames, c. 1946. Molded plywood dining chair in original aniline dye finish; 20 inches wide × 21 inches deep × 29 inches high; very good condition; $650.

"DCW," designed by Charles Eames, c. 1946. Molded plywood dining chair in original walnut; early Evans label; 20 inches wide × 21 inches deep × 29 inches high; excellent condition; $475.

"DCWs" (pair), designed by Charles Eames, c. 1946. Molded plywood dining chairs in original red aniline dye finish; 20 inches wide × 21 inches deep × 29 inches high; excellent condition; $1,500/set.

"DCW," designed by Charles Eames, c. 1946. Molded plywood dining chair in original birch finish; early Evans label; 20 inches wide × 21 inches deep × 29 inches high; excellent condition; $450.

Molded Plywood Dining Chairs (pair), designed by Charles Eames. Molded ash plywood back and seat on frame; original black stain; seat 18 inches high; $700/set.

Dining Chairs (set of four), designed by George Nelson, c. 1950s. Simple architectural black lacquered frame with bright blue original wool; 17 inches wide × 17 inches deep × 29 inches high; very good condition; $260/set.

"LCW" Black Lacquered Plywood Chair, designed by Charles and Ray Eames, c. 1945. Assembled from five separately finished elements; curved legs supporting a wide seat, a curved element joining them to the back; 26½ inches high × 21¾ inches wide × 22 inches deep; $660.

"Low Rod Base Lounge" Chair, designed by Charles Eames. Orange fiberglass armchair with black wire "cradle" base; Herman Miller label; 24 inches wide × 24 inches deep × 24 inches high; very good condition; $250.

"LCW," designed by Charles Eames. Molded plywood lounge chair in original black aniline dye; early Evans label; 22 inches wide × 22 inches deep × 26 inches high; normal wear, minor scratches; very good condition; $600.

Lounge Chair and Ottoman, designed by Charles Eames. Black leather cushions joined to three molded rosewood shells mounted on a cast-aluminum, five-pronged base; a classic Eames design; chair 34 inches wide × 28 inches deep × 33 inches high; ottoman 26 inches wide × 24 inches deep × 16 inches high; excellent condition; $2,300/set.

Lounge Chair, designed by Charles Eames. "Cradle" base; charcoal fiberglass shell with black leather; black wire base; original finish; 24 inches wide × 24 inches deep × 24 inches high; excellent condition; $650.

"LCW," designed by Charles Eames, c. 1945. Molded plywood lounge chair in original black aniline dye; early Evans label; 22 inches wide × 22 inches deep × 26 inches high; very good condition; $650.

"RAR" Fiberglass Metal and Wood Rocking Chair, designed by Charles and Ray Eames, c. 1950. Red fiberglass shell on a wire metal base supported by two curved birch runners; company's paper label; 27 inches high × 24⅞ inches wide × 27 inches deep; $440.

RAR Rocking Chair, designed by Charles and Ray Eames for Herman Miller Furniture Company, c. 1950. Gray-blue fiberglass shell on wire base with curved birch rockers, impressed marks and paper label; 28 inches high x 25 inches wide; $351. *Courtesy of Skinner Inc., Boston/Bolton, MA.*

Rocker, designed by Charles Eames. Charcoal fiberglass seats; beige upholstery; steel base; blonde runners; 25 inches wide × 17 inches deep × 26 inches high; excellent condition; $450.

"LCW" Black Lacquered Plywood Chair, designed by Charles and Ray Eames, c. 1945. Assembled from five separately finished elements; curved legs supporting a wide seat, a curved element joining them to the back; 26½ inches high × 22 inches wide × 22 inches deep; $262.

Dowel Base Chair, designed by Charles Eames. Walnut dowel base with black X-shaped metal supports; armless wire caged seat; original orange Naugahyde bikini cover; 19 inches wide × 21 inches deep × 31 inches high; excellent condition; $350.

Low Wire Chair, designed by Charles Eames, c. 1951. Fiberglass shell frame on welded painted steel wire base; $200.

Chair and Ottoman, designed by Charles Eames, c. 1958. Frame, base, and arms polished cast aluminum; vinyl foam cushions and nylon suspension members covered in burgundy wool; chair 26 inches wide × 29 inches deep × 38 inches high; ottoman 21 inches wide × 22 inches deep × 18 inches high; excellent condition; $700/set.

Chair and Ottoman, designed by George Nelson Cantenary group, c. 1963. Architecturally inspired frame construction of chrome-plated steel cables; seat and back of black-leather-covered steel pans; chair 29 inches wide × 28 inches deep × 28 inches high; ottoman 30 inches wide × 23 inches deep × 16 inches high; very good condition; $1,700/set.

Mahogany Open-Arm Chairs (set of three), designed by George Nelson. $100/set.

Desks

Birch, Chromium-Plated Steel, and Masonite Desk with L-Shaped Side Table, designed by Charles and Ray Eames, c. 1952. Part of the Eames storage units; desk with rectangular birch top supported on the right-hand side by two deep drawers in black Masonite with white side panels, on a chrome-plated steel frame, 29½ inches high × 60 inches wide × 28 inches deep; L-shaped side table with a birch rectangular top holding an aluminum frame, with three drawers on the left-hand side, stamped "AUG101954," 26¼ inches high × 47 inches wide × 15¾ inches deep; $2,860/set.

Child's Desk, designed by George Nelson. Four drawers; walnut finish; chrome pulls; tubular chrome frame on casters; Herman Miller/G. Nelson label; 34 inches wide × 16 inches deep × 26 inches high; some scratches; good condition; $160.

Desk, designed by George Nelson. Re-covered Naugahyde top and doors; walnut finish; aluminum legs and perforated file basket; floating organizer; back of drop-leaf typewriter space drilled to house electric typewriter; 58 inches wide × 24 inches deep × 41 inches high; extremely rare; good condition; $2,000.

"ESU" Desk, designed by Charles Eames, c. 1950. Earliest version of the Eames storage unit system, which eventually was enlarged and equipped with drawers and filing system; primary-colored Masonite panels; zinc angled-iron legs; birch top; early Herman Miller label; 46 inches wide × 28 inches deep × 29 inches high; very good condition; $3,500.

Sideboards/Buffets

Sideboard/Buffet, designed by George Nelson. Elegant and functional unit with four exterior drawers; three doors that open to reveal flatware drawer, pull-out server, and adjustable shelves; round wood-and-aluminum pulls; black ebonized walnut-finish base; 80 inches wide × 19 inches deep × 31 inches high; one aluminum pull replaced; very good condition; $550.

Sofas

Sofa, designed by George Nelson, c. 1950. Colorful piece with wedge back in green-and-gold houndstooth fabric; platform seat on aluminum legs; in orange, chartreuse, and turquoise; original Herman Miller fabric by Alexander Girard; 90 inches long × 30 inches deep × 27 inches high; excellent condition; $1,700.

Marshmallow Sofa, designed by Irving Harper, manufactured from 1955–1965 in a variety of Herman Miller fabrics. Brightly colored vinyl cushions; $8,000–$11,000.

Storage Units

Storage Cube, designed by Charles Eames, c. 1951. Blond wood top; black laminate bottom; blue Masonite side and open front with X-crossed braced side and back; early production; 24 inches wide × 16 inches deep × 20 inches high; excellent condition; $1,800.

Storage Unit, designed by Charles Eames. Two-tiered unit with early production zinc angled-iron legs; laminated birch top; black aniline-dyed shelves; primary-colored Masonite back panels; monotone sides with replaced sliding wood and fiberglass doors; early label; 47 inches wide × 16 inches deep × 33 inches high; very good condition; $3,750.

Tables/Stands

"LTR," designed by Charles Eames. Early production; laminated plywood; walnut; zinc low wire base; early Herman Miller label; 15 inches wide × 13 inches deep × 10 inches high; very good condition; $500.

"ETR Surfboard" Table, designed by Charles Eames, c. 1951. Black laminate top with laminated plywood beveled sides; original black wire cage legs; 30 inches wide × 90 inches long × 10 inches high; minor chips to top, small repair in top; good condition; $950.

Leather and Wood End Table, designed by George Nelson, c. 1948. Rectangular with a drawer on one side; top covered with beige leather; supported by four ebonized legs; 22 inches high × 19 inches wide × 30 inches deep; $440.

Wood and Chromium-Plated Metal Table (Model 8430-X), designed by George Nelson, c. 1948. Rectangular wood top supported by two X-shaped brushed-chromium-plated metal legs; 28½ inches high × 83¼ inches wide × 36 inches deep; $1,760.

Wood Gateleg Table, designed by George Nelson, c. 1948. Rectangular top with wide aprons having special wood hinges; on four straight legs joined by side stretchers and a central panel; closed 29½ inches high × 18½ inches wide × 40 inches deep; fully extended 65 inches wide; $825.

Nightstands (pair), designed by George Nelson, c. 1951. Rosewood exteriors and drawers; white lacquered interior with adjustable shelf; white porcelain pulls; tapered steel legs; 23 inches high; excellent condition; $600/set.

Swag-Legged Side Table, designed by George Nelson. Highly polished chrome base; black laminate top has beveled edge; 17 inches in diameter × 16 inches high; excellent condition; $300.

Coconut Chair, designed by George Nelson for Herman Miller Furniture Company, c. 1956. Unsigned, unupholstered, finish wear; 40 inches high x 31 inches wide; $468. *Courtesy of Skinner Inc., Boston/Bolton, MA.*

Table, designed by George Nelson, c. 1950s. Primavera sides and legs; black leather top; small drawer; Herman Miller tag; 39 inches wide × 19 inches deep × 22 inches high; exceptional original condition; $550.

Gate-Legged Table, designed by George Nelson, c. 1950s. Primavera finish; open 66 inches long × 29 inches wide × 40 inches high; excellent condition; $1,100.

Coffee Table, designed by Isamu Noguchi, c. 1944. Two-part movable base in walnut; 50 inches wide × 36 inches deep × 16 inches high; triangular plate glass has small chip; very good condition; $2,000.

Rudder Coffee Table, designed by Isamu Noguchi, manufactured by Herman Miller Furniture Company, c. 1949. Extremely rare, re-ebonized birch top supported on two parabolic bent metal legs, one solid leg; 15 inches high x 36 inches deep x 50 inches wide; $1,500. *Courtesy of Toomey-Treadway Galleries, Oak Park, IL.*

Coffee Table, designed by Isamu Noguchi, c. 1944. Two-part adjustable base in black painted ash; rounded triangular glass; 50 inches wide × 36 inches deep × 16 inches high; excellent condition; $2,500.

Coffee Table, designed by Isamu Noguchi, c. 1950s. Two-part adjustable base in painted ash; rounded triangular glass; 50 inches wide × 36 inches deep × 16 inches high; excellent condition; $2,400.

Walnut and Plate Glass Coffee Table, designed by Isamu Noguchi, c. 1944. Plate glass top on two-part adjustable base; 15 inches high × 44 inches wide × 43 inches deep; $500.

Wood and Glass Coffee Table, designed by Isamu Noguchi, c. 1944. Ebonized walnut base of two amorphous interlocking forms holding a triangular glass top with rounded corners; 17¾ inches high × 49¼ inches wide × 35¼ inches deep; $880.

Dining Table, designed by Isamu Noguchi, c. 1949. Birch and chrome-plated steel; "rudder table"; birch top supported on two parabolic bent metal legs and one solid birch leg; extremely rare, very few ever produced; refinished top and leg; 50 inches wide × 36 inches deep × 27 inches high; very good condition; $1,400.

Cloud Table, designed by Gilbert Rohde. Burled walnut top; exotic walnut sides; leather-studded legs; top refinished; 27 inches long × 23 inches deep × 27 inches high; very good condition; $1,000.

Side Table, designed by Gilbert Rohde, c. 1940s. Architectural geometric form of two wooden rectangles supported by tubular aluminum bar; two drawers in top; original finish; 32 inches wide × 15 inches deep × 19 inches high; very good condition; $475.

Telephone Stand, designed by Gilbert Rohde, c. 1940s. Streamline design in walnut with rounded corners and floating geometric planes; one drawer in top; door opens to reveal sculptural bookshelf; original finish; 32 inches wide × 12 inches deep × 28 inches high; excellent condition; $850.

Miscellaneous

Five-Piece Bedroom Set, designed by George Nelson, c. 1950. Two twin headboards, can lock together to make king with adjustable backrests and built-in nightstands; one large chest of drawers and two small chests that fit together as one, primavera tops and sides, black lacquer fronts, satin chrome pulls; original finish; headboards 40 inches wide × 12 inches deep × 42 inches high; small chests 24 inches wide × 19 inches deep × 30 inches high; large chest 56 inches wide × 19 inches deep × 30 inches high; very good condition; $2,200/set.

Dinette Set, designed by Charles Eames, c. 1950s. White enameled pedestal base, white laminate top, blond sides with built-in lazy Susan; "Eiffel Tower" base chairs with white metal cage seat, black "Eiffel Tower" base, white plastic cap feet, original black Naugahyde covers; table 47 inches in diameter × 29 inches high; chairs 19 inches wide × 20 inches deep × 34 inches high; excellent condition; $1,000/set.

HEYWOOD-WAKEFIELD

While the name Heywood-Wakefield has been most closely associated with woven reed and bentwood furniture, it is their 1940s and 1950s pieces that are appealing to budget-conscious modern collectors. As early as the 1930s the company was influenced by the Scandinavian use of light woods, such as birch, and the Modern look popularized by the Swedish Exhibition (held in London in 1930). In 1931 Heywood-Wakefield commissioned Gilbert Rohde, a New York industrial designer, to create some pieces in the new, light woods for mass production. By the 1940s the company was offering the fashionable blond woods in styles similar to those of contemporary Scandinavian furniture. By the 1950s the light wood furnishings had found their way to hotel rooms. Today, this hotel room furniture, usually refinished, is beginning to come on the market. Prices are modest compared with those for other pieces of the period. Postwar pieces, both those sold retail and for hotel use, had a wood-burned stamp. Pieces that can be attributed to a name designer, such as Russel Wright or Gilbert Rohde, fetch higher prices.

PRICES

Sideboards/Buffets

Buffet with Tilted China Cabinet, c. 1956. China cabinet with angled glass siding panels, one adjustable center shelf on top; buffet with three deep linen drawers at center flanked by vertical cabinet with two adjustable shelves in each; northern birch with wheat finish; 59 inches high × 18 inches deep × 48 inches wide; excellent condition; $550.

Chest of Drawers, by Heywood-Wakefield, from Encore bedroom group. Birch, refinished; 46 inches high x 19 inches deep x 33 inches wide; $575. *Courtesy of South Beach Furniture, FL.*

Tables/Stands

Lazy Susan Coffee Table, c. 1950s. Solid birch circular platform on center threaded pedestal joined by four curved legs; wheat finish; 16 inches high in low position × 32 inches in diameter; excellent condition; $160.

Black Lacquer Drop Leaf Dining Table, c. 1950. Hinged rectangular top with rounded corners; raised on flattened tapering angular legs; 29 inches high × 36 inches wide, length extends to 5 feet; $935.

Poufe for Lady's Vanity, by Heywood-Wakefield. New upholstery; 16 inches high x 20 inches in diameter; $325. *Courtesy of South Beach Furniture, FL.*

VLADIMIR KAGAN (1927-)

Born in Worms am Rhein in Germany in 1927, Vladimir Kagan came to the United States in 1938, and his career spans forty years "as one of the pioneers" of Modern design. He studied architecture at Columbia University and joined his father's woodworking shop in 1947. His earliest success came with his design for the Delegate's Cocktail Lounges for the first United Nations headquarters in Lake Success, New York (1947–1948). In 1949 he opened his showroom in New York City. Over the years his company opened showrooms throughout America and became the preeminent haute couture design and custom furniture manufacturing facility in this country. At the end of those first forty years, Kagan closed his factory and showrooms to concentrate on his first love: design.

> When I had a chance I worked with architects. I could do details. I had my own factory, Kagan Designs, founded by my father. I began my career in 1939, when we came to America as refugees—and worked as a cabinetmaker. The factory became a custom shop that took pride in craftsmanship. Where the Eameses were concerned with industrial and machine-designed pieces, my motivation was craftsmanship.
>
> I began working with organic forms in 1947.

I am best known for my innovative modern designs that I began designing in the early fifties. From organic sculptural modernism I went on to explore the architectural minimalism of the sixties and seventies and continued into the post-modernism and neo-classic designs of the eighties. I consider the 1956 rocking chair and the 1960s Unicorn chair two of my signature pieces. While many of my designs are being reproduced today, these two are out of production. Another innovation was my use of lights as an element in the late 1960s. I used both fluorescent and cold cathode.

Today, Kagan is creating designs inspired by the deconstructionist movement of the nineties tempered with a strong flair for organic sculpturism that was his trademark in the fifties.

His works are in the permanent collections of the Brooklyn Museum, the Vitra Design Museum of Weil am Rhein in Germany, and the Cooper Hewitt Museum in New York. His designs were originally shown in the Museum of Modern Art's "Good Design" exhibit in 1958 and most recently in 1991, at the London Design Museum's Organic Design Show. In 1980, New York's Fashion Institute of Technology (F.I.T.) honored him with a thirty-year retrospective exhibit: "Three Decades of Design."

He has designed furniture for such clients as Marilyn Monroe, and acted as design consultant to such diverse clients as General Electric, Walt Disney, and the Kingdom of Saudi Arabia.

A number of his pieces have been reproduced and copied over the years. I advise collectors to carefully examine the quality of workmanship, which is of the highest quality on original pieces. Study fabrics used in the various periods versus contemporary ones, and compare their quality to cheaper knock-offs of the period. As Kagan points out, "the repros don't use the old upholstery techniques."

Cabinets

File Cabinet/Credenza, c. 1950s. Original design with ten sculpted two-toned drawers of cherry and ebonized wood resting on curved legs; original finish; 80 inches long × 22 inches deep × 32 inches high; very good condition; $4,250.

Chairs/Lounges/Stools

Armchair, c. 1953. Sculptural form of molded walnut with one continuous arm that swoops around chair and jets back to create an extremely elegant exaggerated frame and leg configuration; refinished and reupholstered in white Naugahyde; a rare and desirable form; 29 inches wide × 33 inches deep × 34 inches high; very good condition; $2,200.

Armchair. Sculptural form of molded walnut with tilted, floating armrests; seat and winged backrest upholstered in original bright red wool fabric; 28 inches wide × 28 inches deep × 32 inches high; very good condition; $250.

Chair, c. 1950. Organic armless seat and back on walnut-and-brass swivel pedestal; original nubby beige Dreyfuss fabric; Kagan/Dreyfuss label; 20 inches wide × 30 inches deep × 35 inches high; excellent condition; $225.

Occasional Chairs (pair), c. 1950. High-back upholstered chairs in original nubby beige and gold stripe Dreyfuss material; sculptural wood frame and legs in mahogany finish; 15 inches wide × 24 inches deep × 37 inches high; good condition; $400/set.

Seating Unit, designed by Vladimir Kagan, c. 1950. Aluminum and upholstered wood frame, aerodynamic yet biomorphic form on cast aluminum legs in original Henry Dreyfuss brushed wool fabric, pumpkin color, two sections; repaired leg; one measures 8 feet, 1 inch, the other measures 5 feet, 1 inch, both measure 29 inches high x 31 inches deep; $5,000. *Courtesy of Treadway Gallery, OH.*

Vinyl and Aluminum Triangular Stool, c. 1955. Triangular upholstered seat raised on a three-legged pedestal base; upholstered in hot orange vinyl; $805.

Sofas

Sofa, c. 1960. Unusual biomorphic form with sculpted backrest resting on crisscrossed teak legs in original oatmeal "Zulu" Dreyfuss fabric; 90 inches wide × 30 inches deep × 28 inches high; minor fading to lower back; very good condition; $3,000.

Tables/Stands

Walnut, Marble, and Brass Low Table, c. 1955. Tan travertine triangular marble section within a brass surround intersecting a tapering rectangular walnut section; raised on tapering, canted legs; 5 feet long × 14 inches high × 19¾ inches wide; $1,840.

KNOLL ASSOCIATES

Founded in 1938 by Hans Knoll, this international furniture manufacturer and distributor specialized in Modernist furniture. Over the following decades some of the leading architects and designers worked for the company. Hans Knoll came to America from Germany in 1937. He started the Hans C. Knoll Furniture Company in New York City the following year, hiring another new arrival, Jens Risom, from Denmark. In 1941 Risom designed Knoll's first chair, establishing the simplistic style that would define the Knoll look. The woods featured in their designs were cherry, birch, and walnut.

Florence Shust married Knoll in 1941 and became an important part of the company. She graduated from Cranbrook Academy of Art and had worked for Walter Gropius and Marcel Breuer before working for Knoll.

The impressive roster of designers who worked for Knoll over the years included Isamu Noguchi, Eero Saarinen, and Harry Bertoia.

The firm opened a textile division in 1947, utilizing the talents of such well-known names as Marianne Stengell and, later, Eszter Haraszty.

Upon the death of Hans Knoll in 1955, Florence Knoll assumed the presidency of the company. Four years later the firm was sold to Art Metal, who manufactured traditional metal office furniture.

In 1969, after ownership had changed hands more than once, the name was changed to Knoll International. In 1977 General Felt Industries took over ownership of the company. It is currently owned by one of the partners of General Felt, Marshall S. Cogan.

PRICES

Chairs/Lounges/Stools

Armchair, designed by Franco Albini. Asymmetrical birch frame with original purple-and-black Danish wool; 22 inches × 23 inches × 31 inches; excellent condition; $50–$85.

Child's Side Chairs (pair), designed by Harry Bertoia. Welded steel wire frame; upholstered seat pads; $200/set.

Children's Chairs (set of four), designed by Harry Bertoia, c. 1950s. Bent metal with frame of welded steel white-coated wire; seat pads upholstered in bright turquoise; 16 inches wide × 15 inches deep × 24 inches high; excellent condition; $500/set.

Wire Metal Child's Chairs (group of three), designed by Harry Bertoia, c. 1952. White painted bent-metal frame with a wire structure forming the backrest and seat; supported by white painted trapezoidal metal feet; 20 inches high × 13¼ inches wide × 12 inches deep; $330/set.

"Diamond" Lounge Chair and Ottoman, designed by Harry Bertoia, c. 1952. Chrome-plated steel rod construction with rubber shock mounts separating seat from frame to rock chair; chair 44 inches wide × 30 inches deep × 28 inches high; ottoman 24 inches wide × 17 inches deep × 14 inches high; excellent condition; $475/set.

"Diamond" Lounge Chair, designed by Harry Bertoia. Chrome-plated steel rod construction with rubber shock mounts separating seat from frame to rock chair; original red Knoll fabric; 28 inches high × 30 inches deep × 44 inches wide; excellent condition; $400.

Welded Wire "Diamond Chair," designed by Harry Bertoia, c. 1952. Flaring tub-form body of trellis design; raised on canted trapezoidal supports; $330.

Side Chair, designed by Donald Knorr, c. 1951. Sculptural

design of repainted yellow zinc-plated steel with seat and back one continuous form; legs of repainted black steel; very few ever produced; 27 inches high × 21 inches deep × 22 inches wide; very good condition; $700.

"Scissor" Lounge Chairs (pair), designed by Pierre Jeanneret, c. 1951. Birch frame with chrome disk support; canvas straps; original black, white, and beige tweed fabric; 21 inches wide × 31 inches deep × 29 inches high; excellent condition; $1,300/set.

Birch and Chromed-Steel Rocking Stool, designed by Isamu Noguchi, c. 1955. Shaped circular seat supported by intersecting V-shaped struts supported by a circular rocking base; rare; $9,200.

Armchair, designed by Ralph Rapson. Shaped and continuous back and seat side rails with leather webbing; on frame with shaped arms; unsigned; 29½ inches high × 24 inches wide × 20 inches deep; wear; $165.

Lounge Chair, designed by Jens Risom, manufactured by Knoll Associates, Inc., c. 1941. Bent beech frame with khaki-colored web upholstery, raised on tapered angular feet with Knoll Assoc. Inc. decal (later webbing); 30 inches high; $250. *Courtesy of Treadway Gallery, OH.*

Lounge Chair, designed by Jens Risom, c. 1941. Sculptural form of molded birch; seat and back of natural leather strap webbing; one of the first chairs introduced by Knoll; 20 inches wide × 30 inches deep × 29 inches high; excellent condition; $1,700.

Lounge Chair, designed by Ralph Rapson, c. 1945. Rare and early lounge chair of cantilevered birch reupholstered in charcoal gray Knoll fabric; produced for only several years; 28 inches wide × 28 inches deep × 38 inches high; very good condition; $350.

Grasshopper Chair, designed by Eero Saarinen, c. 1948. Formed seat and back supported by sculptural molded birch plywood arm/legs; seafoam-green wool; original finish; 26 inches wide × 32 inches deep × 34 inches high; slightly soiled; very good condition; $3,500.

"Womb" Chair and Ottoman, designed by Eero Saarinen. Organic form of molded fiberglass shell; foam padding; reupholstered in mauve Knoll fabric; frame and legs of chrome-plated steel; chair 36 inches high × 34 inches deep × 36 inches wide; ottoman 15 inches high × 21 inches deep × 25 inches wide; very good condition; $950/set.

Outdoor Chaise Longue, designed by Richard Schultz. White enamel cast-aluminum frame with adjustable back of vinyl straps and woven mesh; 35 inches high × 76 inches deep × 25 inches wide; excellent condition; $240.

Desks

Desk, designed by Florence Knoll. Three drawers in birch finish; early Knoll label; 29 inches high × 24 inches deep × 48 inches wide; excellent condition; $130.

Sofas

"Womb" Sofa, designed by Eero Saarinen. Extremely rare sofa version of the classic "womb" chair that even further exaggerates the organic sculptural form; original green Knoll fabric; black steel frame; 60 inches wide × 35 inches deep × 35 inches high; very good condition; $2,700.

Storage Units

Modular Storage System, designed by Florence Knoll. Walnut; four pieces consisting of a three-drawer case, drop leaf desk, and display case with sliding glass doors floating on a wood-and-steel bench; 72 inches wide × 18 inches deep × 43 inches high; very good condition; $950/set.

Three-Piece Modular Storage System. Two separate units in recent walnut finish with burlap-covered sliding doors and leather pulls floating on walnut bench with tubular steel legs; 18 inches wide × 72 inches deep × 29 inches high; very good condition; $425/set.

Tables/Stands

Walnut and Metal Occasional Table, mid-twentieth century. Petal-shape walnut top forming eight segments on cylindrical support in fused-white finish; eight prongs form base; paper label; 19⅛ inches high × 16 inches in diameter; $150.

Popsicle Stick Table, designed by Hans Bellman, c. 1945. Round birch plywood top; painted ash legs pierce through top; collapsible; top refinished; 20 inches high × 23 inches in diameter; very good condition; $280.

Conference or Dining Table, designed by Florence Knoll, c. 1961. Walnut; oval top; chrome-plated steel base; original finish; 78 inches long × 28 inches deep × 28 inches high; excellent condition; $1,000.

Marble and Chromium-Plated Steel Table, designed by Florence Knoll. 17 inches high × 27 inches wide × 27 inches deep; $121.

Children's Table, designed by Isamu Noguchi, c. 1950. Low wire base table; chrome-plated crisscrossed rods; white Formica top; laminated and beveled; very rare; original finish; 24 inches wide × 20 inches high; excellent condition; $1,100.

Dinette Table, designed by Isamu Noguchi. Rare breakfast size of the classic dining table with chrome-plated crisscrossed wire rod base construction; circular cut-out black iron base; laminated plywood sides and white Formica top; Knoll label; 29 inches high × 36 inches in diameter; very good condition; $900.

Cocktail Table, designed by Warren Platner. Steel wire cage base in nickel finish; beveled glass top; 15 inches high × 42 inches in diameter; very good condition; $425.

Side Table, designed by Eero Saarinen. Elegant pedestal form of white enameled aluminum base; beveled walnut top; Knoll label; 21 inches high × 20 inches in diameter; excellent condition; $250.

Miscellaneous

Organizers. Two molded plywood organizers that adjust on a plated steel pin; 12 inches wide × 15 inches deep × 7 inches high; excellent condition; $110/set.

Dining Set, designed by Eero Saarinen, c. 1950s. Repainted white cast-aluminum base; round top of Rosso Collenandima marble; arm and side chairs of molded fiberglass; reinforced plastic shell on white cast-aluminum base; Naugahyde seats in brown and yellow; table 30 inches high × 54 inches in diameter; armchair 34 inches high × 22 inches deep × 26 inches wide; side chair 32 inches high × 21 inches deep × 19 inches wide; very good condition; $950/set.

Pedestal Base Table, Four Armchairs, and Four Stools, designed by Eero Saarinen, c. 1956. Table with white fused finish on cast metal base with circular white marble top; four armchairs of fiberglass reinforced plastic in white lacquer finish, beige cushions, cast-aluminum base; four round stools in beige upholstery on cast metal base in white fused finish; with manufacturer's mark; finish wear; tabletop 52 inches in diameter; $650/set.

PAUL McCOBB (1917–1969)

McCobb is an American furniture and furnishings designer who brought low-priced, high quality modern furniture to the middle American market with his "Planner" group, manufactured by Winchenon Furniture Company of Michigan. It featured modular pieces pioneered by George Nelson. During the early 1950s, McCobb was also known for his textiles in brightly colored "contemporary" patterns.

PRICES

Chairs/Lounges/Stools

Dining Chairs (set of four). Sculptural form of black rod iron frame/legs; horizontal dowel back and molded plywood seat in recent birch finish; 18 inches wide × 19 inches deep × 39 inches high; very good condition; $700/set.

Dining Chairs (set of eight). Walnut and upholstered chairs; $90/set.

Side Chair. Whimsical form with black rod iron frame; molded plywood seat and top; spindle back; walnut finish; 34 inches high × 24 inches deep × 18 inches wide; one spindle repaired; very good condition; $100.

Desks

Burled Wood Desk. Trapezoidal top supported on one end by a trapezoidal foot and on the other by a cabinet with three drawers; 29¾ inches high × 63 inches wide × 30 inches deep; $935.

Sideboards/Buffets

Walnut and Marble Sideboard. Rectangular top over cupboard drawers opening to shelves and drawers; 32 inches high × 71 inches wide × 19 inches deep; $450.

Tables/Stands

Walnut Dining Table. Banded rectangular top set on square tapering legs; one leaf; 29 inches high × 29 inches wide × 42 inches deep, leaf 21 inches; $400.

GEORGE NAKASHIMA (1905-1990)

He has a B.A. in architecture from the University of Washington, 1929; a diploma from Ecole Americaine des Beaux Arts Fountainbleau, 1929; and an M.A. in architecture from the Massachusetts Institute of Technology, 1930. His works are included in the collections of the Museum of Fine Arts, Boston; the Philadelphia Museum of Art; the American Craft Museum, New York City; and the Victoria and Albert Museum, London.

PRICES

Cabinets

Dressing Cabinets. Walnut; 5 feet long × 31¾ inches high × 20 inches wide; $2,000.

Chairs/Lounges

Side Chairs (six), designed for Widdicomb Furniture, c. 1955. Comb-shaped crest rail over nine vertical spindles; plank seat flared and shaped; raised on four canted legs; branded "George Nakashima 2711"; 36 inches high; $1,400/set.

"New" Chairs (group of four). Two armchairs and two side chairs; cantilevered seat with spindled back and curved crest rail; armchair 39 inches high × 23¾ inches wide × 16½ inches deep; side chair 36 inches high × 18¾ inches wide × 16½ inches deep; $3,080/set.

Sideboards/Buffets

Wall Mounted Sideboard, designed for Widdicomb Furniture, c. 1955. Overhanging top with angular ends; two sliding glass doors of burled and darker wood veneer; interior of cabinet shows the hearts of the wood; 16¼ inches high × 79¾ inches wide × 15½ inches deep; $1,200.

Sideboard. Rectangular top with four circular pegs in its center with dovetailed edges; two sliding doors covering four graduated drawers on one side and two adjustable shelves on the other; 32 inches high × 60 inches wide × 20 inches deep; $1,760.

Tables/Stands

Coffee Table, designed for Widdicomb Furniture, c. 1955. Rectangular top with recessed panel for glass; bank of two drawers with metal pulls at one end; opposing two tapering ovoid-shaped legs; textile Widdicomb label; glass not included; 17¾ inches high × 54 inches wide × 17¼ inches deep; $650.

Coffee Table, designed by George Nakashima for Widdicomb Furniture, Grand Rapids, MI, c. 1955. Rectangular top with recessed panel for glass, bank of two drawers with metal pulls at one end, textile Widdicomb label, glass not included; 17¾ inches high x 17¼ inches deep x 54 inches wide; $650. *Courtesy of Skinner Inc., Boston/Bolton, MA.*

Drop Leaf Table, designed for Widdicomb Furniture, c. 1955. Asymmetrical top on shaped supports; keyed tenons joining four tapered legs; hinged leaf with sliding leg support; 29¼ inches high × 73¾ inches wide × 38 inches deep; leaf 26 inches deep; $700.

Miscellaneous

Bookcase Headboard. Walnut; 30⅛ inches high × 54 inches long × 12 inches wide; $1,700.

Dining Table and Four Chairs. Walnut and ash; 28½ inches high × 6 feet long × 36 inches wide; $7,000/set.

GEORGE NELSON (1908–1986) (SEE ALSO HERMAN MILLER FURNITURE COMPANY)

Nelson, best known for his furniture designs, studied to be an architect at Yale University. He also became a writer and teacher. While co-managing editor of *Architectural Forum* from 1943 to 1944, he was influenced by the work of International Style architects such as Alvar Aalto. In 1946 he became design director of the Herman Miller Furniture Company, where he remained until his death in 1986. Many of his designs, along with those of his many staff members, are still considered unique. Among them are the Coconut chair (1956), the Sling sofa (1964), and the first pole system in America, Omni (1956), designed for Aluminum Extrusions. In 1947 he opened his own design studio, while continuing to work for Herman Miller. He authored many important books on design over the years.

PRICES

Benches

Black Slat Bench, c. 1955. Rectangular top composed of slats; raised on U-form supports; 6 feet long × 14¼ inches high × 18½ inches wide; $1,840.

Black Slat Bench, c. 1955. Rectangular top composed of slats; raised on U-form supports; 56½ inches long × 14¼ inches high × 18½ inches wide; $1,495.

Black Slat Bench, c. 1955. Rectangular top composed of slats; raised on U-form supports; 4 feet long × 14¼ inches high × 18½ inches wide; $1,380.

Platform Bench. Multifunctional slat bench with primavera top; black ebonized base; 68 inches wide × 18 inches deep × 14 inches high; good condition; $500.

Platform Bench, c. 1947. Rare; three-foot variation of the classic slat bench; re-ebonized finish; 36 inches wide × 19 inches deep × 4 inches high; very good condition; $500.

Cabinets

Cabinet with Matching Bookcase. Dark walnut finish with original forest green lacquered fronts; black ebonized base; turned brushed-steel handles; tops refinished; cabinet 56 inches wide × 18 inches deep × 29 inches high; bookcase 56 inches wide × 12 inches deep × 29 inches high; good condition; $650/set.

Chairs/Lounges

Dining Chairs (ten), c. 1955. Two armchairs originally designed by John Pile for George Nelson and eight side chairs; curved chair rail; open arms and back over circular seat with orange upholstered cushions; raised on four bentwood legs; unsigned; 30 inches high; $3,300/set.

Coconut Chair with Ottoman. Sculptural molded steel shell; cast-aluminum legs; chrome-plated steel leg braces; reupholstered in red Herman Miller fabric; rare version with ottoman, very few ever produced; chair 40 inches wide × 34 inches deep × 33 inches high; ottoman 23 inches wide × 17 inches deep × 14 inches high; very good condition; $3,000/set.

Fiberglass, Chromed and Painted Metal Platypus Chair, c. 1958. Molded seat and back raised on a metal X-form pedestal base; base painted black; $1,150.

Laminated Wood Pretzel Chair, c. 1952. Dished circular seat raised on tapered legs; $2,587.

Laminated Wood Pretzel Chair, designed in 1952. Dished circular seat raised on tapering legs; back and arms a continuous piece of bent laminated rail; $4,887.

Miscellaneous

Daybed. Frame of primavera finish; hairpin legs and back support in brushed aluminum; original teal Alexander Girard fabric; 75 inches wide × 34 inches deep × 27 inches high; excellent condition; $1,800.

Wood-and-Metal Daybed, c. 1955. Rectangular seat frame with metal springs and back rail support; raised on bent metal legs; 75 inches long; $3,450.

Isamu Noguchi (1904–1988)
(see also Knoll Associates, and Herman Miller Furniture Company)

Noguchi is considered one of the most important American sculptors of the twentieth century, and he contributed many designs for furniture and decorative arts that are equally noteworthy. His influences came from both his Japanese father and his American mother, and from the education he received in both countries. In the late forties he made a series of sculptures in the new biomorphic forms. His first furniture was also biomorphic (1939). In 1944 he designed biomorphic furniture for the Herman Miller Furniture Company. In later years he created his Akari lamps (1951), versions of traditional Japanese lanterns. He designed various versions of the Akari lamps for the next twenty-five years. In 1985 his Isamu Noguchi Garden Museum in Long Island City opened, displaying his work in rough, primal stone. His sculptural garden was clearly influenced by a Japanese sensibility.

PRICES

Chairs/Lounges/Stools

Laminated Wood and Metal "Fin" Stool, c. 1946–1947. Molded circular seat raised on a single tapering wood leg and two cylindrical metal legs; the seat for this rare prototype stool was adapted from a Charles Eames–designed chair seat; $12,650.

GILBERT ROHDE (1894–1944)

American. A leading industrial and furnishings designer who is newly appreciated for his contributions to Art Deco and 1940s Modern design. An avant garde in designs, he not only designed commissions for wealthy clients, but mass-produced pieces for the Herman Miller Company; and he created modern designs for children's furniture for Kroehler. He also created furniture lines for Heywood Wakefield, John Widdicomb, and others.

PRICES

Cabinets

Cabinet, c. 1940. Elegant walnut cabinet with inlaid blond wood stripe on top and sides; asymmetrically placed Lucite handles and legs; original finish; label inside drawer; 40 inches wide × 16 inches deep × 38 inches high; excellent condition; $700.

Tables/Stands

Cloud Cocktail Table. Designed by Gilbert Rohde, manufactured by Herman Miller, c. 1940s. Elegant freeform top of exotic palaqdeo supported by four tapered legs in black lacquer finish.

Original protective glass top, refinished. 44 inches wide × 44 inches deep × 15 inches high. Very good condition. $1,300.

Cocktail Table, c. 1940. Four tapered, fluted wooden legs; two floating glass circular surfaces; brass caps top legs; 17 inches high × 30 inches in diameter; a very beautifully designed table, excellent condition; $375.

End Table, c. 1940. Three tapered, fluted wooden legs; two floating glass circular surfaces; brass caps top legs; 26 inches high × 20 inches in diameter; excellent condition; $275.

JENS RISOM (1916-) (SEE ALSO KNOLL ASSOCIATES)

Risom studied in his native Copenhagen before coming in 1939 to the United States, where he continued his study of furniture and interior design. He later applied the simple lines he studied to his furniture designs. Risom met Hans Knoll in 1941, was asked to design fifteen pieces that exemplified the look of Scandinavian Modern. They included chairs, tables, and cabinets. In 1946 he became the sole designer for his own company, Jens Risom Design, Inc. The influence was always Scandinavian and the work included both home furnishings and textiles. By the 1970s he was also designing office furniture.

PRICES

Miscellaneous

Chest, c. 1955. Four long drawers over four long drawers; square brass rod pulls; raised on rectangular frame with four tapered legs; paper decal; 56¾ inches high × 36⅛ inches wide × 21 inches deep; $325.

Walnut Veneer Low Chests on Frame (pair), c. 1955. On rectangular frame with four tapered legs; one chest with four long drawers, the other with three; square brass rod-shape pulls; paper decal; 31½ inches high × 36 inches wide × 21 inches deep; $200/set.

EERO SAARINEN (1910-1961) (SEE ALSO KNOLL ASSOCIATES)

Most experts agree that Saarinen's talent came naturally. His father, Finnish architect Eliel Saarinen, helped establish and then became president of the Cranbrook Academy of Art in Bloomfield Hills, Michigan. His mother was a respected textile designer.

The family came to the United States from Finland in 1923. Eero began designing furniture from 1929 to 1933 for the neighboring Kingwood School for Girls (designed by his father). From 1939 to 1942 Eero acted as assistant in the Department of Architecture at Cranbrook. After collaborating with Charles Eames he won two prizes for introducing three-dimensionally molded shell and modular furniture. In 1943 Saarinen began designing furniture for Knoll Associates.

His first chair for Knoll was of bent plywood (1943). In 1946 he designed the first fiberglass chair to be mass-produced in the United States, the #70 lounge chair (1946–1948). The most important of his designs utilized his architectural and furniture knowledge in combination with new materials. The pedestal chair series, designed for Knoll (1955–1957), used the molded shell concept. The chairs were aluminum with a fused plastic finish and fiberglass and nylon upholstery.

Many copies of the pedestal armchair were made during the 1950s and 1960s. Collectors should study the beauty of his original proportions, not found in the copies. The side chairs and tables in the pedestal line are still produced by Knoll.

PRICES

Miscellaneous

Modular Furniture Group, designed by Eero Saarinen and Charles Eames for Red Lion Furniture Company. Cabinet and bench; winner of the Organic Design Competition 1940–1941; extremely rare, very few ever produced; original finish; cabinet 18 inches wide × 18 inches deep × 22 inches high; bench 34 inches wide × 18 inches deep × 13 inches high; $4,250/set.

Grasshopper Chair, designed by Eero Saarinen. Sculptural seat and back of one continuous form, supported by laminated and molded plywood arm/leg configuration in original birch finish, back and Knoll fabric; 34 inches high x 32 inches deep x 26 inches wide; $1,100. *Courtesy of Toomey-Treadway Galleries, Oak Park, IL.*

FRANK LLOYD WRIGHT (1867-1959)

The "father of American architecture," Wright developed the concept of an organic architecture. His later Usonian houses (1936) were relatively inexpensive, because the furniture for the most part was built into the walls and could be completed at the same time as the house, thereby saving on labor and materials. However, in this book we are concerned with the furniture designed in the 1940s and 1950s, not only that made for luxury houses but also the mass-produced, commercial line designed for Heritage Henredon Furniture Company. Fabrics and wallpapers for F. Schumacher and Company are addressed in other sections. The mass-produced lines were offered to the public in 1955.

PRICES

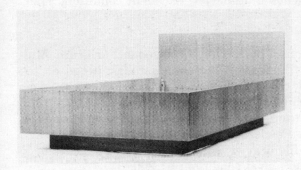

Bed Frame, designed by Frank Lloyd Wright, c. 1950. Spruce, platform, original finish; 24 inches high x 82 inches long x 42 wide; $770. *Courtesy of Toomey-Treadway Galleries, Oak Park, IL.*

Chairs/Lounges/Stools

Upholstered Armchairs (two), manufactured by Heritage Henredon Furniture. Angled arms and original green print fabric over foam cushions. 29 inches wide × 31 inches deep × 27 inches high; excellent condition; $1,200–$1,300.

Upholstered Aluminum Armchair, designed for the Pryce Company Tower, Bartlesville, Oklahoma, c. 1952. Hexagonal swiveling back flanked by sloping shaped arms; hexagonal seat, raised on a molded platform base; frame painted in silver paint; upholstered in red leather; $10,925.

Plywood Upholstered Armchair, designed for the Sonderen House, Kansas City, Missouri, c. 1940. Shaped cantilevered arms flank a rectangular back and seat; raised on a trapezoidal base; $9,775.

Plywood Upholstered Side Chair, designed for Trier House, Des Moines, Iowa, c. 1956. Rectangular back pierced with geometric designs fronted by a rectangular seat with central leg; fitted with seat cushions upholstered in beige fabric; $10,350.

Upholstered Plywood Side Chair, designed for the Sonderen House, Kansas City, Missouri, c. 1940; $7,475.

Side Chair, manufactured by Heritage Henredon Furniture. Low chair with green upholstered seat and octagonal back; front and back legs connect to form rectangle; seat is cantilevered; 21 inches wide × 21 inches deep × 28 inches high; excellent condition; $275.

Stool, manufactured by Heritage Henredon Furniture. Swivel seat in gray velour on cruciform base; original finish; 17 inches high × 17 inches in diameter; excellent condition; $425.

Desks

Desk, manufactured by Heritage Henredon Furniture. Multiple drawers; one file drawer; recessed handles; detail on top edge; top refinished; numbered; 52 inches wide × 20 inches deep × 24 inches high; chips to edges, good condition; $2,700.

Usonian Desk, from the Thomas E. Keys House, Rochester, Minnesota, c. 1951. Ponderosa pine top on a tri-form base and three drawers; one file drawer; 48 inches wide × 26 inches deep × 28 inches high; very good condition; $1,200.

Sideboards/Buffets

Buffet, manufactured by Heritage Henredon Furniture. Double cabinet and eight drawers on cruciform base; original finish; red monogram; 66 inches wide × 20 inches deep × 34½ inches high; $2,500.

Sofas

Sectional Sofa Piece, manufactured by Heritage Henredon Furniture. Left arm original off-white fabric echoes carved edge on base; 27 inches wide × 31 inches deep × 30½ inches high; very good condition; $1,000.

Settee, manufactured by Heritage Henredon Furniture.

Curved button-tufted back and cushion on block legs carved with modified Greek key design; 96 inches long; $1,000.

Tables, designed by Frank Lloyd Wright for Heritage Henredon, model 452, c. 1955. Carved, square low tables, branded HENREDON HERITAGE BY FRANK LLOYD WRIGHT; $1,870. *Courtesy of Butterfield and Butterfield Auctioneers, CA.*

Tables/Stands

Dining Table, manufactured by Heritage Henredon Furniture. Table 29 inches high × 48 inches in diameter; three leaves, 16 inches each; very good condition; $1,500.

Dining Table, manufactured by Heritage Henredon Furniture. Round form with copper decorative edging; three 16-inch leaves; open cruciform base, refinished; 29 inches high × 48 inches in diameter; very good condition; $1,600.

End Table, manufactured by Heritage Henredon Furniture. Hexagonal top on tri-form base; original finish; branded and numbered; 20 inches wide × 20 inches deep × 17 inches high; excellent condition; $1,300.

Vanity or Typing Table, manufactured by Heritage Henredon Furniture. Original finish; 24 inches wide × 20 inches deep × 24 inches high; good condition; $650.

Night Table, manufactured by Heritage Henredon Furniture. 25½ inches wide × 21½ inches deep × 18 inches high; $600.

Miscellaneous

Bookcase/Room Divider, manufactured by Heritage Henredon Furniture. Used alone or in combination with a buffet or coffee table; four open shelves on each side of a four-pane glass cabinet; original finish; monogrammed; 62 inches wide × 16 inches deep × 50 inches high; excellent condition; $2,500.

Dining Suite, manufactured by Heritage Henredon Furniture, Model 2001, c. 1955. Dining table and six side chairs; circular table with brass-banded edge, raised on four geometric edge-carved legs joined by base stretchers, one leaf; chairs decorated en suite; table 24¼ inches high × 54 inches in diameter; $1,760/set.

Mahogany Table and Four Stools, designed for the Arch Oboler House, Malibu, California, c. 1954. Rectangular top with triangular veneer sections at either end mirroring the rectangular legs joined at 45-degree angles by a central medial shelf; four square stools of steeped section fitted with yellow vinyl cushions; table 95½ inches long × 45 inches wide × 25 inches high; stools 15 inches high; $19,300/set.

Dining chairs (four side chairs and two armchairs), manufactured by Heritage Henredon Furniture. Refinished; upholstered backs and seats; side chairs 20 inches wide × 22 inches deep × 32 inches high; armchairs 23 inches wide × 23 inches deep × 32 inches high; very good condition; $1,200/set.

RUSSEL WRIGHT (1904–1976) (SEE ALSO HEYWOOD-WAKEFIELD)

This foremost Modernist designer is mentioned in detail elsewhere in this book for his important ceramic designs. However, he also designed furniture, beginning in the 1930s, for such manufacturers as Heywood-Wakefield Company and Conant Ball. Periodically his pieces from the 1940s and the postwar period come to market. They include both decorative and functional furnishings.

PRICES

Chairs/Lounges/Stools

Armchair, c. 1940s. Molded birch arms and legs; slat back with loose cushions in original fabric of beige, brown, and green architectural print; 27 inches wide × 33 inches deep × 32 inches high; excellent condition; $800.

Tray, by Mary Wright, 1940s. Wood tray with plastic over wood handles, rare example by Russel Wright's wife, signed; 24 x 10 inches; $300. *Courtesy of Al and Kim Eiber Collection.*

PRICES

Chairs/Lounges/Stools

Wire Mesh Armchairs (two), c. 1955. Sculpted back and arms in aqua paint; metal rod base; unsigned; indoor or outdoor use; 27½ inches high; $250/set.

Folding Armchairs (four), designed by Warren McArthur, manufactured by Mayfair Industries, c. 1955. Tubular aluminum construction; black upholstered seat, back, and arms; $950/set.

Bent Walnut Desk Chair, Plycraft. Sculptural back support and arm that scroll in form of ram's horn; black Naugahyde disk seat; 28 inches high; seat 17 inches in diameter; excellent condition; $220.

Arm Rocker, c. 1958. Black wire mesh on bent tubing; 26 inches wide × 30 inches deep × 29 inches high; excellent condition; $90.

Tall Swivel Chair, attributed to Paul Goldman, Lawrence, Massachusetts, c. 1955. Teardrop-shape-waisted backrest; white upholstery; four tall laminated and bentwood legs; unmarked; 38 inches high; $300.

Wood and Vinyl Stacking Footstools (pair), c. 1955. Circular top on curved legs; $40/set.

Desks

Desk, manufactured by the Plymold Corporation. Streamline design of molded plywood in original walnut finish; 30 inches high × 23 inches deep × 44 inches wide; excellent condition; $250.

Sofas

Sofa, c. 1940s. Early biomorphic form in the style of Vladimir Kagan; original textured black fabric; minor fading; 27 inches high × 41 inches deep × 100 inches wide; very good condition; $1,700.

Sofa, designed by Ross Littell, William Katauolos, and Douglas Kelly, manufactured by Cadsana, c. 1953. Chrome-and-steel base; upholstered seat and back; 63 inches wide; $500.

Sofa, designed by Stendig, mid-twentieth century. Continuous chrome arm and back rail over three vertical rails ending in disk feet; black wooden seat with black matte front apron; tan geometric cushions and pillows; 20¾ inches high × 86 inches long × 31 inches deep; $1,100.

Tables/Stands

Glass-and-Wood Coffee Table, c. 1955. Rectangular top; hinged X-form base with serpentine supports and arched legs; 17 inches high × 28¼ inches long × 15 inches wide; $175.

Modern Coffee Table and End Table, c. 1950. Coffee table has overhanging rectangular top on U-shaped base raised on platform, unsigned, 16½ inches high × 36 inches wide × 18¼ inches deep; end table has rectangular top on U-shaped base raised on platform, unsigned, 22 inches high × 26¾ inches wide × 12¼ inches deep; $330/set.

Modern End Tables (pair), c. 1950. G-shaped, two-tier tables on platform base with blond finish; unsigned; 26 inches high × 12¼ inches wide × 26¾ inches deep; $247/set.

Chrome and Laminated Kitchen Table, c. 1940. Oval top with blond faux grain laminate over deep apron highlighted by metal banding against black ground raised on four double-tubular chrome legs; includes single leaf; 54 inches in diameter; $75.

Limed Oak End Table, manufactured by Ranch Oak and Company. Rectangular top over single drawer with bent horseshoe pull; triangular-shaped panel ends with square wooden pegs; joined by lower median shelf over arched skirt; branded mark; registered patent; 26 inches high × 20 inches wide × 15 inches deep; $85.

Chair, c. 1950. Western-style chair with modern design upholstery; 30 inches high x 3 feet deep x 28 inches wide; $450. *Courtesy of Skank World, CA.*

Hardwood-and-Glass Low Table, artist designed and executed, third quarter twentieth century. Rectangular reticulated hardwood base with glass surface; unsigned; 15 inches high × 45 inches long × 23½ inches deep; $500.

Metal and Formica Telephone/Typewriter Table, designed by Eliot Noyes, c. 1950. Rectangular black Formica-topped surface hiding a metal open drawer; supported by a tripod metal base on ball rolling feet; 23 inches high × 15½ inches wide × 13½ inches deep; $462.

Occasional Stands (two), in the style of Charles Eames. Round dish-shaped top of blond wood supported by three black rod legs with wooden ball feet; 18¼ inches high × 9 inches in diameter; $75/set.

Miscellaneous

Dinette Set, designed by Thayden Jordan, c. 1940s. Table, buffet, four chairs; birch molded-plywood set with geometric cutouts; buffet has detachable display top; leaf for table; chairs 34 inches high × 20 inches deep × 17 inches wide; buffet 54 inches high × 18 inches deep × 49 inches wide; table 29 inches high × 44 inches deep × 32 inches wide without leaf, 58 inches deep with leaf; excellent condition; $800/set.

Laminated Wood Headboard, designed by architect David Barnes, c. 1945. Oversized and custom; long rectangular backboard flanked by cylindrical shelving and mounted with tubular metal lamps; 32 inches high × 116 inches long × 13 inches deep; $225.

Cocktail Bar with Matching Stools (three), c. 1950s. Rattan, wood with formica top, pink vinyl on front, seats; 4 feet ½ inch high x 5 feet long; $485. *Courtesy of Mark Bickford Antiques, Chicago, IL.*

Bent Plywood Tea Cart, mid-twentieth century. Rectangular (rounded corner) top fitted with beverage holder; center tray; bent wood legs joined by lower median shelf with bottle rack; two wooden wheels with rubber tires; 27 inches high × 20 inches wide × 27 inches deep; $250.

▨ SCANDINAVIA ▨

Many of the important Scandinavian designers of the Art Deco period continued to influence furniture design in the 1940s and 1950s. Chief among them was Finnish architect and designer Alvar Aalto. He was among the first to work with tubular steel furniture in the early Art Deco period, but it was his continual experimentation with the use of molded plywood that made him a leader in the Modern design era, influencing a new generation internationally. Ilmari Tarpiovaara is another noted Finnish furniture designer. He worked mostly on industrial pieces for manufacturers, and is best known for the prefabricated chairs he designed for a local school. The design was called the Daddy Long Legs, because of its spindly metal legs; the seat was made of plywood.

Tarpiovaara and Tapio Wirkkala were among the noteworthy designers who worked for Asko Finnternational, Finland's first mass-production furniture factory. Scandinavian designs were internationally popular in 1956, and Asko was their largest producer.

Even the furniture manufactured by the Stockmann department store was designed by a leading designer, Olof Ottelin.

As a group, however, Danish designers were the most influential. Hans Wegner's classic design, "The Chair," was in keeping with the new organic philosophy; it was sculpted to fit the contours of the human body. Another Dane, Arne Jacobsen, took the organic style one step further with his Series 7 group, which began with the concept of his Ant chair, constructed entirely of plywood. A lesser-known designer, Poul Kjaerholm, was a minimalist whose chairs used a flattened bent steel bar as the frame and taut string, woven cane, or leather as upholstery.

Rosewood used in Modern design cabinets, bedroom suites, and dining sets, was mass-produced. The simple designs and the

Danish oil finish set a trend for oil-finished furniture in the United States and Europe. It was especially popular because scratches could be sanded and oiled. Though the design was up-scale, it was moderately priced and of good quality.

Manufacturers worth looking for include France and Sons, Soren Willadsens, Soborg Mobel-fabrik, and P. Jeppesens.

In Sweden, important designers such as Folke Ohlsson and Carl-Axel Acking designed for the many manufacturers who made moderately-priced furniture.

ALVAR AALTO (1898–1976) FINLAND (SEE ALSO ARTEK OY)

Considered one of the most important architects of the Modern movement, Alvar Aalto is equally important to collectors for his many contributions in the design of furniture, glass, and lighting.

His architecture first came to the attention of Americans at the 1933 New York World's Fair, with his design for the Finnish Pavilion, which featured a beautiful orchestration of natural materials and organic shapes.

Aalto's experimentation with laminated wood in the 30s laid the foundation for some of the most avant-garde furniture designs of Modernism. His armchair, model number 179, designed in 1932, used the strong, but easy-to-mold, native birch. The resulting chair had graceful, flowing lines, with the seat and back made from a single piece of plywood. It was one of his many furniture designs to be produced by Artek (Helsinki). They first manufactured this chair in 1935, and they continue to produce it today.

ARTEK OY

Founded in 1935 in Helsinki, Finland, Artek Oy was planned as "a centre for modern furniture and housefittings and an exhibition space for art and industrial art." Alvar and Aino Aalto were principal shareholders, and Nils-Gustav Hahl and Maire Gullichsen were partners. The name was a combination of the words *art* and *technology*. The emphasis was on plywood furniture designed by Aalto, but Venini glassware and Calder sculptures were among the many items displayed. Aalto's furniture was popular in Great Britain from its introduction, and the response to its appearance in the United States in 1947 was the same.

Cabinets

Cabinet #810, designed by Alvar Aalto. Simple architectural form of rectangular birch two-door case with multiple compartments inside supported by four tall molded plywood legs; extremely rare; signed "Aalto Design, Made in Sweden"; 38 inches wide × 16 inches deep × 39 inches high; excellent condition; $1,700.

Chairs/Lounges/Stools

Side Chairs #62 (set of six), designed by Alvar Aalto. Molded birch plywood legs and back supports with seat and back upholstered in original purple-and-black Danish wool; 19 inches wide × 17 inches deep × 31 inches high; excellent condition; $900/set.

Stool #11, designed by Alvar Aalto. Round birch top in original red finish supported by three legs of laminated molded birch; signed "Aalto Design Artek, Made in Sweden #60"; 18 inches high × 13 inches in diameter; excellent condition; $290.

Stacking Stools #66–1 (pair), designed by Alvar Aalto. Round birch top with three molded birch plywood legs; 18 inches high × 15 inches in diameter; excellent condition; $280/set.

Stacking Stools (set of four), designed by Alvar Aalto. Black lacquered tops; legs of laminated and molded birch; original finish; 17 inches high × 15 inches in diameter; excellent condition; $650/set.

Side Table, designed by Alvar Aalto, made in Sweden for Artek, #75-2. Two tiers of molded plywood and two molded birch plywood legs of one continuous form, signed AALTO DESIGN #75, refinished, recent white lacquer; 24 inches high x 19 inches deep x 24 inches wide; $180. *Courtesy of Toomey-Treadway Galleries, Oak Park, IL.*

X Stools (two), designed by Alvar Aalto, c. 1954. Each leg of five laminated pieces of ash jointed at seat; upholstered in leather; traces of original label; 18 inches high × 18½ inches wide; $385/set.

Tables/Stands

Side Table #75–2, designed by Alvar Aalto. Two tiers of molded plywood in original black lacquer finish and two molded birch plywood legs of one continuous form; 24 inches wide × 19 inches deep × 24 inches high; excellent condition; $950.

ARNE JACOBSEN (1902–1971) DENMARK

His most influential designs, notably his chairs, were designed for Fritz Hansen's Eft and produced in the postwar decades. His training, initially as a craftsman, gave him an appreciation of materials. Later he became an architect, and then a designer of furniture. His early design influences were Charles and Ray Eames, Alvar Aalto, and Eero Saarinen.

Jacobsen first gained international attention with his Ant side chair, designed in 1952. Its organic form was the inspiration for the name. Designed for the canteen of the Novo Pharmaceutical Company in Copenhagen, it was mass-produced by Fritz Hansen in the early 1950s. It was made of teak-faced beech plywood molded in three dimensions, steel, plastic sheathing, and rubber. The fact that it was lightweight, stackable, and inexpensive made it right for the times.

In 1957 his two most important designs, the Swan and Egg chairs, became instantly popular. They have been continuously produced ever since, with many variations. Originally they were leather, with a plastic shell and padded with foam rubber. Variations included coverings of vinyl or fabric. They were mounted on chromed steel pedestals.

PRICES

Chairs/Lounges/Stools

Egg Chair, designed for Fritz Hansen, c. 1958. Foam-injected molded fiberglass shell upholstered in vibrant purple Danish wool on aluminum swivel base; original finish; 35 inches

---

wide × 30 inches deep × 40 inches high; excellent condition; $1,100.

Danish Swan Chair and Ottoman, c. 1955. Gray upholstery; $170/set.

Ottoman, designed for Fritz Hansen. Black Danish wool upholstered over polyurethane foam-injected shell; aluminum base; 22 inches wide × 16 inches deep × 14 inches high; excellent condition; $600.

Swan Chair, designed by Arne Jacobsen for Fritz Hansen, Denmark, c. 1952. Orange-colored upholstery on molded fiberglass shell raised on four-legged, star-shaped base of polished aluminum, label DANISH FURNITURE MAKERS CONTROL; 29½ inches high x 18 inches deep x 28½ inches wide; $100. *Courtesy of Skinner, Inc., Boston/Bolton, MA.*

BRUNO MATHSSON (1907–1988) SWEDEN

Like other Scandinavian architects, Mathsson was fascinated with the design possibilities of the chair. His early training began in the family cabinetmaking workshop, where he was employed from 1923 to 1931. Like other architects, he was influenced by the functional designs of Mies van der Rohe, Le Corbusier, and Marcel Breuer, and he explored the possibilities offered by laminated wood. His first three chairs, made between 1933 and 1936, featured laminated bentwood frames and webbed seats. He was unable to sell them to the larger Swedish manufacturers, so they were made by his father's firm, Firma Karl Mathsson. The chairs were designed to follow the contours of the human body. The first was called "the working chair," based on his idea that it is easier to work in a relaxed position. Other designs included an armchair and a lounge chair.

PRICES

Chairs/Lounges/Stools

Working Armchair and Footstool, c. 1941. Laminated bentwood and solid wood with attached arms and webbed fabric up-

---

holstery; branded marks; chair 35½ inches high × 39 inches long × 25¼ inches wide; stool 15¾ inches high × 25 inches long × 19¾ inches wide; $990/set.

Chaise Longue, c. 1940s. Organic form of molded and laminated birch plywood upholstered in original red paper webbing; detachable headrest; label says "Bruno Mathsson firma Karl Mathsson made in Varnamo Sweden"; 25 inches wide × 65 inches deep × 37 inches high; excellent condition; $2,100.

Lounge Chair and Ottoman, c. 1940s. Two-piece armless version of the classic chaise in laminated molded birch plywood; reupholstered in original Mathsson hemp webbing; original detachable headrest; chair 40 inches wide × 20 inches deep × 32 inches high; ottoman 20 inches wide × 25 inches deep × 17 inches high; very good condition; $2,000/set.

Sofas

Loveseat, c. 1940s. Organic form of laminated and molded birch plywood in original blue and natural paper webbing; water stains to webbing; 45 inches wide × 24 inches deep × 35 inches high; very good condition; $700.

Tables/Stands

Occasional Table. Round top of bird's-eye maple supported by three sculptural molded birch legs; 25 inches high × 34 inches in diameter; very good condition; $325.

VERNER PANTON (1926–) DENMARK

An industrial designer of many talents, Panton is recognized primarily for his chair designs, made from a variety of materials. However, his design creativity extended to textiles, lighting, and other products as well. This Danish architect's cone chair design in 1958 brought him early recognition in the world of contemporary design. After studying at the Royal Danish Academy of Fine Arts, Copenhagen, from 1947 to 1951, he became an associate with Arne Jacobsen (1950–1952) and went on to form his own architectural and design office in Denmark (1955–1962). In 1963 he moved his work to Binningen, Switzerland.

He is known for making the first single-piece plastic chair. It was designed in 1960, but because of technical production problems it wasn't actually made until 1968, when Vitra GmbH (Basel, Switzerland) produced it for Herman Miller International, New York. This side chair was manufactured from 1968 to 1979. It became popular as part of the Pop designs of the 1960s.

PRICES

Cone chair. Conical form of bent sheet metal construction; upholstered in pale gray wool; 32 inches high × 24 inches deep × 23 inches wide; excellent condition; $750.

Left: Cone Chair, designed by Verner Panton, c. 1959. Bent chromium steel cage construction, ponyskin seat; 30 inches high x 24 inches deep x 23 inches wide; $1,700. *Right:* Cone Chair, designed by Verner Panton, c. 1959. Bright orange upholstery, bent sheet metal construction; 32 inches high x 24 inches deep x 23 inches wide; $1,100. *Far right:* Swag-legged Side Table, designed by George Nelson for Herman Miller Furniture Company, Inc. Highly polished chrome base, black laminate top has beveled edge; 16 inches high x 17 inches in diameter; $300. *All are courtesy of Treadway Gallery, OH.*

HANS JORGENSEN WEGNER (1914–) DENMARK

This important furniture designer started out as an apprentice to a cabinetmaker at fourteen. By 1938 he was on his way in the office of Arne Jacobsen and Eric Moller. He became a designer of repute in the late 1940s with a series of chair forms. At age thirty-three he was recognized as a leader of Denmark's craftsmen-designers. His first important design was the peacock (model number JH 550) armchair, from 1947. It was, as many of his designs were to be, the reworking of a traditional wooden chair, in this case, the Windsor. It was another first in Danish furniture design, using a light-colored, attenuated wood frame with a natural finish. However, it was his 1949 design of the round chair (model number JH 501) that is considered his most important contribution. Over the years he has modified and adapted it into many models using a variety of materials.

In 1949 he created a well-known design for a wide, low lounge chair, inspired by Eero Saarinen's Womb chair of 1946–1948. In 1950 he designed a number of chairs using molded plywood shells; others had metal frames and bases with string upholstery. Through the 1950s and 1960s his work included case pieces, office systems, and upholstered furniture, with an emphasis on metal and molded plywood. These later pieces are not considered as fine as his simple wooden chair designs.

PRICES

Chairs/Lounges/Stools

Ash Armchairs (pair). Shaped elliptical back with wide through tenons joined to the shaped frame; original rush seat; one chair stamped "DESIGNER HANS J. WEGNER MADE IN DENMARK BY CARL HANSEN & SON ODENSE DENMARK BB65"; 27 inches high × 28 inches wide × 25 inches deep; $990/set.

Bear Chair and Ottoman. Tufted back in reupholstered black fabric; winged arms with teak armrest and legs; chair 35 inches wide × 33 inches deep × 36 inches high; ottoman 27 inches wide × 15 inches high; very good condition; $700/set.

Stacking Chairs (pair), manufactured by Fritz Hansen, Denmark, c. 1952. Birch frame and leg pierced through triangular walnut seat; 29 inches high × 16 inches deep × 20 inches wide; very good condition; $425/set.

Miscellaneous

Ash Dining Table and Four Chairs. Side chairs with shaped seats, X-form bowed backs, and Y-form legs; drop leaf dining table with curving X-form legs, branded "FABREKAT ANOR TUCK ARKITEKT HANS J. WEGNER DENMARK"; table with leaves open 28 inches high × 34 inches wide × 93 inches long; $2,090/set.

Danish Modern Dining Table and Four Chairs, manufactured by Fritz Hansen, c. 1950. Table with circular laminated top on three cylindrical legs; chairs with narrow concave crest rail over triangular seat on tapering legs; stackable; manufacturer's label; table 47 inches high × 47 inches in diameter; chair 28½ inches high; $500/set.

Chairs/Lounges/Stools

Chromium-Plated Metal, Leather, and Wood Armchair, designed by Poul Kjaerholm, Denmark, c. 1957. Vertical brushed-chromium-plated steel legs joined by a semicircular laminated ash backrest; semicircular leather seat; 25¾ inches high × 25 inches wide × 16¾ inches deep; $880.

Swedish "Kurva" Laminated Plywood Armchair with Ottoman, designed by Yngve Ekstrom, c. 1945. En suite with the above; 39¾ inches high × 27½ inches wide × 29 inches deep; $1,320/set.

Danish Modern Teak Slat-Back Armchair. Three vertical back slats in frame flaring to tapered legs; curved arms attached to arched seat rails and pierced below by single side rails; black vinyl seat; partial branded mark on seat rail "Made in Denmark by K . . ."; seat branded "Made in Denmark"; American materials regulating tag indicating "sold by Scandinavian Design"; back 38 inches high; seat 18 inches high; $100.

Sofas

Rosewood-and-Leather Sofa and Ottoman, Scandinavia, c. 1958. Black leather upholstered seat tied and accented by wooden buttons fitted into rosewood framework; approximately 31½ inches high × 75 inches long × 28½ inches deep; $700/set.

▒ ITALY ▒

Several distinctive furniture designs came out of Italy following World War II. One of them was adjustable furniture using the new distinctively Modern concepts and materials. One of the important designers who emerged in this era was Osvaldo Borsani, previously known for his work in Traditional furniture. The new adjustable pieces were manufactured beginning in 1954 by Techno S.p.A., the firm owned by the Borsani family. Osvaldo's first adjustable design was divan bed D70, made with metal frames and polyfoam upholstery. It was unique for its multiple functions, which included transformation from a seat to a bed or a storage piece. His next piece, the P40 lounge chair, offered even more complicated mechanical options, and included organic curves that softened the look. For the ultimate in comfort it shifted to three positions.

Techno Chair, designed by Osvaldo Borsani, c. 1954; $3,000.
Courtesy of Al and Kim Eiber Collection.

Marco Zanusco, a contemporary of Borsani, created his Lady chair in 1951, originating a new form of upholstered furniture. It used rubber webbing that supported foam rubber cushions. Another of his firsts was the Sleep-O-Matic sofa bed. It was constructed in 1954 with the same tubular steel frame and upholstery as his earlier easy chair. These and later Zanusco pieces were manufactured by Arflex.

Another contributor to postwar furniture design was Carlo Mollino, whose experiments with form led to such classics as his biomorphic table, Arabesco. Trained as an architect, he originally designed furniture for specific clients. The Arabesco was one such piece, and was originally treated as both furniture and sculpture.

PIERO FORNASETTI (1913–1988)
This Italian was a self-taught artist who used modern techniques in designs for a variety of objects, including ceramics, furniture, and decorative arts. He also designed complete interiors. However, he enjoyed the decoration more than the form of objects.

His screens are among the most widely sought of his 1950s designs. Many were hand-colored lithographs on wood panels.

PRICES

Tables/Stands

Cocktail Table. Classic Roman coin series with various size coins illustrating classical Roman figures in gold and black marbleized background; 39 inches in diameter × 13 inches high; very good condition; $375.

Table. Surrealistic collage composition with book theme; black-and-yellow marbleized background; brilliant red, blue, yellow, and green design; 40 inches wide × 19 inches deep × 16 inches high; very good condition; $600.

Giovanni (Gio) Ponti (1891-1979)

This versatile architect and designer is considered one of Italy's most important creative influences. He led Italy back to prominence in the design world with his post–World War II glass and furniture works. His decorative objects and furniture can be recognized by their distinctive sleek, tapering, and curving forms. In the 1940s and 1950s he created vividly colored glassware for Venini. Among his interior designs for Italian ships were those he executed for the S.S. *Andrea Doria*. In the field of furniture he created pieces for Knoll, Arflex, Cassina, and Techno in the 1950s and 1960s. They are noted for their simplistic elegance. His side chair (model number 699) Superleggera, meaning extra light, is an example of his use of traditional design translated into Modern form. It combines ash, rush, and steel glides.

PRICES

Tables/Stands

Coffee Table, manufactured in Italy for the Singer Company, c. 1950. Black ebonized blade-shaped legs with brass tips; bentwood-and-brass base supports original tempered glass top with controlled air bubble around edge to prevent shattering; 39 inches wide × 14 inches high; excellent condition; $800.

Cocktail Table, manufactured in Italy for the Singer Company. Sculptural geometric construction in walnut; tapered legs with brass tips; original tempered glass top with controlled air bubble around edge; 41 inches deep × 14 inches high; excellent condition; $550.

Dining Table, c. 1950s. Collapsible ebonized wood base in the form of an oversized jack; replaced glass top; 29 inches high × 48 inches in diameter; very good condition; $700.

Miscellaneous

Hall Console, c. 1950. Exotic walnut; tall tapered legs with brass tips and stretchers; floating drawers; asymmetrical sides; original finish; 61 inches wide × 20 inches deep × 34 inches high; excellent condition; $3,750.

Various Italian Designs

PRICES

Chairs/Lounges/Stools

"Lady" Green Fabric and Brass Armchair, designed by Marco Zanusco for Arflex, c. 1951. Wide chair with bean-shaped armrests; upholstered in green; supported by four brass feet; 31 inches high × 31 inches wide × 31 inches deep; $2,090.

Gray Fabric and Brass Armchairs (group of three), design attributed to Marco Zanusco for Arflex, c. 1951. Wide seat and slightly curved backrest; flanked by triangular pierced armrests; four brass legs; 33 inches high × 28½ inches wide × 34 inches deep; $3,300/set.

Giltwood Tall Ladderback Chair, Italy, c. 1955. Tapering back with seven-shaped rungs over trapezoidal seat on turned legs; back 51½ inches high; seat 16 inches high × 17½ inches wide; gilt wear; $225.

Lounge Chair, designed by Osvaldo Borsani, manufactured by Tecno, c. 1955. Organic sculptural form with high-tech use of materials; unusual rubber tension-suspended arms; original black wool upholstery; 34 inches wide × 28 inches deep × 45 inches high; very good condition; $750.

Lounge Chairs (pair), designed by Franco Albini, manufactured by Vittorio Bonacina and Company, c. 1950. Three-legged black metal frame/support; optical seat and back of molded Indian cane and malacca cane; 34 inches wide × 36 inches deep × 36 inches high; excellent condition; $550/set.

"Mezzadro" Stool, designed by Achille and Pier Giacomo Castiglioni, manufactured by Zanotta, c. 1957. Chrome-plated steel tractor seat form with natural beech footrest; 20 inches high × 20 inches deep × 19 inches wide; excellent condition; $325.

Desks

Olivetti "Spazio" Painted Metal Office Desk, designed by the group BBPR (Gianluigi Banfi, Lodovico Barbiano di Belgiojoso, Enrico Peressutti, and Ernesto N. Rogers), c. 1956. Rectangular black painted metal top with cantilevered corners; supported by a metallic structure holding a filing cabinet on the left side; plastic cabinet door stamped "OLIVETTI ARREDAMENTI METALUCU"; 29 inches high × 63 inches wide × 31½ inches deep; $935.

Sofas

Silk-and-Wood Sofa, designed by Ico Parisi, c. 1948. Three-seat sofa with three arched backrests; upholstered with pastel green silk; set within a wooden frame signed "ICO PARISI 1948"; 29 inches high × 74½ inches wide × 26½ inches deep; $2,640.

Tables/Stands

Occasional Table. Elegant tapered legs with ball feet supporting a floating glass disk with asymmetrical oval handle; dark walnut finish; 17 inches wide × 17 inches deep × 25 inches high; excellent condition; $850.

Miscellaneous

Trolley, designed by Cesare Lacca, c. 1955. Plate glass shelf supported by sculptural frame of solid mahogany with brass mounts and castors; 28 inches wide × 17 inches deep × 33 inches high; excellent condition; $600.

OTHER EUROPEAN FURNITURE DESIGNS

PRICES

Chairs/Lounges/Stools

Lacquered Wood and Green Upholstered Armchairs (pair), designed by Jean Royere, c. 1950. Green upholstered trapezoidal seat and back; black painted armrests and tapering legs; 32¼ inches high × 20½ inches wide × 17¾ inches deep; $3,080/set.

Chair and Ottoman, designed by Pierre Paulin, manufactured by Artifort, c. 1950s. Sculptural molded fiberglass form upholstered in original turquoise purple tweed fabric; chrome-plated solid steel legs; black rubber pod feet; chair 35 inches wide × 27 inches deep × 33 inches high; ottoman 28 inches wide × 19 inches deep × 13 inches high; some wear, very good condition; $600/set.

Black Painted and Drilled Metal Chairs (group of six), attributed to Mathieu Matégot, c. 1950. Drilled black painted sheet iron back and seat in a tubular black painted metal continuing to two front feet; inverted V-shaped back legs joined at the seat level to hold the back; 31 inches high × 15⅜ inches wide × 14 inches deep; $1,320/set.

Bentwood Chauffeuses (pair), designed by Charlotte Perrinad, produced by the Steph Simon Gallery, Paris, c. 1954. Low elongated frame with slats; boomerang shaped legs; each with two cushions; 17 inches high × 30 inches long × 18 inches wide; $880/set.

Chairs (pair), Jacobs/Kandya, England. Animated forms with black base and trim, seats, and backs; original finish; very good condition; $120/set.

Steel and Plywood Antelope Chairs (group of nine), designed by Ernest Race, c. 1950. Steel rod frame on four tubular legs supporting a drilled plywood seat; three chairs painted in ecru, three in blue, and three in green; 31 inches high × 22 inches wide × 18 inches deep; $176/set.

Desks

"Compas" Wood-and-Metal Desk, designed by Jean Prouve, c. 1948. Inverted V-shaped black lacquered legs supporting a rectangular oak top with a steel drawer on each side; 29 inches high × 62½ inches wide × 27½ inches deep; $3,300.

Through most of history, glass-work was considered a craft. Its purpose was primarily functional. Even though it evolved in the Middle Ages to include the making of stained-glass windows, largely for cathedrals, it was not thought of as an art form. Louis Comfort Tiffany elevated glass production to another level with his art glass, as did other glassmakers, such as Galle and Lalique. Rene Lalique treated glass as sculpture. Some of his most memorable pieces date from the Art Deco period. By the 1940s European glass artists in Czechoslovakia, Italy, and Scandinavia were taking glass one step further, often experimenting with small sculptural pieces.

In the postwar years the Italians and the Scandinavians dominated and exemplified the field of modern glass production. Fluid forms employed as early as the 1930s were enhanced by new techniques. Bubbled glass was a popular form that became associated with Scandinavian designers such as the Finn Gunnel Nyland. As early as 1936 another Finnish designer, Alvar Aalto, experimented with free-form glass designs. One of his organic pieces, vase model number 3031, has been in production

Glass

153

continuously since its design. While Scandinavian designers for the most part used clear glass, in keeping with a Modern statement, the Italians used ever more vibrant colors, patterns, and designs. Earlier traditional latticino work was also incorporated in the new forms. So much glass was produced in the postwar period in Italy that today it has all but taken over the auction and dealer market.

Tip: Many of the most popular Venini figures are still in production and are often passed off as older, more valuable, pieces. They even show up in consignment shops—without labels, of course.

In the United States, where exciting designs in furniture, ceramics, and jewelry burgeoned, modern glass forms generally lagged behind. Steuben and Blenko were exceptions. Steuben slowly introduced new designs into their line and Blenko made decorative giftware items in free-form shapes and new colors such as chartreuse. Examples of Blenko work can be found for just a few dollars in many thrift shops.

It was individual glass designers working around the country who experimented with colors, shapes, and techniques. Many continue to employ contemporary methods in their work today. The works of Harvey K. Littleton and Maurice Heaton are highly collectible when they come to market. Michael and Frances Higgins are still active, and many of their pieces are in museums and private collections. Working with fused glass, they have been—and continue to be—prolific artists and craftspeople. Perhaps this is one of the reasons their work is still underpriced. While they design one-of-a-kind objects, they also designed a commercial line of trays, plates, and ashtrays, most often in orange and gilt designs. Their finest pieces rarely come to auction.

An overlooked area for collectors is Czechoslovakian art glass. These distinctive pieces feature designs on the surface of the glass made with a variety of media, including enamel. When pieces do come to market, they are apt to be unrecognized as important additions to Modern art glass.

Note that price listings are primarily from auctions, unless otherwise stated.

MAURICE HEATON (1900–)

Born in Neuchâtel, Switzerland, Heaton later attended the Stevens Institute of Technology in Hoboken, New Jersey. His works are in museum collections at the Metropolitan Museum of Art and the Museum of Contemporary Crafts, both in New York City, and elsewhere.

PRICES

Kiln-formed glass, untitled, executed c. 1959. Powdered glass-enamel decoration; 14¾ inches in diameter; $1,300.

MICHAEL HIGGINS (1908–)
FRANCES HIGGINS (1912–)

A lifelong shared career as glass artists began for Michael and Frances Higgins over forty years ago while both were university teachers. For Frances glasswork began as a hobby in 1942, when she became interested in working with sheet glass. Shortly after she and Michael married they began experimenting in fused enameled sheet glass, which was an innovation in art glass at the time. Now in their eighties, they continue to experiment with new forms and techniques. Collectors have discovered what museums have known for years—that their work is of the highest quality. Both have always created their own designs; Frances specializes in jewelry and decorative pieces, while Michael is recognized for his bowls and plaques. One of his pieces, a plaque titled "The Medieval Naval Dockyard," is in the Victoria and Albert Museum. A retrospective book of their pieces is in the works.

In early experiments they worked with clear glass, fusing up to three layers together. They later copyrighted these pieces. By 1959 they were using enamels. Their first retail customers were Marshall Field's and C. D. Peacocks in Chicago.

Through the years they have produced a wide variety of objects from earrings to a 500-square-foot curtain of glass. Their work is in many museum collections and there is a renewed interest in the work they did many years ago, including their mobiles. Under the stimulus of what the antiques trade is unearthing of their early designs and techniques, the Higginses are reviving and adapting some early works. As far as they know, there is no selling of such pieces by dealers as "antiques." Naturally, the Higginses would not lend themselves to any chicanery of that kind.

Michael organized the Midwest Designer Craftsmen, a society of glass artisans. Their well-respected and innovative designs have been the basis of many imitations.

For the last thirty-four years, usually a plain "Higgins" in the handwriting of Frances or Michael identifies their work. For quite early and one-of-a-kind studio pieces, the name is engraved on the back of the rim. For pieces produced in quantity during their period under contract with the Dearborn Glass Company of Bedford Park, Illinois, their name is either printed in gold luster on top of the rim or is incorporated in the enameled decor inside the piece.

PRICES

Bowls

Art Glass Bowl, c. 1950. Radiating violet-and-blue bubbled pattern with painted gold highlights; 12 inches in diameter; $110.

Square Glass Dish, designed by Michael Higgins, c. 1950s. Radiating blue, green, yellow, etched script signature HIGGINS; 10 x 10 inches; $125. *Courtesy of Al and Kim Eiber Collection.*

Enameled Slumped Glass Bull Masque Bowl, c. 1955. Irregular form; composed of two layers of glass with patterned oxides in gray, white, and brick-red melted in between; signed "higgins" with monogram; 20¼ inches long; $4,600.

Dishes/Plates

Chargers (two). Round charger of pale lavender clear glass with internal enameled peacock feather decoration in blues and purples, gold spiral painted center and rim, signed "Higgins" in gold paint; round charger of textured pale lavender glass with irregular triangles applied that have internal triangular enamel decorations in green and blue; both 1 inch high × 17 inches in diameter; both mint condition; $190/set.

Enameled Glass Platter, c. 1950s. Clear glass; circular platter with a radiating design in yellow and white; heightened with platinum luster; inscribed "higgins"; 15 inches in diameter; $287.

Art Glass Tray. Abstract design in vibrant blues and gold; 10 inches wide × 14 inches long; $180.

Miscellaneous

Glass Ashtray. Orange, black, and gold abstract decoration; 7 inches wide × 10 inches long; mint condition; $60.

Glass Ashtray and Bowl. Square form with green-and-blue stylized decoration; together with a frosted glass square bowl; tray 7 inches × 7 inches; $110/set.

Wall Sculpture. Wire stick figures trapped between layers of glass with multiple colors and mesh screen; very rare; glass 7 inches wide × 14 inches high; dimensions with frame 24 inches wide × 30 inches high; excellent condition; $1,400.

Glass Charger and Bowl, designed by Michael Higgins. Charger of amethyst with chartreuse and blue geometric inclusions, signed in gold HIGGINS; 17 inches in diameter. Speckled bowl of green and aqua with three white and yellow circular design elements highlighted in gold, signed HIGGINS; 2½ inches high x 8¼ inches in diameter. $193/set. *Courtesy of Skinner Inc., Boston/Bolton, MA.*

STEUBEN

Steuben glassworks was founded in 1903 by Frederick Carder. It was a time of new ideas and the growth of art glass on both sides of the Atlantic. Carder came to Corning, New York, from England at the same time Louis Comfort Tiffany was developing his new concepts in American art glass. Color and the way it was used in new techniques were all-important to the glass developed at Steuben. During the thirty years Steuben was under the direction of Carder, hundreds of different colors and thousands of forms were produced. However, by the end of World War II new techniques originated at Orrefors and Kosta glassworks in Sweden began to influence modern glass production. They explored the optical properties of glass and the newly popular geometric and other forms.

When Arthur A. Houghton, Jr., became president of Steuben in 1933, he banished color, and with a team of architects and artists combined Scandinavian techniques with a newly developed optical glass composition that offered an unusual brilliance. By 1935 a series of decorative pieces by Sidney Waugh were produced, using copper wheel and diamond-point engraving, similar to the Swedish style.

A 1937 Paris meeting of architect John Gates and Henri Matisse led to the production of a Steuben piece that featured an engraving with a Matisse drawing. Gates went on to commission drawings from other important European and American painters and sculptors that became the Steuben Series "Design in Glass by Twenty-seven Contemporary Artists."

Like many American companies, Steuben found that its output was changed by America's participation in World War II. Not until the 1950s did Steuben regain its place as an innovator of quality, with such important designers as Sidney Waugh, Donald Pollard, Don Wier, George Thompson, and Lloyd Atkins leading the way.

In the 50s, Arthur Houghton commissioned internationally renowned artists to design for Steuben. In the years from 1954 to 1955 artists from the Near East and Far East created a series of designs that were displayed in an exhibit at the National Gallery of Art in Washington called "Asian Artists in Crystal."

The same decade saw the manufacture of major ornamental pieces. In 1959 a group of thirty-one "collector's pieces" in engraved crystal were made to showcase Steuben's own designers. In a sense, this glass from the 50s began a new form of American art glass. The pieces were always high-priced and produced in limited number. When they come to market, and that's a rare occasion, they still go for top dollar.

More affordable are tableware, barware, and nonengraved decorative pieces. Their beauty relies on their form, often freeform shapes or undulating curves of the Modern design era. Many of these pieces were designed by Donald Pollard, who also created important limited edition engraved pieces.

From the mid-fifties through the seventies Steuben produced free sculptural forms of crystal and animal and bird figures.

Mid-century Steuben pieces offer good collecting opportunities that have not been fully appreciated and explored.

PRICES

Bowls

Crystal Low Bowl, designed by John Dreves, c. 1941. Circular rim tapering to narrow circular foot; signed "Steuben"; 7⅝ inches in diameter; $100.

Crystal Trefoil Bowl, designed by Lloyd Atkins, c. 1950. Circular rim tapering to trefoil base; signed "Steuben"; 6⅝ inches in diameter; $200.

Martini Glasses (set of six), 1950s. Tear drop, signed STEUBEN; $650/set. *Courtesy of Skinner Inc., Boston/ Bolton, MA.*

Crystal Free-Form Bowl. Signed; 5½ inches in diameter; $110.

Dishes/Plates
Crystal Nut Dish, designed by George Thompson, c. 1949. Signed "Steuben"; 11 inches high; $130.
Crystal Canapé Plate, designed by Lloyd Atkins, c. 1953. Signed "Steuben"; 6½ inches in diameter; $160.

Urns/Vases/Vessels
Crystal Vase. Tapering cylindrical form on circular foot; signed "Steuben"; 7 inches high; $300.
Crystal Bouquet Vase, designed by George Thompson, c. 1951. Signed "Steuben"; $225.
Crystal Pitcher, designed by George Thompson, c. 1950. Signed "Steuben"; 11 inches high; $200.
Crystal Pitcher, designed by Lloyd Atkins, c. 1955. Ovoid form with double loop handles; signed "Steuben"; 10 inches high; $275.

Miscellaneous
Crystal Massive Ashtrays (pair), designed by George Thompson, c. 1946. Signed "Steuben"; $200.
Set of Crystal Stemware. Teardrop stems; includes 14 water goblets, 14 champagne glasses, 5 white wine glasses, 8 red wine glasses, 6 sauterne glasses, and 6 cordials; $1,900/set.

▣ ITALIAN STUDIO GLASS DESIGNERS ▣

AVEM (ARTE VETRARIA MURANESE),
FOUNDED IN 1932

PRICES

Urns/Vases/Vessels
Vase, probably designed by Giorgio Ferro, c. 1950. Clear heavy body with internal layer of blue and large pulled hole in a Streamline form; unsigned; 12½ inches high; mint condition; $325.

Vase, probably designed by Ansolo Fuga, c. 1955. Clear heavy body with internal dark amethyst stripes; fine gold leaf and opaque white; pulled hole; unsigned; 15½ inches high; mint condition; $2,500.

Vase, probably designed by Ansolo Fuga, c. 1955. Clear with internal random patchwork design of opaque white, red, blue, yellow, amethyst, and green overlaid with gold leaf; unsigned; 13¾ inches high; mint condition; $2,900.

Miscellaneous

Swans (pair), c. 1950. Figurines with complicated bit work; dappled opaque white bodies and polychrome applications; paper label (MURANO MADE IN ITALY); tallest is 8¼ inches high; mint condition; $425.

Glass Figure, AVEM, c. 1940. Female skier, clear with opaque white applications, paper label: AVEM MURANO MADE IN ITALY; 10 inches high; $150. *Courtesy of Toomey-Treadway Galleries, Oak Park, IL.*

BAROVIER AND TOSO

This firm began producing colorful glass in a variety of textures and abstract designs in 1942. Ercole Barovier (1889–1974) and his son, Angelo Barovier (1927–   ), are considered among the important designers of Modern glass. Their designs used abstract sculptural forms with minute bubbles and spots of color within the glass.

PRICES

Bowls

"Zebrata" Bowl, designed by Ercole Barovier, c. 1950. Clear with dark amethyst spiral overlaid with heavy gold leaf; unsigned; 4¾ inches in diameter; mint condition; $150.

"Spuma Di Mare" Bowl, designed by Ercole Barovier, c.

1947. Heavy clear glass with "sommerso" striations of very fine bubbles, large bubbles, and black powders; overlaid with gold leaf and a clear layer with tinted aquamarine edges; unsigned; 8¼ inches in diameter; mint condition; $650.

"Rugiadose" Leaf-Form Bowl, designed by Ercole Barovier, c. 1940. Large clear molded leaf form with applied crushed pink glass and applied clear ball feet; unsigned; 16½ inches wide; mint condition; $150.

Glass Bowl, c. 1948. Variation on the clam form; transparent glass with internal gold decoration; 13 inches wide × 6 inches high; mint condition; $210.

Small Glass Bowl, c. 1950. Classic clam form in jewel-tone red with heavy stripes; 6 inches wide × 3 inches high; mint condition; $100.

Venetian Glass Bowl, attributed to Barovier. Dark burgundy and cream stripes within amber glass walls; 3 inches high × 7 inches in diameter; $325.

Bowl. Gold striped decoration; pointed rim; 9 inches wide × 4 inches high; mint condition; $180.

Urns/Vases/Vessels

"Graffito Barbarico" Vase, designed by Ercole Barovier, c. 1952. Clear with enclosed blue-and-opal decoration under a gold profusion; unsigned; 9¼ inches high; mint condition; $1,400.

"Eugenei" Vase, designed by Ercole Barovier, c. 1951. Clear iridescent body with internal decoration of blue and metallic inclusions; two pulled handles and applied foot; unsigned; 13½ inches high; mint condition; $2,500.

"Graffito Lattimo" Vase, designed by Ercole Barovier, c. 1952. Clear with enclosed opaque white swags encompassing controlled form bubbles; unsigned; 10⅞ inches high; mint condition; $1,200.

"Tessere Ambra" Glass Vase, designed by Ercole Barovier, c. 1957. Squat bulbous vessel internally decorated with a patchwork motif in butterscotch, white, and deep amethyst; 6¼ inches high; $3,740.

Patchwork Vase, designed by Ercole Barovier, c. 1957. Cylindrical vessel composed of rectangles of opalescent glass edged in purple with faint overlays of gilt; unsigned; 9⅞ inches high; $4,025.

Glass Vase, designed by Ercole Barovier, c. 1940. Rectangular vessel in clear glass decorated with overlapping layers of multicolored canes with silver foil inclusions; 7¼ inches high; $517.

Glass Vase, designed by Dino Martens, c. 1950s. Bulbous tapered form of colorless glass with internal spiral decoration of white, purple, and copper threaded bands creating many different optical patterns as they intersect; 12 inches high × 6 inches in diameter; mint condition; $425.

Glass Vase, attributed to Dino Martens, c. 1950. Pink, purple, and white stripe decoration with pulled and coiled top; 7 inches wide × 11 inches high; mint condition; $300.

"Nerox" Vase, designed by Ermanno Toso, c. 1956. Clear inlaid with bright orange and pink murrines; unsigned; 16 inches high; mint condition; $750.

"Nerox" Vase, designed by Ermanno Toso, c. 1956. Black heavy iridescent body inlaid with bright orange and pink murrines; unsigned; 4 inches high; mint condition; $250.

"Murrina" Vase, designed by Ermanno Toso, c. 1959. Opaque white with aqua blue spiraled murrines; paper label (MURANO GLASS MADE IN ITALY); 8¼ inches high; mint condition; $6,500.

Glass Vase. Cylindrical transparent form with green and gold applied seaweed decoration; unsigned; 9 inches high × 4 inches in diameter; mint condition; $200.

Glass Vase, c. 1950. Heavy gold overlay background with brilliant red-and-green drip decoration; 12 inches high; mint condition; $800.

Vase. Irregular conical form of colorless glass with internal skeletal stripe decoration in blue, green, and white; 6 inches wide × 5 inches deep × 11 inches high; mint condition; $275.

Glass Vase, designed by Dino Martens, from the Oriente series, produced by Aureliano Toso, Murano, c. 1948. Irregular gourd-form vessel with elongated neck; clear glass with enclosed powders of red, royal blue, yellow, white, and turquoise; latticino patches; a large star-shaped murrina and gold foil inclusions; 14½ inches high; $7,762.

Blown Glass Vase, Il Burlesco, designed by Pablo Picasso, blown by Lado Bon, produced by Aureliano Toso, Murano, c. 1955. Ovoid vessel with trumpet-form neck atop a bulbous body flanked by handles; raised on a trumpet-form base; clear glass decorated with black paste glass to depict a face; signed "Picasso"; 12¼ inches high; $10,925.

Miscellaneous

Bottle, c. 1950. Vertical ribbed body of turquoise-blue overlaid with gold leaf and controlled bubbles then cased clear; unsigned; 21 inches high; mint condition; $160.

Bottle, designed by Ermanno Toso, c. 1959. Clear body with applied vertical canes of alternating gray and white; unsigned; 17½ inches high; mint condition; $450.

Bottle, designed by Ermanno Toso, c. 1959. Clear body with applied vertical canes of pink and white latticino; unsigned; 18¾ inches high; mint condition; $300.

Bottle, designed by Ermanno Toso, c. 1959. Clear body with applied vertical canes of pink and gold latticino; paper label (MURANO GLASS MADE IN ITALY); 18¼ inches high; mint condition; $300.

FULVIO BIANCONI (1915–) (SEE ALSO VENINI)

Fulvio Bianconi is regarded as one of the most important Italian glass designers of the postwar years. After the war he began designing perfume bottles and graphics. His meeting in 1948 with Paolo Venini resulted in his decision to join the Venini glasshouse. Humorous figurines of commedia del l'arte characters were designed by Bianconi for Venini. Other postwar designs, now considered among his finest, were the handkerchief vase and his Scottish vases featuring plaids of caning.

CENEDESE GLASSWORKS
FOUNDED IN 1945 BY GINO CENEDESE (1907–1973)

PRICES

Bowls

"Sommerso" Bowl, designed by Gino Cenedese, c. 1950. Two clear heavy disks with dark amethyst-tinted edges with an internal figure of a polychrome bird overlaid in gold leaf; paper retailer's label (CAMER GLASS NEW YORK MADE IN ITALY); 10 inches in diameter; mint condition; $250.

Marshmallow Sofa, designed by George Nelson for Herman Miller Furniture Company, 1956. Vinyl naugahyde cushions; 32 inches high x 52 inches wide; $16,500.

Courtesy of John Toomey and Don Treadway, Toomey-Treadway Galleries, Oak Park, IL.

Storage Unit, designed by Charles Eames for Herman Miller Furniture Company, c. 1951. Two-tiered, early production, laminated birch top, primarily colored masonite panels and white siding, fiberglass doors, black laminate shelves and drawers; 33 inches high x 16 inches deep x 47 inches wide; $6,000.

Courtesy of John Toomey and Don Treadway, Toomey-Treadway Galleries, Oak Park, IL.

Children's Stool, designed by Charles Eames, manufactured by Evans Products, c.1945. Laminated birch form, legs are a continuation of the top, originally bright red analine dye, very few produced; refinished; 8 inches high x 11 inches deep x 15 inches wide; $1,600.

Courtesy of John Toomey and Don Treadway, Toomey-Treadway Galleries, Oak Park, IL.

Pretzel Armchairs, designed by George Nelson for Herman Miller Furniture Company. Extremely rare sculptural form of laminated birch and walnut with green wool seat cushion, very few produced; 30 inches high x 27 inches wide x 16 inches deep; $2,800.

Courtesy of John Toomey and Don Treadway, Toomey-Treadway Galleries, Oak Park, IL.

Left: **Coconut Chair**, designed by George Nelson for Herman Miller Furniture Company, c. 1955. Vibrant blue upholstery over brake formed and welded sheet steel shell, cast aluminum alloy legs; reupholstered; 33 inches high x 34 inches deep x 40 inches wide; $3,250. *Right:* **Swan Sofa**, designed by Arne Jacobson/Fritz Hansen (Denmark), c. 1958. Foam-Injected, molded fiberglass shell upholstered in wool, on aluminum base; 29 inches high x 24 inches deep x 56 inches wide; $3,500.

Theater Chair, designed by Carlo Mollino, exclusively for the Hall of Rai Auditorium, Turin, 1951. Biomorphic form in original red velvet, curved brass tubing; 33 inches high; 23 inches deep x 26 inches wide; $2,200. *(Note: Only the orchestra section was replaced; the rest of the theater is still in its original condition. Less than thirty armchairs were removed.)*

Pitcher, designed by Hennin
Koppel, Danish, c. 1952. Sterlin
silver; $24,150

Courtesy of Southeby's Inc.,© 199

Umbrella Stand, O. Rosa/San Paolo,
c. 1950. Ceramic, "totem" abstract
faced in relief; minor damage to
relief coil, otherwise good condi-
tion; 21 inches high x 11 inches in
diameter; $900.

Courtesy of John Toomey and Don Treadway
Toomey-Treadway Galleries, Oak Park, IL.

Left: **Murano Studio Glass Bowl**, designed by Ercole Barovier for Barovier and Toso. "Cathedrale" or "Anthena" series, repeating diamond-shaped and geometric elements, original paper and foil label; 6¼ inches high x 8¼ inches in diameter; $4,400. *Right:* **Vase**, designed by Fulvio Bianconi, c. 1955. Venini Studio Glass Pezzato vase, composed of irregular squares in both opaque and transparent colors, in the Pezzato series, etched mark on base: VENINI MURANO ITALIA; 9½ inches high; $6,600.

Courtesy of Skinner, Inc. Boston/Bolton, MA.

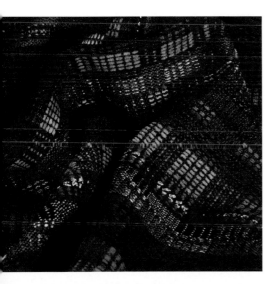

Textile, designed by Jack Lenor Larsen, c. 1954–1955. "Remoulade," wool, cotton, rayon, linen, Mylar, polyethylene, silk, jute, and metallic yarns, warp-faced plain weave, Important as mass-produced textile and hand-woven look; 54 x 48 inches.

Courtesy of Jack Lenor Larsen.

Toy Transportation set, Japan, 1950s. Because of its fragility, it is a rarity. Prices for individual pieces sell from $250 to $18,000 for an extremely rare model.

Courtesy of Carol and Jerry Dinelli.

Beaded Baskets, made by hobbyists, 1940s. American, glass beads; $45/each.

Courtesy of Triple Pier Show.

Poster, "Le Parisien," by Phili, c. 1944; 63 x 47 inches; $800.

Courtesy of Poster Graphics, Inc.

Travel Poster, c. 1948. For Mexico, signed by ESPERY; 28 x 40 inches; $200.

Courtesy of Miscellaneous Man, New Freedom, PA.

Urns/Vases/Vessels

"Sommerso" Bowl, attributed to Gino Cenedese studio. Thick flattened oval of radon yellow-green with internal blue shading of unusual clarity; 13 inches high; $303.

Miscellaneous

Figural "Sommerso" Block, designed by Gino Cenedese, c. 1950. Two clear heavy blocks fused together with aqua-blue-tinted bases and internal sea life decoration, including a large crab; unsigned; 13½ inches wide × 9 inches high; mint condition; $1,800.

"Corroso" Ducks (pair), designed by Alfredo Barbini, c. 1948. Dark amethyst cores cased in clear and heavily frosted glass with black frosted beaks and feet; unsigned; 9¼ inches high; $200/set.

Glass-and-Bronze Sconce, c. 1950. Irregular shield-shaped shade in clear glass enclosing fractured multicolored glass fragments; within an oval bronze mount held by a simple arm; unsigned; 12¾ inches high × 9 inches wide; $575.

ARCHIMEDE SEGUSO (1909–)

Born in the glassmaking city of Murano, Archimede Seguso is considered a premier glassblower. He began blowing glass at the age of thirteen. By 1929 he was making his own items, using a small furnace in the family fireplace. His professional life began when he and others founded Seguso Vetri d'Arte in 1934, where he acted as master glassblower. In 1947 he founded his own company, Vetreria Archimede Seguso. After the war he became known for his variations of the traditional Venetian latticino glass, among them are his lace and feather vases. Many of his creations were tabletop decorations, others were sculptures and chandeliers. He continues his work today.

PRICES

Bowls

Eye-Shaped Bowl. Green interior and gold overlay exterior; controlled bubble decoration throughout; 11 inches wide × 4 inches high; mint condition; $350.

Glass Bowls (two). Green pulegoso quatraform bowl with

acid-stamped mark "Venini/Murano/Made in Italy"; and swirled Seguso-type pink, green, and amber heavy-walled bowl with scalloped edge, unsigned; 3 inches high and 3 inches high × 6¼ inches in diameter, respectively; $330/set.

Glass Latticino Bowl, attributed to Archimede Seguso. Flattened decorative serving piece of colorless glass with white meshed threads spiraling from gold-flecked maroon, blue, and green center; unsigned; 19½ inches long × 15¼ inches wide; $357.

Latticino Bowl, probably executed by Archimede Seguso, c. 1954. Clear body with internal decoration of dark amethyst, white, and gold latticino; cut and polished at top and one end; unsigned; 7 inches wide × 2¾ inches high; mint condition; $50.

Merietto Bowl, c. 1955. Clear with internal coral-colored and shaped lacework; unsigned; 7¼ inches wide; mint condition; $500.

Merietto Bowl, c. 1955. Free-form; clear with internal paths of white lacework and a green border; unsigned; largest 6½ inches wide; mint condition; $1,300.

Free-Form Bowl, c. 1952. Clear with opaque pink spoked bands overlaid with gold leaf; unsigned; 9½ inches wide × 3 inches high; mint condition; $85.

Latticino Bowl, c. 1954. Clear with inlaid spiraled red thread pattern; unsigned; 7 inches in diameter; mint condition; $300.

Bullicante Leaf-Form Bowl. Cranberry interior overlaid with gold leaf and fine bubbles cased clear; paper labels (ARCHIMEDE SEGUSO MURANO MADE IN ITALY); 11 inches wide × 3¾ inches high; mint condition; $150.

Free-Form Bowl, c. 1952. Opaque black with opaque white spoked bands overlaid with gold leaf and cased clear; unsigned; 9½ inches wide × 3 inches high; mint condition; $75.

Leaf-Form Bowl, c. 1954. Ribbed form of translucent green with burst open gold layer, amethyst specks, and iridescent surface; unsigned; 7½ inches wide; mint condition; $180.

Dishes/Plates

Covered Dish. White threaded glass with gold flecks in handle; unusual; 5 inches high; mint condition; $300.

Urns/Vases/Vessels

Vase, probably designed by Archimede Seguso, c. 1955. Heavy clear swirl-ribbed body cased over opaque lime-green with fine gold leaf; unsigned; 12¼ inches high; mint condition; $400.

Opaline Glass Vase, c. 1955. Shouldered ovoid vessel with tapering cylindrical neck in cobalt-blue glass with gold foil inclusions; cased within clear glass molded with thick vertical ribbing; unsigned; 15½ inches high; $3,450.

Seguso Vetri d'Arte Sommerso Vase, designed by Flavio Poli, c. 1955. Clear with internal layers of red and amethyst; unsigned; 13 inches wide; mint condition; $450.

Seguso Vetri d'Arte Sommerso Vase, designed by Flavio Poli, c. 1936. Clear with internal layers of dark amber and green and a large pulled hole; unsigned; 7½ inches high; mint condition; $325.

Seguso Vetri d'Arte Handkerchief Vase (attributed), c. 1950. Clear with amethyst and white latticino; unsigned; 3 inches high; mint condition; $210.

Seguso Vetri d'Arte Handkerchief Vase (attributed), c. 1950. Brilliant orange with controlled bubbles containing gold leaf; unsigned; 4¾ inches high; mint condition, $200.

Seguso Vetri d'Arte Handkerchief Vase, c. 1950. Light green cased over white and overlaid with gold leaf; engraved signature (THE MARAMOR SEGUSO MURANO); 3 inches high; mint condition; $150.

Vase, from the Archimede Seguso studio. Losanghe Italian design of white gridwork squares internally arranged with amethyst-mauve quatraform body; 4¾ inches high × 9 inches in diameter; $1,100.

Opaline Glass Vase, by Archimede Seguso, c. 1955. Shouldered ovoid vessel with tapering cylindrical neck in cobalt-blue glass with gold foil inclusions; cased within clear glass molded with thick vertical ribbing; unsigned; 15½ inches high; mint condition; $3,450.

Vase. Heavy, clear exterior with internal purple free-form

decoration; controlled air bubbles throughout; signed; 5 inches wide × 10 inches high; mint condition; $700.

Vase, c. 1953. Rare vase; heavy body of green shaded to clear with a sommerso layer of very fine bubbles and applied leaves of autumn colors with gold profusion; unsigned; 9¼ inches high; $2,100.

Ribbed Vase, c. 1949. Clear with gold profusion and applied vertical blue ribs; engraved signature (ARCHIMEDE SEGUSO MURANO); 10 inches high; mint condition; $1,100.

Teardrop Vase, designed by Flavio Poli. Blue and green; 10 inches high; $280.

Vase, probably Seguso Vetri d'Arte, designed by Flavio Poli, c. 1950s. Clear cased over green over amber with an internal solid core; unsigned; 6¾ inches high; mint condition; $500.

Miscellaneous

Candle Holders, c. 1940s. Arched stem rose-cased glass with iridescent finish and gold inclusion; each end supporting a concave bobeche with cylindrical candle holder in its center; raised on a domed circular base; acid stamped "MADE IN ITALY"; 5 inches high; $220/set.

Merietto Candlesticks, c. 1955. Solid bodies; clear with green asymmetrical lacework, a rare technique that simulates the appearance of seaweed in water; unsigned; 10¼ inches high; $300.

Figural Couple. In the manner of the Seguso studio; transparent blue glass man and women with applied colorless and gold-infused accoutrements; 12 inches high; $275.

Merietto Dresser Set (four pieces), c. 1955. Clear with internal bright yellow lacework; paper labels (MADE IN MURANO ITALY); largest 6½ inches wide; mint condition; $800/set.

Bullicante Figural Duck. Central teal-blue bird enclosed in gold dust and overlaid in bubbled, colorless glass; partial labels on base; 8¼ inches high; $440.

Glass Ducks (pair), designed by Archimede Seguso, c. 1949. Each bird at rest on a craggy rock-form base; in bullicante glass; internally decorated in sea green with gold leaf; 9 inches high; $690/set.

Elephant Figure. Clear body with iridescent surface; unsigned; 5¾ inches high; mint condition; $85.

Elephant Figure. Solid black body with opaque white spots

on surface; acid-stamped (ARCHIMEDE SEGUSO MURANO); 6¼ inches high; mint condition; $260.

Figural Glass Elephant. Black amethyst glass figure with raised trunk decorated at surface level with white spots and splotches; etched on the foot "ARCHIMEDE SEGUSO MURANO (ITALY)"; 6¼ inches high; $440.

Figures (one dog, two birds). Dog has dappled yellow body overlaid with gold leaf and applied amethyst eyes and nose, paper label (ARCHIMEDE SEGUSO MURANO MADE IN ITALY); 3¾ inches high; birds have dappled yellow bodies overlaid with gold leaf and applied amethyst eyes, beaks, and orange-dappled wings; $80/set.

Figurines. Green glass western cowboy and girl in dancing costumes with applied bandanna and belts; acid stamped "SEGUSO VERONESE ITALIE"; 8¼ inches high; $165/set.

Fish. Elegantly simple design in red with dark blue interior in clear glass; signed "SEGUSO MURANO"; 10 inches long; mint condition; $300.

Perfumes (pair), c. 1953. Triangular twisted forms; clear with enclosed powders of green, amethyst, and gold; clear collar and dauber; paper label (MADE IN MURANO ITALY); 9½ inches high; $700/set.

Vase and Bowl, c. 1954. Lobed form of translucent amethyst and applied green with burst open gold layer; unsigned; vase 4 inches high; mint condition; $100/set.

VENINI S.p.A.

Venini is a familiar name to collectors of Modern glass. The glassworks had its beginnings in 1921 when Paolo Venini (1895–1959), a Milanese lawyer, formed a company with an antiques dealer from a family of glassblowers, and Andrea Rhoda, a Venetian glassmaker. The partnership ended in 1925, but not before they jointly created prize-winning glassware.

Paolo Venini went on to form a new company that created humorous glass animals and potted plants until 1931. In 1946, Gio Ponti began designing pieces for Venini and was later joined by Fulvio Bianconi in 1948. They created many stylized Modern pieces that are eagerly sought by collectors today, among them the series of bottles with anthropomorphic shapes, the handkerchief bowls, biomorphic vases, and stylized figural bottles.

After the death of Paolo Venini, his widow and son-in-law, Ludovico de Santilla, introduced new artists and innovations to the company. Among the artists was Tobia Scarpa, son of architect Carlo Scarpa, who had joined the glassworks in 1932 and revived the "filigrano" technique, which used threads of glass canes. Carlo is recognized as the creator of the Occhi (eyes) series.

Venini is today reproducing many classic designs of the 1940s, 1950s, and 1960s. Included are the commedia del l'arte figures, handerkerchief vases, and bottles. While some original figures were unsigned, collectors are advised to become familiar with the variety of signatures and paper labels Venini did use. The auction catalog "Important Italian Glass," published for the November 15, 1992, specialized auction at John Toomey Gallery in Oak Park, Illinois, shows not only important glassware and prices but various Venini signatures. The catalog is available through Ripley's Antique Galleries.

PRICES

Bowls

Vetro a Spirale Bowl, probably designed by Fulvio Bianconi, c. 1950. Spiraled canes of smoke and opaque white; acid-stamped "Venini Murano Italia" and with paper label; 2¼ inches high × 4½ inches in diameter; $210.

Fasce Orizzontali Bowl, designed by Fulvio Bianconi, c. 1953. Clear body with horizontal stripes of red and amber; acid-stamped "Venini Murano Italia"; 2½ inches high × 5½ inches in diameter; mint condition; $800.

Filigrane Leaf Bowl, design attributed to Fulvio Bianconi. Thread filaments of mauve, brown, and apple green manipulated as pointed leaf design with tooled stem; acid-stamped mark "Venini/Murano/Italia"; 3 inches high × 13¼ inches in diameter; $1,045.

Glass Bowl, designed by Riccardo Licata, c. 1956. Bright blue band at top; white, yellow, and amethyst triple-layered technique with pettine abstract decoration; very rare; 7 inches high × 4 inches in diameter; mint condition; $2,700.

Battuto Bowl, probably designed by Carlo Scarpa, c. 1940. Squared heavy body clear cased over amber with a "beaten" surface; cut by a multigrooved wheel with a flat cut and polished top; unsigned; 7¼ inches wide × 2⅔ inches high; mint condition; $400.

Carved Murrine Glass Bowl, designed by Carlo Scarpa, c. 1940. Shallow circular vessel in red, gray, black, and clear glass murrines; unsigned; 8⅜ inches in diameter; $3,450.

Dishes/Plates

Charger, designed by Paolo Venini, c. 1950. Intricate Zanfirico pattern in celadon green, white, and clear; signed; acid-stamped "Venini Murano Italia"; 10 inches in diameter; mint condition; $200.

Covered Dish. White and clear glass; floral decoration on handle; 5 inches high; mint condition; $110.

Urns/Vases/Vessels

Inciso Glass Decanter, designed by Paolo Venini, c. 1956. Tapered triangular bottle with conical stopper in clear glass cased over red; unsigned; 13⅝ inches high; $4,312.

Inciso Glass Decanter, c. 1950. Flattened shouldered cylindrical vessel with narrow neck in deep purple glass cased in clear; surface carved with a pattern of fine parallel lines; bulbous clear glass stopper; acid-stamped "Venini/Murano/Italia"; 10¾ inches high; $2,012.

Bottiglia Con Fascie Glass Decanter with Stopper, designed by Fulvio Bianconi. Waisted cylinder with tapering neck and conical stopper; decorated with a vertical pattern in black and yellow; acid-stamped "Venini Murano Italia"; 17¾ inches high; $9,350.

Decanter, designed by Paolo Venini. Squashed bulbous form in deep forest green; acid washed and wheel etched; unsigned; 8 inches high × 5 inches in diameter; mint condition; $750.

Glass Decanter, designed by Fulvio Bianconi, c. 1955. Elongated bottle form with conical stopper; clear glass decorated with vertical blue and yellow strips; acid-stamped "Venini/Murano/Italia"; 17⅞ inches high; $3,162.

Glass Vase, designed by Fulvio Bianconi, c. 1955. Elongated cylindrical vessel in clear glass decorated with blue and green vertical canes; acid-stamped "Venini/Murano/Italia"; 15 inches high; $2,587.

Glass Vase, designed by Fulvio Bianconi, c. 1951. Rare vase commonly known as "gatto"; clear body with enclosed decoration of red and black; acid-stamped "Venini Murano Italia"; 9 inches wide × 5½ inches high; mint condition; $20,000.

Fasce Ritorte Vase, designed by Fulvio Bianconi, c. 1952. Fused canes of green, yellow, black, and clear spirally formed; acid-stamped "Venini Murano Italia"; 8¼ inches high; mint condition; $7,500.

Fasce Verticali Vase, designed by Fulvio Bianconi, c. 1955. Fused canes of transparent green and yellow; paper label says "VENINI MURANO VENEZIA NO. 3302 MADE IN ITALY"; 13¼ inches high; mint condition; $1,800.

Glass Handkerchief Vase, designed by Fulvio Bianconi, c. 1948. Pale pink slightly iridescent glass; unsigned; 11 inches high; $1,840.

Glass Handkerchief Vase, designed by Fulvio Bianconi, c. 1948. Deep red glass cased over teal blue; acid-stamped "Venini/Murano/Italia"; 15 inches high; $2,587.

Glass Handkerchief Vase, designed by Fulvio Bianconi, c. 1948. Black glass cased over white; acid-stamped "Venini/Murano/Italia"; 10 inches high; $2,070.

Vetro Pezzato Arlecchino Vase, designed by Fulvio Bianconi. Flaring cylinder with undulating rim; decorated with a patchwork pattern in ruby red, sapphire blue, green, opaque white, and black; acid-stamped "Venini Murano Italia"; 9¼ inches high; $4,180.

Pezzato Vase, designed by Fulvio Bianconi. Flared large trumpet form composed of fused glass patchwork squares in red, blue, green, and opaque black and white; recessed base with acid stamp "Venini Murano Italia"; 9¼ inches high × 6 inches in diameter; $5,500.

Vetro Pezzato Arlecchino Vase, designed by Fulvio Bianconi. Flaring cylinder with flattened sides; patchwork pattern in clear, deep burgundy, green, and sapphire blue; circular paper label; 8½ inches high; $4,620.

Cinesi Vase, designed by Carlo Scarpa, c. 1940. Rare opaque royal blue waisted gourd form; acid-stamped "Venini Murano MADE IN ITALY"; 7¾ inches high; mint condition; $1,500.

Tessuto Vase, designed by Carlo Scarpa, limited edition reissue of a 1940 design. Vertically fused canes of yellow and white and yellow and black cased with clear; entire surface carved to create a fabric effect; engraved signature "venini italia Carlo Scarpa 1984/03"; 13¾ inches high; mint condition; $2,300.

Tessuto Vase, designed by Carlo Scarpa, c. 1940. Teardrop-form vessel with slender neck in yellow and black vertical threads; hammered surface; 13½ inches high; $7,475.

Glass Vase, designed by Paolo Venini. Hourglass form graduating from pale to deep amber, green, and clear; acid washed and wheel etched; "venini" label; acid-stamped "Venini/Murano/Italia"; 10 inches high × 5 inches in diameter; very good condition; $900.

Bottle Vase. Crisp emerald-green cylinder; darker at base; centrally belted by bright red glass ribbon showing white core at joining; acid-stamped "Venini/Murano/Italia"; 10 inches high; $1,045.

Glass Vase, c. 1940s. Oversized brandy snifter form in bright turquoise; early acid stamp signature; 15 inches high × 12 inches in diameter; excellent condition; $375.

Glass Vase. Clear aquamarine-blue; biomorphic shape with elliptical opening off center; original tag; etched "Venini/Murano/Italia"; 12 inches high; mint condition; $1,700.

Glass Vase, 1950. Heavy gourd form with internal white spiral decoration; acid-stamped "Venini/Murano/Italia"; 8 inches high × 5 inches wide; mint condition; $550.

Fazzoletto Vase. Elegant cased pearl-white handkerchief bowl; acid-stamped mark; "Venini/Murano/Italia" on base; 7 inches high; $440.

Sommersi Bottle Vase. Flattened oval form of transparent amber with submerged opaque black glass decoration; acid-stamped "Venini Murano Italia" on base; 9 inches high; $1,210.

Blown Glass Vase, c. 1950. Bulbous vessel with cylindrical neck and flaring rim; pale amethyst glass; decorated with two wraps at the shoulder; remnants of original paper label say "VENINI/MURANO/VENEZIA, NEW YORK/ 125 E. 55TH/MADE IN ITALY"; 17 inches high; $1,725.

Messico Glass Vase, c. 1970. Lattimo glass cylindrical vessel with rounded base and shoulder; deepest amethyst glass with random white trailing cased in clear glass; inscribed "venini/italia" with original paper label; 13¼ inches high; $1,437.

Miscellaneous

Beverage Set (five pieces). Red, yellow, pink, blue, and green transparent alternating stripes on pitcher; four tumblers; acid-stamped "Venini Murano Italia" on pitcher base; 6¾ inches high; $660/set.

Bottle, elongated neck on olive-green bottle fused to white lower half; white to colorless stopper; label on base says "Venini S.A. Murano"; 12¾ inches high; $413.

Battuto Bottle, designed by Carlo Scarpa, c. 1940. Translucent aquamarine shaded to green with a green stopper; the whole surface "beaten" with a carving wheel; paper label says "MADE IN ITALY"; 12 inches high; mint condition; $3,000.

Cinesi Bottle, designed by Carlo Scarpa, c. 1940. Brilliant red cased over white and overlaid with gold leaf; acid-stamped "venini murano MADE IN ITALY"; 5½ inches high; mint condition; $1,500.

Inciso Stoppered Bottle, designed by Paolo Venini, c. 1956. Short ovoid vessel with mushroom-shaped stopper in clear glass cased over red; unsigned; 5¼ inches high; $575.

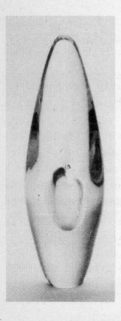

Two-Hole Vase, designed by Fulvio Bianconi, c. 1951. Clear cased glass over blue over lavender with two pierced-through holes, acid-stamped VENINI MURANO ITALIA; 12¼ inches high; $1,900. *Courtesy of Skinner Inc., Boston/Bolton, MA.*

Morandiane Bottle, designed by Gio Ponti, Fulvio Bianconi, and Paolo Venini, c. 1946. Red and white "incalmo" (fused); paper label says "Made in Italy"; 13¾ inches high; mint condition; $750.

Fifteen-Piece Beverage Service, designed by Fulvio Bianconi. Tankard pitcher with applied striped handle; eight flared tumblers; six spherical glasses; each striped with opaque orange, transparent yellow-amber, and clear crystal; pitcher 10½ inches high; $1,760/set.

Glass Figures (two), designed by Fulvio Bianconi, c. 1950. Probably depicting Romeo and Juliet; each with amber glass heads and arms, dressed in Renaissance costumes in various colors; each acid-stamped "Venini/Murano/Italia"; 14 inches high and 13⅝ inches high, respectively; $4,025/set.

La Commedia del l'Arte Figurine of a Head, designed by Fulvio Bianconi, c. 1948. White opaque body with applied red nose, light rose eyes, and a black hat with a red feather; acid-stamped "Venini Murano Italia"; 5⅛ inches high; mint condition; $3,000.

Figurine Modeled as a Chicken, designed by Fulvio Bianconi, c. 1950. Opaque white body of polychrome "variegato" with opaque and translucent application of opaque black base; acid-stamped "Venini Murano Italia"; 7¼ inches high; mint condition; $8,500.

Matched Pair of Figures Modeled as Chickens, designed by Fulvio Bianconi, c. 1950. Opaque white bodies of polychrome "variegato" with opaque and translucent application on opaque black bases; acid-stamped "Venini Murano Italia"; 6¾ inches high; rare; mint condition; $19,000.

Venini Glass Figural Chickens, designed by Fulvio Bianconi. Rooster and hen composed of lattimo and multi-color swirled, hollow, cone bodies, stamped VENINI MURANO ITALIA; 7½ inches high; $5,775. *Courtesy of Skinner Inc., Boston/Bolton, MA.*

Glass Display Plaque, c. 1950. Rectangular, clear glass with impressed facsimile signature in medium relief; unsigned; 3½ inches high × 6¼ inches in diameter; $920.

Glass, Brass, and Wood Hourglass, designed by Paolo Venini, c. 1957. Brilliant red-orange and bottle-green egg chambers supported by "zanfirico" canes around threaded glass rods with circular wood bases; retains original paper label "VENINI/ MURANO/VENEZIA/N. 4901/MADE IN ITALY"; 10½ inches high; $1,437.

Glass Lemonade Set (five pieces), c. 1950. Four glasses and pitcher; unusual form with pinched spout; thin jewel tone stripe decoration; pitcher 7 inches high × 6 inches in diameter; glasses 4 inches high × 3 inches in diameter; excellent condition; $1,000/set.

Center Bowl, designed by Alfredo Barbini. Thick-walled clear glass, air-trapped bubbles around a central well internally accented by a streaked black encircling swirl and lined with segments of gold-leaf; engraved A. BARBINI; 4½ inches high x 11¾ inches in diameter; $880. *Courtesy of Butterfield and Butterfield Auctioneers, CA*

Glass Sculptures (pair). Emerald-green fluted base with transparent conical top and red-and-white spiral decoration; acid-stamped "Venini/Murano/Italia"; 11 inches high × 3 inches in diameter; $550/set.

Sculpture. Emerald-green hexagonal base with oval transparent top; green, yellow, and white internal spiral decoration; unsigned; 7 inches high × 2 inches in diameter; mint condition; $300.

Opaque Glass Three-Part Tiered Cake Stand, c. 1950. Each graduated tier has circular dish with upturned rim raised on a trumpet-form pedestal; lower two tiers in powder blue glass; upper tier in bright yellow with central handle in clear glass; each acid-stamped "Venini/Murano/Italia"; top section retains portion of original paper label; 11 inches high × 9½ inches in diameter; $1,437.

CARLO SCARPA (1906-1978)

Not only was Carlo Scarpa one of Italy's most prominent mid-twentieth-century architects, he was also a multifaceted designer of glass, furniture, and flatware. Some of his finest glass designs were created in the 1940s for Venini glassworks. During those years he designed the Tessuto series, which used a ground with cane patterns. In the same decade he created the Battuto series, with a ground surface that looked like beaten metal. Before leaving the Venini glassworks in 1947 he designed pieces using irregular splashes of colored glass wound around simple shapes. He died in Japan in 1978.

Many of his glass designs were manufactured by the Venini glassworks. Please see Venini listings for price information.

▦ OTHER ITALIAN DESIGNS ▦

PRICES

Bowls

Murano Glass Bowl. Amethyst, green, yellow, and white lattice and ribbon technique; folded lip; 8 inches wide × 7 inches deep × 3 inches high; mint condition; $200.

Murano Glass Bowl. Heavy clear glass with internal red spiral decoration; 7 inches wide × 3 inches high; mint condition; $270.

Murano Glass Bowl, c. 1950s. Thick-walled squashed form in amber; elongated pulled bubble decoration with abstract twisted funnel decoration in between; unusual design; 11 inches wide × 9 inches deep; mint condition; $200.

Salviati Murano Glass Sculpture, design attributed to Luciano Gaspari. Partial label SALVIATI & C. MURANO, MADE IN ITALY; 11 1/4 inches high; $550. *Courtesy of Skinner, Inc., Boston/Bolton, MA.*

Venetian Glass Bowl. Ribbed body with zigzag design in white, orange, and purple; 3 inches high × 6 inches wide; $700.

Art Glass Patchwork Bowl. Heavy-walled crystal folded and tooled as bowl form with cut-out handles; internally decorated in colorful geometric squares of red, yellow, orange, green, blue, amethyst, and white using the layered technique to simulate pezzato work; unsigned; 5½ inches high, 14½ inches deep × 10½ inches wide; $1,100.

Glass Centerpiece Bowl, designed by Luciano Gaspari for Salviati and Company, c. 1950. Sculptural form resembling Surrealistic hand with stylized bent fingertips; transparent; signed "Gaspari/Salviati"; 14 inches high × 16 inches in diameter; mint condition; $375.

Venetian Swirl Decorated Bowl. Symmetrically spiraled wavy stripes of white, amethyst, and gold against colorless ground; rippled exterior surface; applied polished gold-dusted foot; 4½ inches high × 10¼ inches in diameter; $138.

Urns/Vases/Vessels

Venetian Millefiore Decanter. Squared bottle of silver-speckled pale amber randomly decorated with red, blue, and white star canes; conforming hollow ball stopper; unsigned; 13 inches high; $358.

Murano Decanter. In clown form; removable head forms the stopper; rotund body in orange glass with multicolored details; 14 inches high; $900.

Murano Vase, possibly designed by Ercole Barovier, c. 1955. Translucent blue ribbed body with controlled bubbles and an applied clear foot with gold leaf; iridescent; unsigned; 11½ inches high; mint condition; $290.

Salviati Murano Glass Sculpture. Flattened amber and colorless glass coil wrapped as a conical triangular form, raised on colorless rectangular platform base, two partial labels: SALVIATI C. MURANO; 16 inches high; $330. *Courtesy of Skinner Inc., Boston/Bolton, MA.*

Murano Vase, possibly designed by Ercole Barovier, c. 1955. Clear ribbed body with internal layer of fine gold leaf and opaque white; unsigned; 12¼ inches high; mint condition; $190.

Murano Battuto Vase, possibly designed by Carlo Scarpa. Flattened oval form of colorless glass cased to olive-green with sommerso blue; acid-finished exterior; polished lip; 11 inches high; $550.

Murano Glass Vase. Clear with red internal decoration; purple swirl; 8 inches high × 4 inches wide; mint condition; $185.

Murano Glass Vase. Teardrop form in two shades of deep blue; 6½ inches high × 3 inches wide; mint condition; $180.

Murano Glass Vase, c. 1950s. Whimsical form with fluted handkerchief top; lemon-yellow and mint-green stripes; unsigned; 10 inches wide × 10 inches high; mint condition; $450.

Murano Glass Vase, c. 1950. Bulbous bottle form with blue rim and bright green irregular internal decoration; unsigned; 7 inches high × 7 inches wide; mint condition; $210.

Murano Glass Vase. Free-form shape; flared sides and edges; green glass with frosted etched design on outer edge; 3 inches high × 7 inches wide; mint condition; $110.

Murano Glass Vase. Unusual form in transparent blue with deep blue banded stripe; unsigned; 8 inches high × 6 inches wide; mint condition; $170.

Murano Glass Vase. Heavy blue glass bottom with purple internal decoration and top; 10 inches high × 6 inches wide; mint condition; $325.

Murano Glass Vase. Iridescent gourd form with large irregular bubble and wave decoration; 6 inches high × 5 inches wide; mint condition; $310.

Venetian Glass Vase. Swirled design of five white bands separated by wider caramel bands; "Murano" paper label; 7 inches high; $325.

Venetian Glass Vase. Bulbous vase with long tapered neck; purple glass; 21 inches high; mint condition; $160.

Miscellaneous

Murano Dresser Set (five pieces), c. 1950. Lamp, two perfumes, covered bowl, and vase in opaque white with controlled bubbles and fine gold leaf; unsigned; lamp 17 inches high; mint condition; $375/set.

Glass Candlesticks (pair), designed by Luciano Gaspari for Salviati and Company, Murano/Venice, c. 1950. Matching candlesticks in transparent tinted glass; signed "Gaspari/Salviati"; 9 inches wide × 6 inches high; mint condition; $100.

Murano Glass Lamp. Squashed bulbous form in transparent white glass with internal opaque and irregular bubble decoration; unusual design; 14 inches wide × 10 inches deep × 9 inches high; excellent condition; $300.

Murano Glass Double Sea Horse Figurine, c. 1950. Probably designed by Barnini; $500. *Courtesy of Toomey-Treadway Galleries, Oak Park, IL.*

Venetian Long-Stemmed Wineglasses (four). Clear glass with applied blue glass in crisscross line-and-dot design; circle of blue glass on stems; 10 inches high; one with broken band on stem, others mint condition; $250.

Glass Sculpture, manufactured by Salviati, c. 1950. Heavy glass block in brilliant jewel tones depicting underwater scene of fish and plant life; 12 inches wide × 9 inches high; mint condition; $800.

Murano Glass Sculpture, manufactured by Salviati. Flattened amber and colorless glass coil wrapped as conical triangular form; raised on colorless rectangular platform base; two "Salviati C. Murano" partial labels; 16 inches high; $330.

Glass Figurine. Clown holding accordion; green, yellow, red, black, blue, and white glass; mint condition; $70.

Figures of Dancers (pair), manufactured by Salviati, c. 1955. Opaque green, black, and clear with gold leaf; unsigned; 12¼ inches high; mint condition; $650.

Murano Clown, c. 1950. Internally decorated body with polychrome transparent and opaque applications; unsigned; 21½ inches high; mint condition; $500.

Bullicante Figural of Two Fish, designed by Alfredo Barbini, c. 1950. Heavy clear bodies with internal controlled bubbles and aqua-blue core; applied foot and gold leaf applications; unsigned; 16½ inches high; mint condition; $900.

Kosta Two-Hole Glass Vase, designed by Vicke Lindstrand, c. 1955. Engraved LH 1175; 1 inch high; $1,600. *Courtesy of Toomey-Treadway Galleries, Oak Park, IL.*

Bird Sculpture, designed by Alfredo Barbini Studio. Red to amber birds perched in gold-flecked tree branch above pad foot; foil label says "Venetian/Barbini/Murano"; 7 inches high; $165.

Murano Ornamental Bird, designed by Tosi Berto. Blown-glass figure internally colored green, blue, and pink with applied gold-infused colorless beak, comb, and leafy perch; raised on half-round green-and-amber platform foot; engraved signature says "Tosi Berto 1964 Murano"; 8¾ inches high × 17 inches long; $440.

▨ Scandinavian Glass Designs ▨

Much Scandinavian glass, notably pieces from Finland and Sweden, was not made by the designer but by master glassblowers and master engravers.

PRICES

Urns/Vases/Vessels

Savoy Vase, designed by Alvar Aalto. Clear glass free-form vase; marked "Alvar Aalto—3030" on base; 6 inches high; $200.

Savoy Vase, designed by Alvar Aalto. Free-form amber glass; 5½ inches high; $200.

Swedish Glass Vase. Thick-walled clear vessel with pale blue diagonal stripe decoration; unsigned; 7 inches high × 4 inches in diameter; mint condition; $60.

KOSTA BODA

This Swedish firm founded in 1864 is the sister company of Kosta. In 1953 Swedish artist Erik Hoglund (1923–) joined Kosta Boda and totally changed previous concepts of the company's designs. Influenced by Picasso, Hoglund's designs often used primitive motifs. Pieces were sometimes playfully painted; others were deeply engraved with primitive animals and figures. Still other examples of his work were anthropomorphic or colored, and hand-blown with irregular bubbles.

PRICES

Bowls

Bertil Vallien Bowl. Blue crystal flared cylinder internally decorated with controlled black-outlined spiraling bubbles; fully signed and numbered; 3 inches high × 5¼ inches in diameter; $500.

KOSTA GLASBRUK

The oldest of Swedish glassworks and still in existence today, it was founded in 1741. It began making drinking glasses, chandeliers, and windowpanes. By the end of the nineteenth century its works included cameo glass in the manner of Emile Galle. In 1950 the factory hired prominent designer Vicke Lindstrand. He was previously employed by the Orrefors factory. Lindstrand created asymmetrical forms that gained popularity in the postwar period.

PRICES

Bowls

Art Glass Bowl. Blue-and-green paisley decoration; signed "Warff"; 6 inches wide × 4 inches high; mint condition; $170.

Crystal Bowl. Flared cranberry-pink bulbed and flared half-round decorated internally with white gridwork design; signed and numbered; 3½ inches high × 5 inches in diameter; $150.

Cut Overlay Bowl, designed by Ernest Gordon. Flared oval of amethyst layered to clear crystal; cut and etched in geometric repeats of circles and ovals; signed "Ernst Gordon/Kosta" and numbered; 4½ inches high × 7¼ inches in diameter; $200.

Compote Bowl, designed by Vicke Lindstrand. Crystal internally decorated with white swirls complementing the form; etched "Lind/Strand/Kosta"; 7 inches high × 7¼ inches in diameter; $600.

Compote Bowl, designed by Warff. Frosted colorless bowl with green and blue internal swirls; signed "Kosta Unik 683 Warff"; 5½ inches high; $165.

Dishes/Plates

Free-form Dish. Tobacco, gold, and white swirl decoration; 18 inches long × 11 inches wide × 3 inches high; $300.

Urns/Vases/Vessels

Crystal Vase. Heavy-walled oval body internally decorated with amethyst fish net; externally cut and polished to simulate waves and ocean currents; signed and numbered; 5½ inches high; $700.

Crystal Bud Vases (two). Each heavy-walled teardrop form; etched and frosted; one with an archer, the other a kneeling girl; signed "Kosta KK" and numbered; 4½ inches high; $400/set.

Crystal Vase. Heavy-walled colorless flattened oval layered internally with blue-on-green spiral stripe design; signed "Kosta" and numbered; 6¾ inches high; $425.

Glass Vase, designed by Vicke Lindstrand. Heavy-walled colorless cylinder; internally decorated with elongated green and brown grasses as underwater scene; acid-stamped "Lind-strand/ Kosta LU2007"; 13½ inches high; $605.

Glass Vase, designed by Vicke Lindstrand. Flaring flattened form with etched design of trees with leaves and birds; finely detailed; signed on bottom "Kosta, #42268, Lindstrand"; 12 inches high; mint condition; $900.

Glass Vase, designed by Bertil Vallien. Conical form internally decorated with green stripes alternating with white cross devices; signed "Kosta Boda Artist Call B. Vallien 48467"; 5¼ inches high; $165.

Glass Vases (two), designed by Mona Morales Schildt, c. 1959. Each ovoid vessel in faceted glass internally decorated in shades of blue and green; signed and numbered; 8⅝ inches high and 6¾ inches high; $632.

Glass Vase, designed by Vicke Lindstrand, c. 1955. Bulbous

vessel in clear glass internally decorated with a pattern of blue dots against a transparent red ground; acid-stamped "LIND/STRAND/KOSTA"; inscribed "KOSTA LC 10"; 6 inches high; $805.

Miscellaneous

Crystal Owls (two). Rounded obelisks cut and engraved into whimsical owl figures; both signed "Kosta"; smaller also signed "Lindstrand"; 5 inches high and 4 inches high; $400/set.

Orrefors Flared Crystal Vessel, designed by Vicke Lindstrand. Kykaren vase, inscribed ORREFORS LINDSTRAND 1342 A3R; 11¼ inches high; $935. *Courtesy of Skinner Inc., Boston/Bolton, MA.*

Crystal Sculpture. Free-form green-tinted block with polished face; etched with an elk at a brook; signed "Kosta, V. Lindstrand"; 7 inches high; $600.

ORREFORS GLASBRUK AB

Founded in 1726 in the Swedish province of Amaland, Orrefors was originally an ironworks. It wasn't until 1913 that the company hired skilled glassworkers and began producing cameo glass. Over the years Orrefors established a reputation for quality engraved glass. In postwar Sweden, Nils Landberg created designs in the Modern manner for Orrefors. Especially noteworthy are his Tulip goblets. They were blown from a single pull of glass, with elongated thin stems. Of cased glass, they used gradations of colors. Another important Orrefors glass designer to look for was Ingeborg Lundin.

VIKTOR EMANUEL (VICKE) LINDSTRAND (1904–1983)

One of Sweden's most famous glass designers, his avantgarde designs were recognized as early as 1935, at an important Stockholm exhibition. As a designer for Orrefors Glasbruk, he initially produced designs in the Moderne classicism style. In the 1940s his vases with nudes clearly showed influence from the work of Matisse, while those with animals were more abstract. In 1950 he became artistic director at Kosta Glasbruk, where he worked until his retirement in 1971.

The forms of his vases were asymmetric and used internal color threads. In the late 50s he used a thicker crystal. Many of his vases are biomorphic, some with shallow holes on one side.

PRICES

Orrefors Graal Glass Fish Vases, designed by Edward Hald, c. 1950s. *Left: signed* ORREFORS SWEDEN/GRAAL NO. *9940/EDWARD HALD; 5¾ inches high; $440. Right: inscribed* ORREFORS GRAAL NR. *217B EDWARD HALD; 5¼ inches high; $770. Courtesy of Skinner Inc., Boston/Bolton , MA.*

Bowls

Graal Art Glass Bowl. Heavy-walled colorless crystal squared bowl with enclosed decoration of green and black fish amid sea grasses; signed "Orrefors Graal/299L/Edward Hald"; 3 inches deep × 5½ inches wide × 5¾ inches high; $500.

Ravena Glass Bowl, designed by Sven Palmquist, c. 1955. Narrow curved vessel internally decorated with red and blue overlapping designs; inscribed "ORREFORS/RAVENA 533/Sven Palmquist"; 7¾ inches long; $2,300.

Urns/Vases/Vessels

Ariel Vase, designed by Ingeborg Lundin, c. 1955. Bulbous ovoid vessel in thick clear glass; internally decorated with controlled air bubbles in cobalt blue; signed "Orrefors/Ariel Nu 334 M/Ingeborg Lundin"; 5¾ inches high; $1,150.

Ariel Vases (pair). Heavy-walled teardrop-form colorless crystal internally decorated with blue crosshatch pattern centering controlled bubbles against yellow ground; signed "Orrefors/ Sven Palmquist" and numbered; each 8 inches high; $900/set.

Decorated Graal Fish Vase. Heavy-walled oval crystal with

internal layer of brown monochromatic fish and aquatic plants; signed "Orrefors Sweden Graal/Edward Hald"; 4¾ inches high; $425.

Orrefors Crystal Vase. Lindstrand-designed cone with sailboat and gulls, one inscribed ORREFORS L1355 A1S, the other marked ORREFORS; 10¼ inches high; $330. *Courtesy of Skinner Inc., Boston/Bolton, MA.*

Graal Fish Vase. Heavy-walled colorless crystal oval with internal decoration of green and black fish swimming among marine vegetation; signed "Orrefors Graal"; numbered and signed "Edward Hald"; 6½ inches high; $750.

Crystal Vase. Squared colorless oval etched with a stylized Romeo on obverse, Juliet on balcony at reverse; signed and numbered on base; 7¾ inches high; $150.

Graal Vase. Heavy paperweight technique with green underwater scene of deep-sea diver meeting mermaid; inscribed "Orrefors Graal-301B"; 5½ inches high; $412.

Crystal Vases (two), designed by Vicke Lindstrand. Cone with engraved sailboat and gulls above brilliant green foot, inscribed "Orrefors L1355 A1S"; and oval cylinder with child diving, marked "Orrefors N3676D2 AR"; each 10¼ inches high; $330/set.

Kykaren Vase, designed by Vicke Lindstrand, c. 1930. One of series of three designed by Lindstrand including also Shark Killer and Pearl Fishers; flared crystal vessel with engraved naked male diver viewed through rippled "waves" with bubbles; applied black foot; inscribed "Orrefors Lindstrand 1343 A3R"; 11¼ inches high; $935.

Graal-Fish Vase, designed by Edward Hald, c. 1950. Bulbous faceted vessel in clear glass; internally decorated with tropical fish among aquatic plants in shades of green; signed "ORREFORS/SWEDEN/GRAAL/Na 454/B/Edward Hald"; 6 inches high; $517.

Jellyfish Graal Glass Vase, designed by Edward Hald, c. 1955. Bulbous ovoid vessel in thick clear glass; internally decorated in shades of green with jellyfish floating among aquatic plants; signed "Orrefors/Sueve/Graal Nu. 619/Edward Hald"; 6¾ inches high; $1,380.

▨ VARIOUS SCANDINAVIAN GLASS DESIGNS ▨

PRICES

Dishes/Plates

Engraved Glass Dish, designed by Tapio Wirkkala for Ittala, c. 1955. Clear glass; leaf-form vessel finely engraved with opposing parallel lines; inscribed "TAPIO WIRKKALA ITTALA 3337"; 10 inches long; $920.

Urns/Vases/Vessels

Norwegian Plus Vase, designed by Benny Motzfeldt. Colorless cylinder internally decorated with brilliant blue bubble-filled layer banded with free-form black; acid-stamped "Plus BM"; 10½ inches high; $220.

Norwegian Art Glass Vases (two). A Hadeland green jardiniere, designed by Willy Johansson; and an internally decorated cylinder with blue birds in flight against a brown, white, and yellow sky, designed by Severin Brorb; 6½ inches high × 8¾ inches in diameter and 8¾ inches high, respectively; $247/set.

Finnish Molded Glass Vase, designed by Heinrik Krisula, c. 1950s. Inscribed HEINRIK KRISULA, HUMPPILA FINLAND, sold with paperweight signed LEVOY; 6¼ inches high; $440/set. *Courtesy of Butterfield and Butterfield Auctioneers, CA.*

Finnish Engraved Art Glass Vase. Amber vessel with nude woman diving among fish and marine plants; signed "Kumela 55-56"; 10½ inches high; $330.

Finnish Art Glass Serpentine Vase, designed by Gunnel Nyman for Nuutajarvi in 1947. Heavy-walled crystal oval with internal white spiral; fully signed; 16 inches high; $1,210.

Glass Vases (three), designed by Timo Sarpaneva, 1957–1958. Spherical form in smoke-gray glass; bullet-form two-tone vase with clear and smoke-gray glass; egg-shaped purple glass; signed "TIMO SARPANEVA/ITTALA/57 AND 58"; range of heights 5¼ inches to 8 inches; $690/set.

Orchid Vase, designed by Timo Sarpaneva, made for Ittala, c. 1954. Colorless hand-blown sculptural form; winner of Finnish section in Milan Triennale, 1954, as well as being named "the most significant object of the year" by *House Beautiful,* 1954; 12 inches high × 4 inches in diameter; mint condition; $700.

Glass Vases (two) and Glass Rosebud Holder, designed by Tapio Wirkkala and Timo Sarpaneva, c. 1955. First vase flattened ovoid form in white glass, cased in clear glass, signed "TAPIO WIRKKALA 3636"; second vase a rosebud holder of swollen cylindrical form, solid clear glass with opening forming internal decoration, signed "TAPIO WIRKKALA 57"; rosebud holder signed "TIMO SARPANEVA/ITTALIA 55"; vases 10 inches high and 5 inches high; $920/set.

Kantarelli Crystal Vase, designed by Tapio Wirkkala. Jack-in-the-pulpit for Finnish-Iittala, inscribed on base TAPIO WIRKKALA IITTALA; 5½ inches high; $440. *Courtesy of Skinner Inc., Boston/Bolton, MA.*

Glass Vase, designed by Nancy Still, c. 1955. Ovoid spherical vessel with narrow neck and broad flat platter-form circular rim; in pale lavender glass; signed "Nancy Still/Ruhimalen La 610Y"; 8½ inches in diameter; $230.

▣ CZECHOSLOVAKIAN GLASS DESIGNS ▣

In the 1940s and 1950s many of the top Czech artists both designed and created art glass. It took exhibits at the 1957 Milan Triennale and the Brussels World Fair of 1958 to expose the unique talents of Czech glass artists and their contributions to the rest of the world. Czech glass design differed from other modern styles in its use of enameling and other surface techniques. Toward the end of the 50s Czech artists were influenced by growing interest in abstract paintings, and used brightly colored enamels to create abstract patterns.

Because these artists and their work are still generally underrecognized today, they offer collectors a real opportunity. Unlike the glass of Scandinavia and Italy, Czech art glass rarely comes to auction. When it does, prices are generally low.

Some designers to look for include the following.

PAVEL HLAVA (1924–)
used prismatic cutting to create geometrical faceted sculptural objects in colored underlay glass.

STANISLAV LIBENSKY (1921–)
used very thin glass and almost transparent, pastel enamels to achieve designs that resemble watercolor paintings. He achieved another novel effect by using enamel painting with engraving.

RENÉ ROUBICEK (1922–)
used glass as if it were crystal; his sculptural, carved pieces used in-depth relief cutting. Figures resemble stone carvings.

VLADIMIR KOPECKY (1931–)
used a distinctive technique that utilized glass as a painter uses canvas, with heavy use of enamels forming patterns.

OTHER ARTISTS
include Jiri Harcuba (1928–), Karel Wunsch (1932–), Adolph Matura (1921–1978), and Ludvika Smrckova (1903–).

PRICES
Skrolovice Blown-Glass Vase. Heavy clear body shaded to light green with well-applied layers that form a V at each side and contain trapped air bubbles; paper label; 12 inches high; mint condition; $40.

Britain, still not fully recovered from World War II by the 50s, didn't enjoy the same creative development in glass design as Italy and Scandinavia. While those countries experimented with new forms and techniques, the British concentrated on surface designs, using engraving to achieve the Modern style.

Artists to look for include the following.

JOHN HUTTON (1906–1978)

considered one of the most important artists working in the 50s. Hutton created a new method of engraving on glass with a hand-held wheel. His designs exaggerated the lines of his figures and objects. He is best-known for his engraved glass screens created for Coventry Cathedral.

DAVID PEACE (1915–)

did work that can be recognized by his use of a fluid wheel—and diamond-engraved calligraphic inscriptions.

HELEN MUNRO-TURNER (1901–1977)

also used wheel engraving in her designs.

Collectors will want to look for the work of Lawrence Whistler (1921–) as well.

Jewelry made in the 1940s and 1950s offers an opportunity for collectors to get in on the ground floor. Remember what happened to Art Deco and Art Nouveau jewelry? Once, fine examples from these periods could be found inexpensively. These days even reproductions are expensive.

Keep in mind that this is a different type of jewelry market; pieces don't require precious stones to give them value. Knowing the market is a matter of becoming familiar with the important designers' names—names you have probably never heard before—and recognizing their styles. In the not-too-distant future you can expect reproductions and forgeries of their work. For now, you can browse at your own pace for prices in your range. Whenever possible examine the jewelry sold at auctions and in antiques shops. Since this is a relatively new area of collecting you can find bargains in shops and estate sales—just about anywhere. Generalized auctions with a smattering of jewelry can be treasure troves. Study the photos and examine the descriptions. Be choosy while you can.

From the late 1940s to the end of the 1950s, designs exemplifying the various Modern movements were defined in

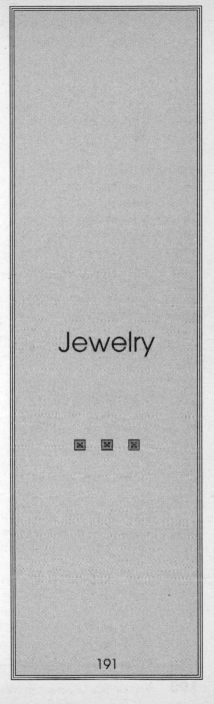

Jewelry

191

jewelry, often using new techniques. The forms were undulating, biomorphic, surrealistic, or organic. Many were closely related to sculpture; other pieces relate to the mobile concept of Alexander Calder and give the appearance of movement. This was particularly true in jewelry designs of the United States, Denmark, and Italy.

A radical change from the sharp, geometric lines of Art Deco jewelry, its free forms were yet another break from prewar traditions. While sterling silver was the metal of choice, it was often combined with totally unconventional materials. These included plain glass, minerals, and semiprecious stones. The use of these materials was especially prevalent with avant-garde American designers such as Sam Kramer. Others relied on form and the metal they used to convey the Modern look. Harry Bertoia achieved exciting effects using brass. Another American sculptor, Ibram Lassaw, worked first through the medium of jewelry. His work is highly collectible, and uses sculptural techniques with metals not usually employed in jewelry design, such as gilt bronze.

The use of gold also broke away from tradition with dimensional forms and surface techniques. Russian-born Irena Brynner learned her techniques in San Francisco, where she became known for her baroque and textured gold rings. She is generally credited with starting the fashion of wearing several rings on one finger or on several fingers of the same hand.

In Denmark, Henning Koppel made innovative silver pieces for Georg Jensen Silversmith that included jewelry. They changed the Jensen style from floral or fruit motifs to the dramatic, Modern motifs we now think of as the "Jensen look." His necklaces and brooches done from the mid-forties to mid-fifties have a distinctly sculptural look.

American-born architect William Spratling moved to Mexico, where he used yet another approach to "modern": ethnic revivalism. Collectors have been buying up examples of his Aztec- and Mayan-influenced jewelry for several years.

Less well-known silversmiths who worked mid-century in Mexico are "sleepers." Among them is Sigfredo Pineda, who signed his work "Sigi." Mexican artist Margot de Taxco is another who used the quality silver from Taxco in her designs. They and Spratling were well known in the 1930s and their Art

Deco–influenced pieces sell at auction for anywhere from the high hundreds to over a thousand dollars. Contrast that to the lower prices for their Modern designs at current auctions. Unsigned modern pieces simply marked "Taxco" or "made in Mexico" sell for a couple of hundred dollars. Mexican silver is marked "925 sterling."

The following listings reflect auction values.

HARRY BERTOIA

During the years Bertoia ran the metalworking school at the Cranbrook Academy of Art (1938–1943) his style compared with that of Alexander Calder, with whom he often exhibited. However, in contrast to Calder, Bertoia used rough, irregular textures. Above all his designs show a sculptural look and the effect of motion. Many of his pieces are silver or brass.

PRICES

Brooches/Pins

Stick Pins (pair). Silver stick pins with coil top decoration; de-acquisitioned from the Montreal Museum; 4½ inches long; mint condition; $250.

MARGARET STRONG BIELAWSKI DE PATTA (1903–1964)

This American designer is primarily known for her jewelry, which combined architectonic structuring, kinetics, and transparency. She first began by studying painting at the Academy of Fine Arts in San Diego from 1921 to 1923, followed by studies at the San Francisco School of Fine Arts and the Art Students League in New York City. Returning to San Francisco in 1929, she continued painting, but also became interested in the early Modern movement, particularly in jewelry design. Armin Hairenian, an artisan and jewelry designer (who designed period pieces for Hollywood movies), showed her various techniques. By 1936 she was selling pieces in San Francisco craft stores. The turning point came in 1940, when she met Laszlo Moholy-Nagy and began her study at his School of Design in Chicago, where she stayed until 1941. She experimented with optical effects, light and shadow. After her marriage to Eugene Bielawski, a design teacher at the school, both returned to San Francisco and established a jewelry studio. By 1946 they put her designs into small production. Each piece sold for under fifty dollars. Truly innovative, she received many awards and exhibited both nationally and internationally.

It is difficult to tell her one-of-a kind pieces from her limited-production jewelry. The quality is consistently high, however production pieces weren't as complicated.

PRICES

Brooches/Pins
Silver-and-Crystal Brooch, c. 1955. Formed of geometric shapes in polished and burnished silver; impressed "STERLING" and with maker's mark; 3¼ inches long; $1,840.

Earrings
Silver Earrings, c. 1950. Boomerang contour; impressed "M. DE PATTA" and "STERLING"; $517.

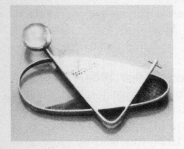

Brooch, designed by Margaret de Patta, c. 1948. Silver and crystal, impressed sterling and maker's mark; 3¼ inches; $1,840. *Courtesy Sotheby's Inc., © 1993.*

Rings
Silver Ring, c. 1955. Face in the form of two opposing leaves centering two spheres; impressed maker's mark; $575.

Silver Ring, c. 1950. Channeled top conjoined by a right-angle bar; impressed "STERLING" and "DE PATTA"; $920.

Silver and Green Stone Ring, c. 1955. Face of rectangular stepped contour centering a rectangular green stone; impressed maker's mark; $690.

SAM KRAMER (1913–1964)

Always avant-garde, Kramer proved almost any material could be incorporated into jewelry design. His parents moved to Southern California during the Depression, and Kramer graduated from the University of Southern California in 1936. While there he took a jewelry course, and shortly after graduation he returned to Pittsburgh, where he worked for a jewelry manufacturer. He developed an interest in Navaho jewelry. After spending a couple of years in Pittsburgh with his wife, Carol, also a jeweler, they moved to New York. In 1939 he studied gemology at New York University and opened a shop on Eighth Street.

Unlike designers of much Modern jewelry, Kramer avoided geometric forms. Instead his pieces had a hint of Surrealism, whether with a red taxidermy glass eye on a sterling silver cuff bracelet or through the use of semiprecious stones. His glass eyes became something of a trademark.

Even though he is considered one of the most innovative and influential American jewelry designers of the Modern movement, his pieces are still priced on the low side of material brought to auction.

PRICES

Bracelets

Bracelet, c. 1950. Silver plaques of various sizes and designs linked together to form a very organic design; impressed "sterling" and maker's mark; 7 inches long; excellent condition; $800.

Brooches/Pins

Brooch, c. 1950. Silver stylized human forms; Kramer monogram; 2 inches long; excellent condition; $275.

Brooch, designed by Sam Kramer, c. 1950. Silver, rose quartz, and sodalite, amorphous contour, set with sodalite and rose quartz cabochons at center, impressed with maker's mark; 2 ¾ inches long; $920. *Courtesy of Sotheby's Inc.,* © *1993.*

Silver-and-Copper Brooch, c. 1950. Copper ring attached to silver elements; impressed "sterling" and maker's mark; 2 inches long; mint condition; $425.

Silver-and-Carnelian Brooch, c. 1950. Caged square of carnelian; oxidized background; impressed "sterling" and maker's mark; 2 inches wide; excellent condition; $400.

Silver-and-Stone Brooch, c. 1950. Conical stone in organic design; Kramer monogram; 2 inches wide; excellent condition; $300.

Silver-and-Glass Brooch, c. 1950. Modeled as an abstracted eye with a brilliant gazing yellow center; impressed "sterling" and maker's mark; 2½ inches wide; $2,860.

Silver Brooch, c. 1950. Modeled in a textured, branchlike motif; set with a stone; stamped with artist's monogram; 3½ inches long; $1,540.

Silver, Rose Quartz, and Sodalite Brooch, c. 1950. Amorphous contour set with sodalite and rose quartz cabochons at center; impressed maker's mark; 2¾ inches long; $920.

Earrings

Silver Earrings, c. 1950. Modeled as an openwork abstracted form; impressed "sterling" and maker's mark; 1⅝ inches long; $990.

Screw-Back Earrings. Silver and copper; biomorphic design linked to copper circle; impressed "sterling" and maker's mark; 1 inch long; excellent condition; $95.

Ear Clips, c. 1950. Silver mobile of hanging shapes; unmarked; 3 inches high; excellent condition; $350.

Necklaces and Pendants

Silver-and-Glass Pendant, c. 1950. Cast with stylized foliage centering an oval glass "cat's eye"; impressed "sterling" and maker's mark; 5¼ inches long; $690.

Rings

Silver-and-Quartz Ring, c. 1950. Oxidized disk with quartz in prong set to band; impressed "sterling" and maker's mark; size 5½; 1 inch wide; excellent condition; $100.

Silver-and-Quartz Ring, c. 1950. Prong-set topaz-colored

quartz; impressed "sterling" and maker's mark; size 5½; 1 inch wide; $105.

Silver and Green Stone Ring, c. 1950. Crude organic design; oval bezel-set green stone; impressed "sterling" and maker's mark; 1 inch high; excellent condition; $200.

Silver and Green Stone Ring, c. 1955. Amorphous with thick band; the body pierced and set with a green cabochon; impressed "sterling" and maker's mark; $1,955.

Silver Ring, c. 1955. In form of Felix the Cat; thick silver band; unmarked; $575.

Miscellaneous

Silver and Tiger's-Eye Cuff Links, c. 1950s. Stylized triangles with bezel-set tiger's-eyes; impressed "sterling" and maker's mark; 2 inches long; excellent condition; $110.

Silver and Iridescent Glass Comb, c. 1955. Set with an oval iridescent glass cabochon; impressed "sterling" and maker's mark; 4½ inches long; $1,035.

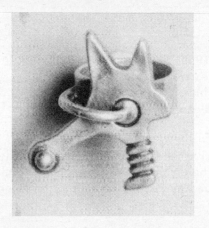 

Ring, designed by Sam Kramer. Sterling, abstract design, stamped maker's mark; $575. *Courtesy of Sotheby's Inc., © 1993.*

Comb, designed by Sam Kramer, c. 1950. Silver and abalone, impressed sterling and maker's mark; 4½ inches long; $1,035. *Courtesy of Sotheby's Inc., © 1993.*

ARTHUR SMITH (1917-1982)

This African-American New York designer expressed his artistic interests early on, and received a scholarship to Cooper Union in 1942. Though he studied architecture, his interests favored three-dimensional sculptural constructions. After graduation, a part-time job as a crafts supervisor led to a job with a black craftswoman who made jewelry from scraps of copper and brass. While he learned the basics from her, it was his own experimentation and designs that brought him to national prominence.

His designs and craftsmanship reflected his African roots and the Modern movement. The pieces are heavy and often use biomorphic forms. Much of his work seems overscale, a result of his work designing costumes and jewelry for the Pearl Primus and Talley Beaty dance companies. Many of his pieces are unmarked, so collectors should familiarize themselves with his craftsmanship. Prices are still comparatively modest . . . awaiting his rediscovery.

PRICES

Earrings

Pierced Earrings, c. 1950. Silver stylized teardrop dangles; unsigned; 2 inches long; excellent condition; $375.

Sterling Pierced Earrings, c. 1950s. Large suspended double hoops; 3½ inches long; mint condition; $475.

Miscellaneous

Copper Earrings and Bracelet, c. 1955. Earrings in the form of corkscrews enclosing balls, unsigned; bracelet cut with an oval at the center conjoined by copper stringing, inscribed "ART SMITH"; $575/set.

ED WIENER (1918–)

Self-taught, Wiener took his only formal training as a jewelry maker in 1945, when he enrolled in a general crafts course at Columbia University. He was intrigued by the neoprimitive shapes being exhibited at that time by Alexander Calder. Shortly afterward he began working out of his home, creating monogram pins from silver wire. In 1946 he and his wife returned to New York and opened a studio, where he sold his own designs along with Mexican jewelry. In 1947 he opened a store, called Arts and Ends, and in 1953 he opened a second one, in Greenwich Village. One of his most important pieces, titled "The Dancer," was inspired by a 1941 photo of dancer Martha Graham. It is cut from sheet silver into a biomorphic shape that defines the dancer's body. One hundred copies were made. His signature, "Ed Wiener," is usually impressed on his work.

PRICES

Earrings

Pierced Earrings, c. 1950. Abstract silver drops; marked "Ed Wiener"; 3 inches long; excellent condition; $325.

Silver-and-Garnet Earrings, c. 1955. Set with garnet cabochons; impressed "ED WIENER" and "STERLING"; $460.

Silver Earrings, c. 1955. Formed of circles and rectangles; impressed "ED WIENER" and "STERLING"; $575.

Necklaces and Pendants

Silver-and-Ceramic Necklace, c. 1950. Irregular contour supporting on one end an ovoid drop set with a ceramic cabochon, on the other six elongated pods; unsigned; $920.

Silver-and-Turquoise Necklace, c. 1950. Arched silver links conjoined by turquoise beads and supporting arched drops and a scarab beetle; stamped "STERLING/ED WIENER"; $575.

Silver-and-Moonstone Pendant, c. 1955. Set with a moonstone; impressed "ED WIENER" and "STERLING"; 1¼ inches long; $172.

Brooch, designed by Ed Wiener, c. 1955. Silver, copper, and amethyst, in the form of a stylized fish, copper stringing, oval amethyst eye; 2½ inches long; $690. *Courtesy of Sotheby's Inc., © 1993.*

Miscellaneous

Silver-and-Copper Belt Buckle, c. 1950. Amorphous form; unsigned; 2¼ inches long; $460.

▦ Various American Jewelry Designs ▦

Bracelets

Wide Bicolored 14K Gold Bracelet, c. 1940s. Triangular domed links; 72.8 pennyweight; $1,760.

14K Yellow Gold Bracelet Watch, c. 1950s. Flexible bracelet with center panel designed as an envelope concealing a watch; 57.2 pennyweight; marked "Daumier"; $880.

Brooches/Pins

Silver Brooch, designed by Betty Cooke, c. 1955. Cast as a sphere conjoined to a parabola; impressed "STERLING" and "COOKE"; 5 inches long; $230.

Brooch, c. 1950s. Sterling silver with natural pearl, handwrought; 2 inches wide x 1⅛ inches deep; $250. *Courtesy of Gillian Hine Antiques.*

Silver and 14K Gold Brooch, designed by Ed Levin, c. 1950. Notched sterling shield with figural designs of gold overlay; signed "Levin sterling/14K"; 3 inches wide; excellent condition; $100.

Silver, Brass, Copper, and Rosewood Brooch, c. 1955. Of early flying machine form; unmarked; 5⅜ inches high; $575.

Silver, Brass, and Copper Brooch, designed by Peter Macchiarini, c. 1955. Constructivist style; stamped "MACCHIARINI"; 3½ inches long; $575.

Mixed-Media Brooch, designed by Peter Macchiarini, c. 1950.

Geometric pin in silver, brass, and copper with ivory inset; signed; 3 inches long × 1¼ inches in diameter; mint condition; $750.

Earrings

Diamond-and-Lucite Hoop Earrings. 18K yellow gold hoops; each set with three oval diamonds encased in Lucite; French hallmarks; $1,760.

Miscellaneous

Sterling Cuff, designed by Ed Levin, c. 1940. Large cuff in flat twisted design; marked "LEVIN Sterling, Venn. VT"; 3 inches long × 2 inches in diameter; mint condition; $250.

Pin and Necklace Set, designed by Paul Lobel, c. 1940s. Silver intertwined twisted circles connected with interesting overlapping links; signed "Lobel, sterling"; pin 1 inch in diameter; necklace 16 inches long; excellent condition; $375.

▦ SCANDINAVIAN JEWELRY DESIGNS ▦

PRICES

Bracelets

Georg Jensen Silver Bangle with Bag. Heavy bangle; wider on one side; marked "Georg Jensen" within oval "925 S Denmark 168"; 2½ inches in diameter interior; $300.

Georg Jensen Silver Bracelet. Cuff decorated with a wide central band of zigzag and cloud motifs between brick borders; $460.

Brooches/Pins

Silver-and-Enamel Brooches (two), designed by Henning Koppel for Georg Jensen, post-1945. Zoomorphic-shaped brooch set with blue/black enamel; abstract pierced brooch with cobalt-blue enamel; stamped with postwar marks and numbers; 2 inches wide and 2½ inches wide, respectively; $990/set.

Georg Jensen Copper-and-Amethyst Brooch (model 479), c. 1955. In the form of a stylized fish set with copper stringing and an oval amethyst eye; 2½ inches long; $690.

Georg Jensen Silver Pin. Round plaque with center cut sup-

Earrings, designed by
Henning Koppel. Sterling
silver, free form, organic
design with cut-out
elements, clip backs,
impressed GEORGE JENSEN
mark in oval, STERLING,
DENMARK 119; 1 inch long;
$325. *Courtesy of
Toomey-Treadway
Galleries, Oak Park, IL.*

porting a black onyx bead; all marked "George Jensen" in a
beaded circle "Sterling, Denmark 336"; $125.

Scandinavian Sterling Pin. Circular with stone-laden bars
extending to the center; impressed "Finland sterling"; 2 inches
in diameter; excellent condition; $120.

Erik Magnussen Pin, c. 1940. Silver-and-enamel multicolored house on green lawn under blue sky in enamel; signed
"Erik Magnussen 1252, sterling, Eneret Denmark"; 3 inches
long; excellent condition; $425.

Modern Age Pin. Elongated boomerang shape impressed
"Sterling Denmark"; 4 inches long; excellent condition; $110.

Necklaces and Pendants

Georg Jensen Sterling Silver Pendant, Copenhagen,
post-1945 design 337A. Marked "Georg Jensen" in a beaded oval
and "925S/Denmark/337A"; 2⅜ inches in diameter on a 29-inch
chain; $150.

Sterling Silver Pendant, c. 1950s. Abstract design 342.
Signed "Georg Jensen"; $192.

Rings

Georg Jensen Sterling Ring. Wide pointed silver wraparound design; impressed "Jensen" circular mark, "925S," and
"#99"; 2 inches long; excellent condition; $110.

Georg Jensen Sterling Silver Ring, Copenhagen, post-1945
design number 130. Marked "Georg Jensen" in a beaded oval
and "925S/Denmark/130"; $85.

Scandinavian Sterling Ring. Six unusual blue lapis balls
raised from flat surface; impressed "Finland sterling"; excellent
condition; $240.

PRICES

Bracelets

Sigi Silver Bracelet. Silver bangle with two oval cabochon quartz obsidian stones set between wishbone ends wrapping to hinge at back; marked "Sterling Hecho en Mexico, sigi, Taxco" with touch mark; 2¾ inches in diameter; $150.

18K Bicolor Gold Bracelet, c. 1940s. Three rows; designed with interlocking fluted cone-shaped links; maker's mark; 55.9 pennyweight; $1,980.

Yellow Gold Mesh Bracelet, c. 1950s. Tapering design highlighted by seven jade-and-diamond bees; hallmark; 25.6 pennyweight; $440.

Bracelet and Pin, c. 1950s. Sterling with cobalt blue enamel, Italian marks; $225/set. *Courtesy of the author.*

Brooches/Pins

14K Yellow Gold Feather Brooch, c. 1940s. Centrally set with channel-set round rubies; 14.0 pennyweight; $880.

14K Bicolor Gold Butterfly Brooch, c. 1940. Stylized polished gold wings; citrines and a tourmaline; diamond eyes and ruby antennae; hallmark "Lester & Co."; $825.

14K Bicolor Gold Bow Pin, c. 1940s. Accented in the center by diamonds and rubies; marked "Eckfeldt & Ackley"; $412.

Taxco Sterling Pin. Design of fish in circle; impressed "Taxco" and "925"; illegible designer's name; 2 inches in diameter; excellent condition; $375.

Sterling Pin. Design of a fish with applied scales; five amber drops hang from waves along his stomach; impressed fish mark, "#1," and "925"; 2 inches long; excellent condition; $150.

Earrings

Salvador Sterling Earrings (pair). Screw backs; unusual figure of a native with arms wrapped around a black stone; marked "Sterling Mexico"; 2 inches; excellent condition; $150.

14K Yellow Gold and Ruby Earclips (pair), c. 1940s. Designed as a stylized flower with ruby centers and radiating gold petals; $1,100.

14K Yellow Gold Earrings (pair), c. 1950s. Flat disks with reed edges and screw backs; hallmarked; 5.2 pennyweight; $110.

18K Yellow Gold Earrings (pair), Guito Knoop. Sculptured triangular form; marked "GK" and "5/8"; 18.1 pennyweight; $1,045.

18K Yellow Gold Flower Earclips, c. 1950s. Stylized petals with diamond tips and center; 16.1 pennyweight; $3,300.

18K Yellow Gold Earclips, c. 1950. Designed as reeded pinwheels; highlighted by sapphire-and-diamond centers; 9.2 pennyweight; $990.

Necklaces and Pendants

Salvador Sterling Necklace. Unusual figure of a native man with arms wrapped around black stone; long hair curves to hold the loop for the chain, which is a series of small circles; marked "Salvador, Sterling Mexico #105"; 14 inches long; excellent condition; $400.

18K Yellow Gold Pendant on Chain, Guito Knoop, made by Emil Schaffner. Sculptured triangular form, marked "GK"; $2,750.

Miscellaneous

Margot Enamel-and-Silver Brooch and Clip Earrings. In the shape of a curling wave highlighted in white enamel; marked "Margot De Brooch; and earrings with clip 1½ inches in diameter, earrings ¾ inch; marked TAXCO; $500/set.

Pin and Curved Hook for Necklace, Mexican. Star design; marked "Taxco, 925 Sterling"; 3 inches wide; excellent condition; $70/set.

William Spratling Silver Belt. Twenty segments, each consisting of a domed circle with rope twisted border flanked at corners by small domes; each link separated by three vertical medium-sized domes; marked in several places "WS" with a circle and "980"; 31¼ inches long; $1,100.

23K Yellow Gold Medallion, Max Ernst, Grande Tete, 1956. Signed and numbered "2/8"; stamped with hallmark of Francois Hugo in a wooden box; 4 inches × 3⅞ inches; $5,500.

▨ COSTUME JEWELRY

It began in New York and spread cross-country as dealers began offering costume jewelry from the 40s and 50s. In 1992 the Victoria and Albert Museum in London exhibited "Jewels of Fantasy," displaying some of the finest costume jewelry designs from the twentieth century. Included were many American-made pieces. The rise in interest and in dealer prices is directly related to the rise in antique gold jewelry prices and the fact that few people can afford jewelry made with real gems.

The appeal of these pieces lies in their sometimes outrageous designs, made of everything from plastic to rhinestones. While the costume jewelry designs of Miriam Haskell and Coco Chanel are well known and command top dollar, many other designers remain relative unknowns but are worth collecting. Inexpensive, mass-produced jewelry was marketed by Trifari, Coro, Napier, and Monet, to mention just a few. Until recently it was known as "junk jewelry" and was sometimes sold by the bag at flea markets. Of course, not all "junk jewelry" was created equal. Developing a discriminating eye is imperative.

The traveling London museum show opened in February 1991 in Milan, then moved to Zurich, Switzerland. Visitors were often transformed into collectors, as they saw and became enamored of designs from Christian Dior, Schiaparelli, Karl Lagerfeld, Kenneth Jay Lane, and others. Items on display included cuffs, bangles, and hat pins in materials such as lacquer, celluloid, silver, copper, brass, rhinestones, and glass.

If you didn't see the exhibit, you can re-create the experience through the museum catalog, "Jewels of Fantasy," published by Harry Abrams. Other books on the subject are listed in the bibliography.

When pricing such mass-produced items, scarcity determines value, though design of course is also important. In the 40s and 50s the pieces that were considered "high fashion" were physically large, so think "big." If possible, look through some *Vogue* magazines of the time to familiarize yourself with some designs.

Surprisingly, the best pieces will have stones hand-set in prongs, and the stones will be properly sized. Quality workmanship is assured if stones can be identified as Czechoslovakian rhinestones or Swarovski crystal. Check metal edges, which should be smooth. A variety of settings, including silver, were used. Sometimes multiple platings were used, with a gold finish. Also examine pieces for patent numbers or manufacturers' signatures.

You can build a collection in a particular category such as dogs, military symbols, or flowers; or by item such as rings, bracelets, pins, or brooches. Some collectors base their choices on the material used to manufacture the pieces. Plastic in all its many forms is growing in popularity. Remember, there are Andy Warhol carved bangles, which can cost as much as $300 each, waiting to be discovered.

COPPER JEWELRY

During the 1940s and 1950s copper art jewelry, combining copper and enamel, added a new look to costume jewelry. In this field the work of two craftsmen is claiming collectors' attention: Frank Rebajes and Jerry Fels. Rebajes, who emigrated from the Dominican Republic to New York, worked in the primitive style. In his Los Angeles studio, Fels worked in stylized designs popular after World War II.

Manufacturers of copper jewelry worth collecting include Coro and Robert and Sarah Coventry.

Copper jewelry was one of the many crafts popular with hobbyists. Kits with small kilns and materials for making enamel-and-copper jewelry were common in the late 50s. Many of the unsigned pieces that turn up today were made by these home hobbyists.

PLASTIC JEWELRY

Remember what happened to prices for the Bakelite (plastic) jewelry of the 1930s? They skyrocketed along with prices of Art Deco pieces. Now there is growing interest in the plastic jewelry of the 40s and 50s. While some of the pieces are similar in style to examples from the 30s, others are strictly Modern. Some of the early 40s pieces combined metal and plastic, and prewar examples often came from Germany.

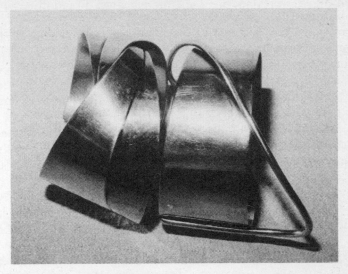

Copper Bracelet, c. 1950s. Signed REBAJES (Frank Rebajes); $125. *Courtesy of Gillian Hine Antiques.*

Bracelet, c. 1950s. Bakelite set with mirrors; $150. *Courtesy of Gillian Hine Antiques.*

Lord and Taylor acted on an Oriental influence of the late 40s and sponsored a benefit for Chinese war orphans. They featured plastic reproductions of Chinese carved medallions in colors of jade, lapis lazuli, and carnelian.

By the 1950s Americans were buying mass-produced plastic jewelry in Woolworth's as well as Saks Fifth Avenue. Beads of all kinds were popular, especially the so called "pop-it" beads. The fun came in mixing and matching, shortening or lengthening your own design with beads that fit together, forming chains. Colors were pastels and frosted.

American jewelry craftsman Bill Smith was one of the first to create one-of-a-kind, hand-dyed acrylic costume jewelry in Modern chunky style. Examples of his work can only go up in value.

Pop-it beads, frosted.	$2
Necklace. Lucite. Yellow and orange.	$15
Acrylic pin, red in square. Modern style.	$10
Green acrylic ring designed by Bill Smith. Modern style.	$50

Bracelet, c. 1950s. Orange plastic with rhinestone; $110. *Courtesy of Gillian Hine Antiques.*

Earrings (two pairs), c. 1950s. Clip on, plastic with red rhinestones; $25/set. *Courtesy of Gillian Hine Antiques.*

◼ AMERICAN LIGHTING DESIGNS

Many exciting new ideas for lighting were devised beginning in the 1950s, in both the United States and other countries. Chief among them was the bubble lantern. It was first designed by George Nelson in 1952 for Herman Miller. Its original form was adapted by various designers well into the 1960s. Nelson's "bubble" was made by spraying a cocoon of vinyl over metal ribs. This technique was originally used by the military for rust-proofing. The lanterns were lightweight and the plastic covering created a soft, diffused light.

Lighting
Designs

◼ ◼ ◼

PRICES

Bubble Lamp, designed by George Nelson, manufactured by Howard Miller. Oval form of self-webbing white vinyl spray over steel wire skeletal frame; 10 inches in diameter × 16 inches high; very good condition; $190.

Bubble Lamp, designed by George Nelson, manufactured by Howard Miller. Large saucer form of self-webbing white vinyl spray over steel wire skeletal frame; 24 inches in diameter × 10 inches high; excellent condition; $325.

Bubble Lamp, designed by George Nelson. Large ten-sided form of self-webbing white vinyl spray over steel wire skeletal frame; rare and unusual configuration; 25 inches in diameter × 23 inches high; excellent condition; $250.

Bubble Lamp, designed by George Nelson, manufactured by Howard Miller. Smaller version of the ten-sided form of self-webbing white vinyl spray over steel wire skeletal frame; 14 inches in diameter × 12 inches high; excellent condition; $190.

Bubble Lamp, designed by George Nelson, manufactured by Howard Miller, c. 1952. Large hourglass form of self-webbing white vinyl spray over steel wire skeletal frame; rare and unusual configuration; 20 inches in diameter × 21 inches high; excellent condition; $425.

Bubble Lamp, designed by George Nelson, manufactured by Howard Miller. Enormous saucer form of self-webbing white vinyl spray over steel wire skeletal frame; 36 inches in diameter × 18 inches high; excellent condition; $220.

Bubble Lamp, designed by George Nelson, manufactured by Howard Miller. Oval form of self-webbing white vinyl spray over steel wire skeletal frame; 11 inches in diameter × 16 inches high; excellent condition; $50.

Bubble Lamp, designed by George Nelson, manufactured by Howard Miller. Oversized zeppelin form of self-webbing white vinyl spray over steel wire skeletal frame; 14 inches in diameter × 34 inches high; very good condition; $110.

Bubble Lamp, designed by George Nelson, manufactured by Howard Miller. Round ball form of white vinyl self-webbing spray over steel wire skeletal frame; 12 inches in diameter; excellent condition; $50.

Bubble Lamp, designed by George Nelson, manufactured by Howard Miller. 24-sided hourglass form of white vinyl self-webbing spray over steel wire skeletal frame; original Howard Miller label; never used; 12 inches in diameter × 12 inches high; excellent condition; $50.

Modern Table Lamp, c. 1953. Two tapering cylindrical shades in woven natural fiber on a diagonal over V-shaped standard joined at base; in black plastic raised on rectangular platform base of white plastic; base light; 31 inches high; $90.

Brass-and-Bamboo Torch Lamps (pair), designed by Russel Wright, c. 1955. Brass trumpet with ball-shaped light switch on bundled vertical bamboo-standard held by brass wire at the top, middle, and bottom; raised on domed circular brass foot; 66⅛ inches high; some wear; $175.

Painted Paper and Wood Lamp, c. 1950. Eliptical black painted wooden arms embracing a conical parchmentlike paper shade covered with "dripping" paint; 40½ inches high; $770.

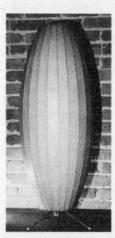 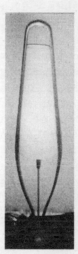

Floor Lamp, designed by George Nelson, manufactured by Herman Miller Furniture Company, c. 1950s. Elliptical wire cage and bubbled shade supported by chrome plated steel rod tripod base; 38 Inches high x 13 inches deep x 13 inches wide; $550. *Courtesy of Toomey-Treadway Galleries, Oak Park, IL.*

Floor Lamp, manufactured by Modeline of California , c. 1950s. Solid wood; 62 inches high; $200. *Courtesy of South Beach Furniture.*

Standing Floor Lamp, designed by Phillip Johnson and Richard Kelly, produced by Edison Price, Inc. Bronze frame; painted aluminum light source and shade; 38 inches wide × 25 inches deep × 25 inches high; excellent condition; $2,800.

Table Lamp, designed by Isamu Noguchi, manufactured by Knoll Associates, c. 1950s. Legs of cherry wood; floating cylindrical shade of fiberglass-reinforced polyvinylchloride and steel; 16 inches high; excellent condition; $850.

Rock Lamp, designed by Isamu Noguchi, c. 1949. Rock-shaped iron base; bamboo shaft; original paper shade; some small tears to shade; 53 inches high; good condition; $110.

Dore Lamps (pair), designed by Clark Voorhees, manufactured by Hansen Lamp Company, c. 1950. Ebonized wood with design of a bird in flight; 27 inches high; excellent condition; $375.

Lamp, c. 1950s. Whimsical kitsch form in chartreuse painted wood with oversized coral fabric shade; 29 inches high × 16 inches deep × 27 inches wide; excellent condition; $80.

Lamp, designed by Ed Weinberg. Abstract brass base; black lacquered wood top; cylindrical fiberglass and gold fleck shade; 7 inches in diameter × 26 inches high; excellent condition; $450.

Floor Lamp, designed by Von Nessen, c. 1940s. Industrial design in spun aluminum with fiberglass shade that can adjust for up or down lighting; shade 17 inches in diameter, total height 62 inches; excellent condition; $230.

Polaroid Study Lamp, designed by Walter Dorwin Teague, c. 1940s. Stylized brown and white marbleized plastic form with copper decoration; 13 inches high, base measures 5 inches in diameter; $220. *Courtesy of Toomey-Treadway Galleries, Oak Park, IL.*

Pair of Table Lamps, manufactured by Fine Arts in Plastics, Brooklyn, N.Y., c. 1950s. Stylized male and female forms in black painted plaster composition with painted fiberglass shade; 29 inches high × 10 inches deep × 10 inches wide; very good condition; $95/set.

Desk Lamp, manufactured by Lightolier, c. 1950s. Two-part adjustable form of pale gray metal that functions as a stabile by balancing off the edge of the surface with weighted brass ball; 34 inches high × 12 inches deep × 7 inches wide; excellent condition; $60.

Floor Lamp, designed by Thomas Moser, manufactured by Lightolier, c. 1955. Wooden and brass shaft attached to brass and metal base with three adjustable arms at top of shaft; white enamel beaker-shaped metal shades pivot to adjust light source; each has concentric circular light diffuser; 78 inches high × 27 inches deep × 27 inches wide; excellent condition; $210.

Table Lamp, designed by Hefitz. Limed oak body with biomorphic leaf-shaped copper overlay on black ebonized base; original fiberglass shade; 24 inches high × 7 inches deep × 5 inches wide; excellent condition; $80.

Table Lamp (pair), c. 1950s. One male and one female figure, marked F>A>I>P>, new paint, new hand-painted shade; 22 inches high, including shade; $245. *Courtesy of South Beach Furniture.*

Floor Lamp, by Modeline of California. Solid wood with brass trim, original finish and parchment shade; 60 1/2 inches high; $135. *Courtesy of South Beach Furniture.*

▦ INTERNATIONAL LIGHTING DESIGNS

▦ JAPAN ▦

Akari Associates is a subsidiary of the Isamu Noguchi Foundation, which manages and coordinates worldwide sales of a line of electric lamps known as Akari. Since 1951 they have represented work based on the designs of sculptor Isamu Noguchi. The pieces are manufactured in Gifu, Japan, by Ozeki and Company, Ltd. The first Akari lamps were small-scale table models. In 1961 standing lamps were made with fluorescent tubes. Due to the number of cheap copies made by imitators, Noguchi created signed limited editions of thirty new designs in 1969. More than sixty Akari styles are still produced, from the earliest to the current line of pyramidal modules.

▦ ITALY ▦

Italian designers took a totally new approach to Modern lighting, often treating it as a sculptural form. Among the most important lighting designers was Gino Sarfatti, a lighting engineer. With Arteluc, the company, began in 1939. They produced hundreds of lighting fixtures in the Modern style, among them table lamps, ceiling fixtures, and floor lamps. Sarfatti adapted the Calder mobile to his unusual ceiling fixture, known as the "pendant" lamp. Colored enamels, metals, and even neon were used to create different lighting effects.

The Castiglioni brothers, Achille and Pier, are among the most important designers of the Modernist period who worked not only on lighting but also on furniture, interiors, and industrial products. They designed lighting for many Italian companies, constantly experimenting with new forms. One of their most famous creations is the Luminator floor lamp, model number B9. Designed in 1955, it is the ultimate simplistic design, well deserving of the Modern term "aesthetic minimalism." Basically, it is a steel tub mounted on a tripod with a light bulb on top. In its time it was considered revolutionary. Another noteworthy design is their Taraxacum lamp shade, made from spun fiberglass tightly stretched over a wire frame.

The hanging glass light fixtures designed by Massimo Vignelli for the Venini glassworks in the early 1950s took a different tack. These fixtures were both functional, reducing glare, and beautiful, with colorful striped borders framing solid colors. Vignelli also created lighting fixtures from inverted Venini vases.

Another important designer, born in Austria but educated in Italy, was Ettore Sottsas. In the late 1950s this architect and designer tried many techniques in lighting, among other fields. He designed tripod lamp tables, novel enameled metal shades strung together with threads, and lamp shades of folded and bent aluminum sheets.

Italian lamps and shades are easily identified by manufacturers' names. They include Artluce, Fontana Arte, New Style, Arredoluce, O-luce, Azucena, and Flos.

Glass Hanging Lamp Shades (pair), designed by Fulvio Bianconi for Venin Pezzato, c. 1950s. $2,070/set. *Courtesy of Sotheby's Inc., © 1993.*

PRICES

Floor Lamp. Unusual configuration with brass pole attached to a weighted white enamel steel base with three detachable brass arms; functions like a Tinker Toy that can fit into any of seven separate spaces to adjust the light source; three conical enamel shades in yellow, green, and white; 72 inches high × 40 inches deep × 36 inches wide; excellent condition; $700.

Desk Lamp, c. 1950s. Repainted metal red shade; blue base; 26 inches high; rewired; good condition; $100.

Desk Lamp. Architectural form with black enamel weighted base; brass-plated arms with individual pivot mechanisms; conical shades in black, orange, and yellow; 19 inches high × 23 inches deep × 22 inches wide; excellent condition; $350.

Lamp Base, designed by Fantoni. Classic bottle form with four whimsical figures in green, blues, and blacks; signed on front and bottom; factory drill on side and bottom; 16 inches high × 5 inches deep × 6 inches wide; mint condition; $250.

Hanging Glass Lamp Shades (two), designed by Fulvio Bianconi, manufactured by Venini Pezzato, c. 1951. Each swollen, elongated domical shade in clear glass with patchwork decoration in pink, blue, and purple; cased over with white glass; unsigned; together with a pen-and-ink drawing by Fulvio Bianconi; 13⅝ inches; $1,150/set.

Ceiling Fixture, manufactured by Venini. Glass; large white globe with irregular wide orange band around center; chrome fitting; 19 inches in diameter; excellent condition; $275.

▨ OTHER EUROPEAN LIGHTING DESIGNS ▨

PRICES

Cerf-Volant Drilled Metal Floor Lamp, designed by Pierre Guariche for Pierre Disderot Luminaires, c. 1950. V-shaped brass arms on black metal fork-shaped feet; black painted metal shade covered with a drilled white painted bent metal sheet; 59 inches high; $1,100.

Metal Light Fixture, designed by Pierre Guariche, c. 1955. Black painted angled tubular metal wall bracket supporting a swivel jointed arm with double up and down lamps at one end and a weighted sphere at the other; shades painted yellow; unsigned; 32½ inches high × 17¾ inches in diameter; $2,012.

Metal Adjustable Lamp, designed by Serge Mouille, c. 1955. U-form clamp supporting an angular tubular rod ending in an adjustable eyeball shade; painted black; unsigned; 22½ inches high; $920.

Metal Desk Lamp, designed by Serge Mouille, c. 1955. Similar to above; painted black; unsigned; 28 inches high; $1,035.

Sculpted Aluminum Floor Lamp, designed by Serge Mouille, c. 1955. Painted black; on triangular spike base; slender shaft supporting a pivoting, rounded, conical shade; 62 inches high; $4,950.

Antony Sculpted Metal Table Lamp, designed by Serge Mouille, c. 1950. Painted black; sculpted helmet metal shade on a base with circular foot; 17¼ inches high; $1,540.

Wall Sconces (pair), designed by Serge Mouille, c. 1950. Elegant sculptural forms with black matte exterior; white interior; lower conical form reading light above uplighting; original finish; each 11 inches high × 11 inches in diameter; $1,500/set.

Wall Sconce, designed by Jean Royere. Black painted undulating metal mount issuing three straight arms, each supporting a light fixture; 54½ inches wide; $2,200.

George Theofiles founded his unique mail-order firm Miscellaneous Man in 1970, specializing in vintage posters and other graphic memorabilia. His firm sells no new items or reproductions. His interest began at age eight with the purchase of his first poster, "I WANT YOU FOR U.S. ARMY," for seventy-five cents. It is now worth over $1,000. He has since become an expert in the ever-growing field of graphics history preservation. He is willing to share his knowledge with collectors, who can contact him at his gallery in New Freedom, Pennsylvania.

World War II was a period of great inspiration for poster artists, though often slogans such as "Loose Lips Sink Ships" made as strong an impression in the memory as any picture. Many designs withstood the test of time and still help to define history. Among the most influential designers were the French émigré artist Jean Carlu, who rendered an early classic, "America's Answer— PRODUCTION," and Norman Rockwell, who painted the common man's influence and desires in his "Four Freedoms." Over twelve million of the "Four Freedoms" were printed. World War II

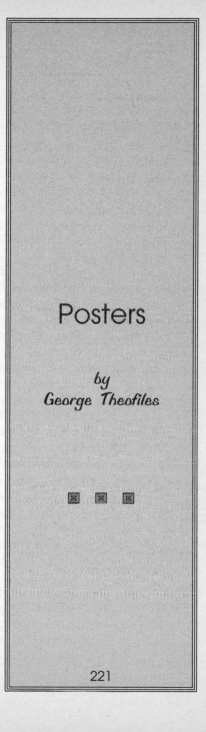

Posters

by
George Theofiles

posters have a wide range of values, from under $25 to over $1,000.

An interesting departure from war propaganda—American or European—took place in Switzerland in the 1940s. Switzerland remained neutral throughout the duration of the war, and poster advertising continued unabated. Otto Baumberger, Hans Falk, Donald Brun, and dozens of other posterists produced crisp, clean designs for clothiers like PKZ, which set a standard for postwar advertising. Many of these designs are still underappreciated and can be found for only a few hundred dollars or less. Generally the print runs of these posters were only a few thousand. None were intended as souvenirs to be sold. Many were saved only through the efforts of the Swiss-based design magazine *Graphis,* which offered a poster subscription service in the late 1940s.

As a communications form, the poster began to wane in postwar America. The new dominant communication forms were radio and television. One exception was the film poster. The movie poster, like the product advertising poster, had always been the work of teams at printing firms and was rarely signed by the artist. The 1940s and 1950s brought a relative glut of exceptions, and a dozen or so artists represented in the medium did sign their work. Among these were Marcel Vertes, whose designs bring $75 to $300; and, again, Norman Rockwell, whose 1946 poster for the film *The Razor's Edge* demands upward of $1,000. Saul Bass, a war vet whose first postwar job was designing movie advertising press books, went on to design a number of the most sophisticated movie posters of the 1950s, among them posters for *Vertigo* and *Man with the Golden Arm.*

The 1950s also saw the reemergence of American corporate identity programs. Classic among these were Paul Rand's designs for IBM, which often bring several hundred dollars or more. He and others also designed subway posters.

Travel became a product in the 1950s. New airlines competed for tourist business, marking the end of the era of the great transocean liners. The ocean liner and the airlines did their best to create appealing images for a new, wider audience. Among the best of 50s airline advertising was the work of E. McKnight Kauffer. He was born in Wyoming, but lived in England by choice and pursued his career there. He came often to the United States in the process of designing a series of posters for Pan American Airways from 1947 through 1955. Though many are considered classics, numerous examples are presently priced near $200.

The American "Beat" era of the 1950s produced some experimental poetry and literature, but not a great deal in terms of memorable graphics. This was also the case for dance and theater imagery. The few window cards and the like announcing Jack Kerouac's books and Ferlinghetti's poetry that have survived are desirable as relics but not for their design value. The era produced a harrowing number of beret-wearing, pseudointellectual sycophants whose surroundings were littered with a cheap international look, namely candle-stuck Chianti bottles and the graphic icon of the cause, the bullfight poster. Bullfight posters were originally offered in America as an afterthought by a California entrepreneur who had seized them for an overdue debt from a Spanish printer. He sold sixty thousand of them the first year. They were offered for a dollar each. This is approximately their value today. The bullfight poster did introduce a generation to the idea that commercial art could serve as decor.

Another significant advance in graphics influence was the fine arts exhibition poster. Galerie Maeght in Paris popularized this trend in the early 1950s with posters showing artwork by Picasso and Leger. Museums soon found that the poster could be a source of extra revenue, and the whole trend took off. Thousands of designs were produced worldwide. Most of these works were, in fact, partial images of fine art amid a mediocre design setting and have little value, often $25 or less.

Among the most avidly sought posters of the 1940s and 1950s are those that were music-related, especially those promoting early rock and roll musicians. Though the 1960s would see a sort of poster renaissance in concert posters, the 1950s was filled with images that would lay the groundwork. Early posters for Bill Haley, Buddy Holly, Elvis Presley, and Little Richard are indeed uncommon. The most popular size for music posters of this period was fourteen-by-twenty-two-inch window placards, often relatively crudely printed in two colors. The largest printer of these cards was the Globe Poster Company of Baltimore, Maryland. This field is one of the few of the 1940s and 1950s that is rife with reproductions. These designs are easy to

Poster, c. 1948. *Les Platters,
French; 33 inches x 44 inches;
$60. Courtesy of
Miscellaneous Man, New
Freedom, PA.*

reproduce, and a large number of reproduction posters for Elvis concerts as well as those for Hank Williams and others have surfaced.

"The poster market is bullish, whether old or new," according to Palm Beach dealers Robert Perrin and Peter Langlykke of Poster Graphics Inc. They feel that 40s and 50s travel and automobile posters are currently "sleepers." They also advise putting away 50s poster designs such as the Lido and Moulin Rouge for the future. Another frequently overlooked category is benefit posters with graphic merit.

"Most people don't know what to do with posters when they get dog-eared, so they throw them away," said Perrin. "Yet, often they can be restored by putting linen backing on them."

"If I were a collector I'd go to auto dealers to look for old posters," suggested Langlykke. "Racing posters, such as those promoting auto races from LeMans and Monaco, have exciting graphics and are also worth putting away. After all, just four years ago the Robert Indiana 'Love' poster retailed for $25. Now, if you can find one it would sell for $1,000."

Poster. *Potteries de Picasso, Pablo Picasso, lithographic poster, signed in pen; some foxing and time discoloration; 23¾ inches x 14¾ inches; $450. Courtesy of Freeman Galleries, Philadelphia, PA.*

Both dealers feel that for the most part the large 40s and 50s posters haven't been reproduced.

Prices are based on many factors, among them rarity and artist. The perfect combination of both is a rare 1955 poster by A.M. Cassandre.

▓ AVIATION AND AIRLINES ▓

PRICES

Hawaii—United Air Lines, designed by Frederick Lawier, c. 1947. Grandly stylized imagery of hula dancer amid motif of mountains, tropical fish, and propeller airliner overhead; scarce; 25 inches × 40 inches; overall mint condition; $975.

Hawaii—United Air Lines, designed by Fredrick Lawier, c. 1947. Smiling, attractive wahini presents lei to viewer under glowing sun; airliner and panorama of beach and surfers; 25 inches × 40 inches; overall mint condition; $800.

Fly to Mexico by Clipper, designed by von Arenburg, c. 1949. Pan American World Airways; richly colored image; partially offset, partially silk screened; 25 inches × 40 inches; mint condition; $350.

Colorado—United Air Lines, anonymous designer, c. 1950. Pulp magazine cover colors of mesquite, mesa, and mountains; airliner overhead; 25 inches × 40 inches; mint condition; $350.

"Boac Flies to All Six Continents," designed by Abraham Games, 1954. Translucent color arrows point in all direction in near-cloudless sky; tiny scratch at bottom; 25 inches × 40 inches; near-mint condition; $600.

Australia, anonymous designer, c. 1953. "Fly there by BOAC & Quantas," silk screen of cricket player; 20 inches × 30 inches; mint condition; $275.

Air France—North Africa, 1948. Arabian gentleman enjoys tea amid carpets, palms, exquisite desert setting; looks to prop plane in sky above; 26 inches × 40 inches; near-mint condition, $425.

Chicago—United Air Lines, anonymous designer, c. 1950. Drawbridge opens in foreground in front of dramatic skyscrapers, famed Chicago architecture; airliner flys overhead; 25 inches × 40 inches; overall mint condition; $450.

Air France, 1950. Grand stone lithograph of Corsican mountains and sea with plane overhead; 24 inches × 39 inches; overall mint condition; $325.

Southern California—United Air Lines, anonymous designer, c. 1950. Attractive young lady dances under sun amid background of old and new Los Angeles; airliner overhead; 25 inches × 40 inches; mint and fresh; $600.

President, Pan American World Airways, anonymous designer, 1951. Advertises first-class flights to New York for the German market on the "Blues Band: trans-Atlantic flight"; this poster was done in many languages, including English; shows luxurious dining table, wine stewards, fresh flowers, rich color; 25 inches × 40 inches; near-mint condition; $425.

PRICES

Benny Carter—America's Most Versatile Orchestra, c. 1946. Photo portrait of Carter against black-and-orange background; Carter formed the first interracial jazz band in music history and composed themes for everything from TV's "Mod Squad" to *The Snows of Kilimanjaro;* 14 inches × 22 inches; mint condition; $225.

Billy Eckstine, "The Romantic Singing Maestro," c. 1946. Color photo portrait of Eckstein; 14 inches × 22 inches; mint condition; $175.

Fight Never Ends, Joe Louis, 1948. Scarce group of ten original 8 × 10 black-and-white photographs from the film; most show Louis; most mint condition; $250/set.

Lionel Hampton and His Famous Orchestra, 1947. Smiling photo portrait; pink background; scarce; 14 inches × 22 inches; $275.

Coleman Hawkins, "The All-American Saxophonist and His Orchestra," 1946. Rare photo portrait against blue background; 14 inches × 22 inches; $325.

Hot from Harlem, c. 1947. Color poster for a Black burlesque show; "Brown-Skinned Beauties That Are A Treat! Right Off The Griddle . . . Excitable Music"; imagery of sepia strippers at bottom; very clean; printed on card stock; 22 inches × 28 inches; $250.

House Rent Party, Toddy, c. 1946. Pigmeat Markham, Hohn "Rastus" Murray; set of eight superb color lobby cards with original envelope; frantic doings, dance scenes, all surrounding the hopeful success of "Pigmeat's World Champion Hair Straightener—Straightens Anything—Wire, Nails, Screws"; scarce; each 11 inches × 14 inches; $250/set.

⬛ FILM POSTERS ⬛

A relatively untapped specialty in this field is original movie poster art. One of the few auction sources to date is Illustration

House in New York City (see listing in Sources). Examples of this art would be a natural supplement to any movie poster collection. Prices depend on the popularity of the subject, the actors featured in the poster, and the artist. Prices range from the low hundreds into the thousands. Illustration House offers an illustrated catalog. Poster art is included with other forms of illustration art at these twice-yearly auctions.

Since there are currently a proliferation of books on movie posters and their prices, I have only briefly noted a few examples from the forties and fifties.

PRICES

Bathing Beauty, MGM, 1944. Esther Williams; nice, intense pin-up; background shows Busby Berkeley–style bather scene; 27 inches × 41 inches; near-mint condition; $125.

Brighton Strangler, RKO, 1944. John Loder, June Duprez; crazed Loder terrorizes female co-star amid lurid, intense, pulp magazine–like design; 27 inches × 41 inches; $175.

Blue Dahlia (La Dahlia Bleu), art by Soubie, Paramount, 1947. French; Alan Ladd, Veronica Lake; Ladd looks down, illuminating dahlia with his flashlight amid design of other stars; rare; 47 inches × 62 inches; $600.

Big Stroke, Marx Brothers, MGM, 1941. Original French release of this great comedy classic; lithographic caricature imagery of all three accosting a dress mannequin; fresh and overall mint condition; $1,100.

Berlin Express, RKO, 1948. Merle Oberon, Robert Ryan; "Trapped on a Train of Terror"; 27 inches × 41 inches; mint condition; $150.

Blind Alibi, RKO, 1938. Richard Dix; Morgan lithograph; fine design of star portraits looking over detective scene; 27 inches × 41 inches; $175.

Black Orchid, Paramount, 1959. Sophia Loren, Anthony Quinn; in reds, blacks, and yellow; 27 inches × 41 inches; near-mint condition; $95.

Blackboard Jungle, MGM, 1955. Glenn Ford, Anne Francis; full color; 27 inches × 41 inches; mint condition; $150.

Between Two Worlds, Warner, 1944. John Garfield, Paul

Henreid; printed in red, blue, and black; 27 inches × 41 inches; overall near-mint condition; $200.

Blaze of Noon, Paramount, 1947. Anne Baxter, William Holden; stunt flyer epic; full color; 27 inches × 41 inches; $125.

Blonde Alibi, Universal, 1946. Martha O'Driscoll; great pin-up; fabulous color; 27 inches × 41 inches; very fine condition; $165.

Blonde Inspiration, MGM, 1941. Virginia Grey, a fine Tooker lithograph of beautiful blond in caricature looking at circular vignette of stars; 27 inches × 41 inches; $150.

▦ WESTERN FILMS ▦

PRICES

Bad Man of Deadwood, Republic, 1941. Roy Rogers, Gabby Hayes; Rogers shown in huge portrait over title; Hayes at bottom; $150.

Bells of Coronado, Republic Pictures, 1950. Roy Rogers, Trigger, Dale Evans; great color; 27 inches × 41 inches; $150.

▦ PRODUCT ADVERTISING POSTERS ▦

PRICES

"AMOCO Lubricants—Put Spring in Your Car," from a Lucian Bernhard design, c. 1946. Full-color lithograph of robin against blue background singing on top of Amoco logo; print on good heavy stock; 45 inches × 35 inches; mint condition; $200.

Avalon Cigarettes, c. 1940. "Union Made"; smiling lass with auburn hair; full color; 10 inches × 16 inches; mint condition; $45.

Eptinger Mineral Water, designed by Herbert Leupin, 1959. Humorous imagery in bright blues, reds, and yellows of steamboat bubbling across sea under bright yellow sun; 35 inches × 50 inches; near-mint condition; $375.

Pril Detergent (set of five), designed by Herbert Leupin, c.

1950. All bright; full color; 23 inches × 33 inches; all in near-mint condition; $600/set.

Pepita Grapefruit, designed by Herbert Leupin, c. 1955. Stylized parrot enjoys a glass perched on bright green logo; 35 inches × 50 inches; overall bright and fresh condition; $325.

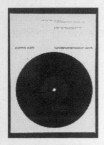

Poster, 1957. First exhibit of record graphics, Kunstgewerbemuseum, Zurich, Switzerland; 26 inches x 41 inches; $250. *Courtesy of Miscellaneous Man, New Freedom, PA.*

Switzerland, The Genuine Swiss Cheese, designed by Herbert Leupin, c. 1959. Cut wheel of cheese; caricature of mountaineer blowing horn; late Leupin classic; 20 inches × 27 inches; overall very fresh condition; $200.

Juicy Fruit, designed by Otis Shepard, c. 1940. "Treat Your Taste to an Exciting Change"; color lithograph card shows two women—one exotic, one not; 28 inches × 11 inches; overall near-mint condition; $176.

Juicy Fruit, designed by Otis Shepard, c. 1940. "Different! Delicious!"; color lithograph card; golfer tees off in office worker's dream; 28 inches × 11 inches; colors fresh; $245.

▩ Sports Posters ▩

PRICES

Daily Express—Boxing, c. 1948. British newspaper poster; vivid lithograph of boxing glove in full color; 20 inches × 30 inches; near-mint condition; $100.

Evening Standard—Programmes, c. 1950. British newspaper poster; photo montage of greyhounds racing; done in red and black; 20 inches × 30 inches; near-mint condition; $76.

Poster, c. 1946. *French Line d'Apres* by Paul Colin, unusual variation on Colins classic French Line poster of the era, showing prow shooting through the design of French tricolor; mint condition; the "d'Apres" is a printer's conceit indicating that the artist did not personally apply the design to the stone, as rarely happened in any case; 25 inches x 30 inches; $500. *Courtesy of the Miscellaneous Man, New Freedom, PA.*

▣ TRAVEL POSTERS ▣

PRICES

Ravello Dele Site, 1950. Floral motif and ornate architecture cleverly form image of a woman; 27 inches × 39 inches; near-mint condition; $50.

Monte Carlo, designed by Sean-Gabriel Domergue, 1946. Hypersensual; elongated blonde nymphette poses on diving board; 25 inches × 39 inches; overall mint condition; $575.

P & O Makes Business Travel a Pleasure—India, Australia, and the East, designed by Thomson, c. 1948. Delightful, strong graphic of happy tourist in lithographed image center; 25 inches × 40 inches; near-mint condition; $275.

Las Vegas—Union Pacific Railroad, c. 1953. "Stop over at exciting Las Vegas"; image of yellow diesel, futuristic station; all illuminated by early, grand neon strip; scarce; great 50s item; 25 inches × 32 inches; mint condition; $350.

Cuba, anonymous designer, c. 1946. "Holiday Isle of the Tropics"; dancer with maracas puts down steps amid palms and verandas; done in a splendid, typically 40s style; 21 inches × 30 inches; overall mint condition; $25.

France—Land of Chateaux, designed by Jean Picarte le Doux, 1950. Classic postwar image of bird statuary and chateaux; very fine and fresh condition; $375.

France—Land of Chateaux, designed by Jean Picarte le Doux, 1950. Classic postwar image of bird statuary and chateaux in a surreal, late-Cassandre style; 24 inches × 40 inches; overall near-mint condition; $175.

Israel (two), c. 1950. "Tiberius" and "Israel"; both lithographed in full color; fresh; overall near-mint condition; $325/set.

Monaco, designed by Jean Cocteau, 1959. Extremely scarce surrealistic image of sailboat emerging as face from sea; done in a stone-lithographic style by Mouriot; mint condition; $1,000.

Acapulco, anonymous designer, c. 1960. Super-rich color; silk screen image of bathing beauty in exotic, fruit-covered straw hat waving to turboprop plane; 26 inches × 33 inches; overall mint condition; $95.

Britain in Winter, designed by Terence Cuneo, 1948. Painterly color rendering of horseman and tourists outside a rustic inn; near-mint condition; $125.

Davos, designed by Herbert Leupin, c. 1955. Caricatured skier shakes hands with huge, smiling, snow-covered pine tree; typical hyperbright Leupin coloration; overall fresh; $200.

Lufthansa, anonymous designer, c. 1955. Poster advertises service to the Orient; brightly colored image of Middle Eastern women, pot atop her burnoose; really vivid color; 24 inches × 39 inches; $175.

Lucerne—Festival of Music 1957, designed by Piatti. Cubist imagery of viola in blocks of red, orange, greens, purple, black, etc.; colors fresh; 25 inches × 40 inches; $250.

▨ WAR POSTERS ▨

PRICES

"Czechoslovaks—Carry On," designed by Peel (Zeman #92), 1942. Issued in the United States by the Czech Information Service; image by English artist of charging Czech in highly stylized, airbrushed art; done in browns, red, white, and blues; 22 inches × 31 inches; mint condition; $150.

"Czechoslovaks—Your Allies," designed by Peel, 1943. Czech and American soldiers shake hands in front of looming Statue of Liberty and American flag in highly stylized, airbrushed art;

done in browns, red, white, and blues; 22 inches × 23 inches; mint condition; $125.

"5000 Danish Seamen Sailing for United Nations," Louise Dahl-Wolfe. Photo montage of merchant seaman against Danish flag; 24 inches × 32 inches; near-mint condition; $125.

"Libertad de Palabra," designed by Alexey Brodovitch, 1942. Anti-Nazi propaganda; produced in America to influence neutral Central American countries during the war; unusually sophisticated image of large face made up of smoke and flames symbolically breaking a swastika in two; pink, red, and black background; scarce; 14 inches × 20 inches; $225.

"China Shall Have Our Help! United China Relief," designed by Martha Sawyers. Imagery of young Chinese family escaping fiery background; done in brilliant colors; 27 inches × 40 inches; very fine condition; $175.

"Liberte . . . Liberte Cherie," designed by Natacha Carlu, 1944. Marianne and Statue of Liberty merge; distributed by the Free French Press in New York for posting in the United States; 30 inches × 23 inches; near-mint condition; $200.

"Libres de Miseria," designed by Alexey Brodovitch, c. 1942. Anti-Nazi imagery; done in United States to influence neutral Central American countries during the war; highly stylized image of one huge hand protecting a family and another hand shackled by swastika; 14 inches × 20 inches; mint condition; $200.

"Greek Children Need Your Help," 1945. Refugees in photo art against blue background; 17 inches × 21 inches; $100.

"To Have and To Hold—War Bonds," c. 1943. Splendid allegory of a soldier with streaming unfurled flag; 20 inches × 28 inches; very fine overall condition; $175.

"Battle Stations! Keep 'Em Fighting," 1942. General Motors factory poster showing naval bugler on gun deck; foreground shows worker at lathe; near-mint condition; 31 inches × 41 inches; $125.

"Buy War Bonds," designed by N. C. Wyeth, 1942. Classic Uncle Sam depiction leading battle; 14 inches × 22 inches; mint condition; $125.

"All Soldiers Can't Be in the Infantry—But . . .", designed by Steele Savage, 1944. Scarce infantry recruiting poster showing charging soldier with bayonet, battle ribbons, and globe; 17 inches × 25 inches; near-mint condition; $125.

"Save Your Cans—Help Pass the Ammunition," designed by McClelland Barclay, c. 1942. "Prepare Your Tin Cans for War"; Salvage Division War Production Board; machine gunners feed empty cans through belts; vivid colors; 25 inches × 33 inches; mint condition; $200.

"SPARs," designed by J. Valentine, 1943. Blonde SPAR salutes in front of allegorical image of pioneer woman and covered wagon; full color; 28 inches × 42 inches; near-mint condition; $200.

"Aviation Cadets—U.S. Army Air Forces," 1943. Tinted photo montage of fighter pilots against fiery orange-and-red background looking past the viewer into sky; 25 inches × 38 inches; near-mint condition; $175.

"Serve Your Country in the WAVES," design by John Faiter, 1944. "I wish I could join, too!"; little girl looks admiringly at photo of a WAVE on table; full color; 28 inches × 40 inches; near-mint condition; $175.

"Someone Talked," designed by Siebel, 1942. A classic of the time period; shows a man about to drown, his huge hand pointing out in accusation to the viewer; 14 inches × 22 inches; near-mint condition; $100.

"Woman's Place in War," designed by Irving Cooper, 1944. "The Army . . . has 239 kinds of jobs for women. The Women's Army Corps"; finely done image of WAC weather observer with instrument; 25 inches × 39 inches; near-mint condition; $125.

"America Calling—Take Your Place in Civilian Defense," designed by Herbert Matter (Zeman #42), 1941. Scarce American piece by Matter showing flying American eagle in front of rays of blue and red; 30 inches × 40 inches; mint condition; $325.

"Americans Will Always Fight for Liberty 1778–1943," designed by Bernard Perlin, 1943. Signed by one artist, but this work is thought to be a collaboration of Koerner and Perlin; infantrymen in winter uniforms march through snow; Colonial patriots from 1778 in background; 28 inches × 40 inches; $90.

"Avenge December 7," designed by Bernard Perlin. Extraordinarily powerful, early 1942 imagery of angered sailor shaking huge fist at stormy sky while U.S.S. *Arizona* explodes at bottom; 22 inches × 28 inches; near-mint condition; $225.

"Can You Look Him in the Eyes When He Comes Back?", designed by Packer, c. 1943. Stark image of wounded vet returning in doorway; 27 inches × 41 inches; very fine condition; $150.

"Dare You Say or Think You Do Not Feel the Bullet . . .", designed by C. C. Beal, 1943. General Cable; grisly image of wounded sailor held by captain aboard a smoke-filled deck; 26 inches × 36 inches; near-mint condition; $125.

"Defense of Our Liberty Begins in the Factory," designed by Ralph Iligan, c. 1942. Beautiful allegorical Statue of Liberty sends rays of light from torch to factory, dry docks, and airplanes below; 16 inches × 20 inches; near-mint condition; $100.

"Attack, Attack, Attack—Buy War Bonds," designed by Ferdinand Warren, 1942. Charging troops, planes overhead, with tanks and ships bringing up the rear; 22 inches × 28 inches; near-mint condition; $75.

"Back 'Em Up—Buy Extra Bonds," 1944. Eisenhower in sepia gravure photo salutes against stars-and-stripes red, white, and blue background; 22 inches × 28 inches; mint condition; $100.

"Back the Attack! Buy War Bonds," designed by Schreiber, 1943. Stalwart paratrooper with Thompson defends comrades landing behind him; dramatic image; 20 inches × 28 inches; near-mint condition; $110.

"Are You a Girl with a Star-Spangled Heart? Join the WAC Now!", designed by Bradshaw Crandell, 1943. Almost unbelievably beautiful WAC gives smoldering look toward the viewer; American flag in background; scarce and extremely fine; 25 inches × 38 inches; near-mint condition; $225.

"Back 'Em Up with Bonds," c. 1942. Retailers for Victory; line of troops in old-style helmets in painterly, vivid rendering; 22 inches × 28 inches; mint condition; $100.

"Britain Must Win—Help Bundles for Britain," designed by McClelland Barclay, 1940. Allegory of muscular man amid rising seas, half hidden by a Union Jack, holding a torch against the darkness; superb imagery by famed American illustrator for British relief; 17 inches × 25 inches stander; near-pristine condition; $200.

"Help China! China Is Helping Us!" designed by James Montgomery Flagg, 1945. Small, intensely colored placard showing Uncle Sam (actually he is a self-portrait of the artist) helping Chinese refugees against flaming background; 11 inches × 14 inches; overall near-mint condition; $100.

"Norway Fights On—American Friends of Norway," designed by McKnight Kauffer, 1943. Norwegian banner floats above stylized blue sea, freighter, and stormy black-and-gray sky; 17 inches × 22 inches; near-mint condition; $150.

"Help Greece Now! Greek War Relief Assn.", c. 1941. Beautiful Greek woman and her child flee amid complex montage of Parthenon statuary and flaming city; colorful; 15 inches × 21 inches; near-mint condition; $95.

"Denmark—Unconquered, Though Captive," 1940. Rich architectural design of the Grundtvig Church in Copenhagen; done in blues, pale green, white, and red; 20 inches × 33 inches; near-mint condition; $125.

"Lutamos Pela Liberdade de Todos," designed by E. McKnight Kauffer for the Inter-American Society, c. 1942. Sleek and crisp design of stylized head of Miss Liberty against shadowy, airbrushed stars and bars; done as a patriotic appeal to influence neutral South American countries; scarce; 14 inches × 20 inches; mint condition; $225.

N.S.F.K. (German National Socialist) Recruiting Poster, designed by Busse, 1941. Handsome and heroic-looking pilot in flying gear smiles toward the blue yonder; N.S.F.K emblem in background at top; space at bottom for text; 23 inches × 33 inches; $425.

"Pour Eux Deux?", c. 1944. Extremely rare French Nazi Occupation propaganda against Britain, referring to England's successful supply blockade; ghostly image of Churchill with glowing cigar looming over airbrushed map of France and fearful mother and child; 31 inches × 48 inches; near-mint condition; $450.

I have listed only a few examples of sculpture that use the forms and materials of the Modern movement. Additional prices can be found in such sources as *Art Auction Index*. While modern artists used traditional sculpture materials such as marble, stone, glass, and metal, they used them in new ways. Biomorphic sculpture—using rounded, undulating forms—was influenced by the art of Jean Arp and paintings of Joan Miró, Fernand Léger, Salvador Dali, and others. As was discussed elsewhere, many sculptors created designs for other mediums that carried out the biomorphic look. Many times there was a fine line dividing sculpture and jewelry. Sculpture became movable art with the creation of the mobile. Other times the form was "abstract" Modern, mixing materials such as glass and metal or metal and ceramics. When such art was viewed on a monumental scale, in the form, say, of a huge sculpture in a public park, the average viewer reacted with comments such as "What's it supposed to be?" Abstract Modern shattered the traditional ideals of what sculpture should look like, just as abstract Modern paintings set new standards in other parts of the art world. While top artists have always

Sculpture

237

found buyers for their work, the lesser known artists and mass-produced adaptations have remained out of favor for the past two decades. Now they are coming out of attics and to auction. Once again they seem fresh, at least to a new generation of buyers. After all, what other type of art goes with Modern furnishings?

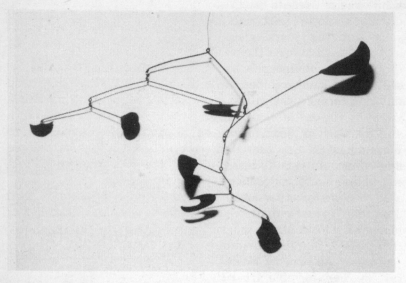

Mobile, c. 1950s. Style of Alexander Calder, red and black; 30 inches high x 22 inches deep x 17 inches wide; $1,200. *Courtesy of Toomey-Treadway Galleries, Oak Park, IL.*

▓ INFLUENTIAL SCULPTORS

As early as the 1920s Jean Arp's sculptures hinted at the organic and amorphous shapes that would define the Modern look. Many pieces of sculpture had a basis in his work.

Even though Constantin Brancusi worked at the beginning of the twentieth century, he was ahead of his time, predating Modern design with his sculptures. His influence was first felt in Finland, where such important designers as Tapio Wirkkala and Timo Sarpaneva adapted his organic forms into their glass designs.

Alexander Calder, a versatile American sculptor best known for his wire mobile and stabile sculptures of tin cans, glass shards, and bits of wire, also designed jewelry, toys, household objects, and pieces that showed whimsical animals. By the late 1940s his designs were being made into textiles and wallpapers.

Henry Moore's sculptures showed the beginnings of organic Modernism as early as the 1930s. By the 1950s his massive sculptures, with their curving organic forms, were influencing every area of Modern design.

PRICES

Ceramic Sculpture, by B. L. Nathe, Los Angeles, c. 1940–1945. Reclining female in bikini with stylized hair and painted nails; 12 inches long × 4 inches high; mint condition; $100.

The Man at Bat, attributed to Manuel Felquerez Barra (Mexican, 1928–   ). Signed "Felquerez" on the figure; painted steel; uniform in colors of cream and blue with number "50"; 11 inches high; good condition; $450.

The Skier, attributed to Manuel Felquerez Barra. Signed "Felquerez" on the figure; painted steel; clothing in shades of gold; 12 inches high; good condition; $250.

Sculpture, c. 1950s. Black plaster figure, biomorphic, signed LEO MIDDLEMAN; 20 x 10 inches; $300. *Courtesy of Decor Moderne.*

Sculpture, late 1950s. "Weight Lifter" signed FELQUEREZ, attributed to Manuel Felquerez Barra (b. 1920, Mexico), painted steel, one of a series of sports figures; 11 inches high; $400. *Courtesy of Decor Moderne.*

The Weight Lifter, attributed to Manuel Felquerez Barra. Signed "Felquerez" on the figure; painted steel; 11 inches high; good condition; $400.

Sunburst/A Sculptural Hanging, by William Bowie (American, 1926–). Unsigned; welded metal spikes with silver, gold, and copper patinas; 36 inches in diameter; very good condition; $200.

Metal-and-Glass Abstract Sculpture, c. 1955. Comprised of wrought iron and used glass; indistinct signature; 18½ inches high; $125.

Mixed Metal Sculpture, by Richard El Filipowski (1933–), mid-twentieth century. Used as a firescreen; 25½ inches high × 4½ inches deep × 53½ inches wide; $300.

Three Figures, by Peter J. Grippe (American, 1912–). Signed and dated "Grippe '58" on the reverse; bronze with gold patina; 8⅝ inches high; very good condition; $325.

Architettura Meccanica Statica, by Silvestre, 1952. Signed and dated; brass and polished steel; 16¾ inches high; $575.

Ruete Dentate Sovrapposte, by Silvestre, 1953. Signed and dated "'53"; polished steel, brass, and aluminum; 25¾ inches high; $460.

Assembloaggio di Reprerti Meccanici, by Silvestre, 1952. Signed and dated "'52"; polished steel and brass; 12¼ inches high; $575.

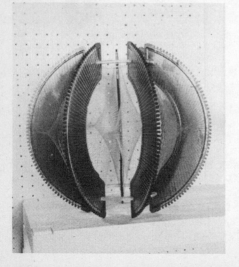

Sculpture, late 1950s. String art and Lucite; 20 x 20 inches; $38. *Courtesy Partners in Time.*

Sculpture, c. 1950s. Bottle-cap figure; $35. *Courtesy of Decades a Go-Go.*

Sculpture, c. 1955. Signed FANTONI, ITALY FOR RAYMOR; cubist ceramic, hand-built and incised figure of a man, hi-glaze decoration, many colors; 18 inches high; $3,800. *Courtesy of Toomey-Treadway Galleries, Oak Park, Il.*

By the mid-1940s, the proponents of Modernism began translating silver into a variety of sculptural forms from jewelry to hollowware, from flatware to decorative pieces. In the early 50s, silversmiths in Scandinavia, Italy, and America were exploring the design possibilities of other metals as well, including stainless steel, copper, brass, and pewter. Designers often combined metals with the newly respectable plastics.

In the United States, John Van Koert was asked by Towle Manufacturing Company to create a line of flatware and hollowware in the Modern idiom. The result was Contour, whose asymmetrical form showed a distinctly Scandinavian influence. The American touch is in his use of melamine handles on the sterling silver teapots and coffeepots. Surprisingly, these designs were considered too radical by the general public. However, from a current collector's standpoint, they are perfect examples of 40s and 50s metal design. Many American silversmiths who worked independently and whose primary work was jewelry created small, custom-made pieces such as bowls and vases that are waiting to be discovered.

In Denmark silversmith Henning Koppel brought a

Silver Designs

new look to the hollowware of Georg Jensen, for whom he was a designer. The biomorphic forms of his pitchers, platters, and wine jugs of the late 1940s can be recognized by their sculptural look.

Finnish designer Tapio Wirkkala used organic motifs in his silver as well as in his glass and wood designs. His silver vases and flatware were inspired by floral and plant forms.

In Sweden important silversmiths working in simple Modern designs included Sigurd Persson and Sven Arne Gillgren, who did many pieces of hollowware that were functional as well as beautiful.

Lino Sabattini is among the most important of the Italian silversmiths whose designs closely followed the postwar Modern of Italian glass and ceramics. One of his most notable designs was the Como tea and coffee service made in 1957, which combined silver-plated brass with plastic cord and raffia handles. It was produced by L'Orfeverie Christofle in Paris. He also designed the Cardinale bud vase using silver-plated brass. It is a stylized version of a Roman Catholic cardinal wearing ecclesiastical robe and miter. It was made in two sizes and is stamped on the underside "Christofle/France," with a square hallmark and pawn facing left.

In England Gerald Benney worked as an independent silversmith in silver and pewter, using the attenuated forms for hollowware and decorative pieces. By the 1960s he had developed a technique for decorating his pieces with an abstract matte-textured surface. Other English silversmiths worth collecting include Robert Welch and David Mellor. Welch worked with stainless steel, creating the Campden dinnerware line, which carried the Modern look, for Old Hall in 1956.

To date, few examples of silver and other metal hollowware have been recorded at auction—with the exception of pieces by Henning Koppel; many remain in private hands, and the few dealers who carry these pieces know they can only go up in value.

PRICES

Sterling Silver Dish, by Tiffany and Company, New York, 1947–1956. Triangular shape with convex sides; downturned rim; on three splayed feet; "S" monogram; 9 inches long; approximately 14½ troy ounces; $110.

Sterling Silver Pitcher, designed by Porter Blanchard. Ebony handle; handmade; 6½ inches high × 8 inches deep; excellent condition; $110.

▓ SCANDINAVIAN SILVER DESIGNS ▓

PRICES

Trays

Silver Tray, designed by Johan Rohde, made by Georg Jensen Silversmithy, c. 1940. Oval form; border scalloped at intervals; two ivory handles with fluted joins and openwork scroll decoration; marked "251B"; 20¾ inches long; 59 ounces; $6,600.

Coffee Service, c. 1956. Mexican, brass and glass tiles, signed SALVADOR TERAN; tray measures 15 inches x 15 inches, pot measures 8 inches high; $400. *Courtesy of Gillian Hine Antiques.*

Miscellaneous

Danish Silver Five-Light Candelabra (pair), designed by Johan Rohde, made by Georg Jensen Silversmithy, Copenhagen, c. 1945–1951. Ten-sided columnar bases topped by leaf, berry, and bud clusters; stamped "Georg Jensen & Wendell A.S." and marked on bases; 17¼ inches high; 118 ounces; $18,400.

Evald Nielsen Sterling Silver Cocktail Shaker and Two Goblets, Denmark. Shaker with ball and tiered foliate finial on swollen cylindrical form; each goblet with cup on foliate and beaded tendril columnar support raised on stepped circular foot; impressed mark; shaker 8½ inches high; goblets 3¼ inches high; approximately 23 troy ounces; $400/set.

Danish Silver Coffee Set (three pieces), made by Georg Jensen Silversmithy, Copenhagen, after 1945. Blossom pattern decorating coffeepot, covered sugar bowl, and creamer; marked on bases; coffeepot 8¾ inches high; 39 ounces gross weight; $4,025/set.

Danish Silver Sauce Boat, made by Georg Jensen Silversmithy, Copenhagen, after 1945. Leaf-and-berry handle; pedestal applied with beads; marked on base; 9¼ inches long; 13 ounces; $1,150.

▦ OTHER SILVER DESIGNS ▦

PRICES

Vases

Italian Sabattini Vase, c. 1950s. Simple elegant form in silver plate; 6 inches square × 17 inches high; mint condition; $200.

Miscellaneous

Mexican Silver Beaker, made by Jean Puiforcat, c. 1945. Of Aztec inspiration; cylindrical with slightly incurved body; applied with four semicircular loops joined by a reeded band; marked on the base and stamped "Jean Puiforcat, Made in Mexico"; 5½ inches high; 9 ounces; $1,265.

Salt-and-Pepper Shakers, by Salvador Teran, mid-1950s. Mexican silver; $300. *Courtesy of Al and Kim Eiber Collection.*

Belgian Silver-Gilt and Cut-Glass Covered Punch Bowl and Stand with Matching Ladle. Maker's mark a boar's head above "W"; almost spherical bowl cut with deep vertical flutes; silver gilt with beaded borders; ladle applied with a grape bunch; stand 15½ inches in diameter; $3,737/set.

Belgian Silver and Enamel Standing Cup, made by Wolfers Freres, Brussels, c. 1942. Octagonal form with gilt interior; decorated with bands of opaque enamel in tones of mottled gold and iron red; marks on the bowl enameled to match hammered surface; collar stamped with the maker's mark and "950 standard"; 10⅝ inches high; 20 ounces gross weight; $3,680.

Antonio Silver Salt and Pepper Shakers (pair), c. 1940. Cast with deeply curved facets; impressed manufacturer's marks; 2¼ inches high; $920/set.

WMF Bowl and Vase. Brushed silver plate with black enamel and polished silver plate triangular decoration; bowl footed with circular disks; signed; bowl 4 inches high × 14 inches in diameter; vase 10 inches high × 6 inches in diameter; very good condition; $150/set.

Jack Larsen is recognized as one of America's foremost textile designers from the mid-twentieth century to the present, and his knowledge of all phases of textile manufacturing has been translated into designs for carpets, leather, and fabrics. Internationally acknowledged for his innovative techniques, he experimented in the late 40s with then-new synthetic fibers, displaying their beauty and elegance. By the end of the 50s his use of color and design were clearly influenced by his extensive travels. Best known were his Indonesian collection of 1959 and his African collection of 1963. He has received many honors and has co-authored several major publications on the use of fibers. He received the Second Annual Brooklyn Museum/Modernism Design Award for Lifetime Achievement in 1993.

Textiles

by
Jack Lenor Larsen

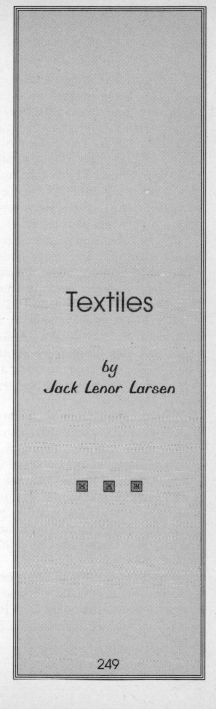

In the brave new years after the war, "new design" was for anyone who cared about it. We liked clean, spare, logical solutions supported by common sense. The new architecture was primarily residential, so was the emphasis of furnishings.

Storage was reconsidered. Overstuffed upholstery was out; so were flowers, wallpaper, clutter, and any reference to ornament. Window walls were draped out with a new fabric, the sheer casement. Color was primary and brash. We saw white walls for the first time.

In textiles the new textures were much admired. We longed for surfaces that were "architectural" and "functional." For the most part these fabrics were inexpensive; so were the cotton, rayon, tow linen, and jute fibers with which they were woven. Novelty yarns emphasized texture; so did cheniles and, for the first time, Lurex. For a decade Peruvian linens dyed luminous shades helped alleviate our appetite for visible texture. The Belgian, then Polish, linens that followed were less durable. Everyday furnishing fabrics were cotton bark cloths and stubby "antique" satins. The square rush floor mat was the typical carpeting, almost as popular as the new white vinyl tile.

At the other end of the price scale, gutsy hand-weaves were locally woven for architects' houses. Patterns were printed, usually simple designs, often showing Swedish influence. The best of them were direct imports from Sweden, drawn by Scandinavian architects isolated and idle during the war. Whether abstractly free-form or geometric, they were graphic and above all architectural. Such leading American print designers as Angelo Testa and Ben Rose were centered in Chicago; in New York, Knoll Associates and Laverne Originals stressed freely drawn linear patterns, which at best were fresh and naive—and sometimes humorous.

The great weavers of the period were led by Dorothy Liebes of San Francisco, who introduced overscaled textures in finger-thick yarns and who reinvented, in her own terms, window blinds of heavy slats supported on warps striped with shimmering contrasts of matte and shiny, rough and smooth, flamboyantly colored materials. Marianne Strengell, weaving more naturalistic textures with a great variety of materials in a muted, Finnish palette, influenced both architectural designers and the many students she educated at Cranbrook Academy of Art in Michigan.

The best fabrics of the period were custom designed and handwoven for specific purposes. Knoll produced some simple power-woven textures by Toni Prestini and Marianne Strengell, and imported hand-prints from the Nordiska Kompaniet in Sweden.

The 1950s were a pivotal decade. Still a child in 1950, the first youth of Modern design was spent before 1960. This was to be the last decade in which American design was dominant. This was the first decade of extensive travel and the rediscovery of the Far East. With it came the first exotic imports. This was a heyday for Thai silks designed by the American architect Jim Thompson in Bangkok. With these simple, lustrous fabrics came glowing colors such as we had never before seen. Knoll imported the first honey-colored tussah silks—or silk burlaps, as they were known in those days. Small California fabric houses introduced Mexican hand-weaves and Norwegian woven straws. Grass cloths for walls were again imported. Jack Lenor Larsen developed hand-spun, wild cottons from Haiti, then hand-spun wools from Colombia and Mexico.

Of the British design studios that geared up after the war, the most influential was Donald Brothers of Dundee, where Peter Simpson developed the leno linen upholstery cloths so successful in New York. Although Lucienne Day, Marianne Straub, and Edinburgh Weavers led a movement to rationally designed, sensibly priced curtainings, appealing to liberated tastes, few found their way to the American market.

In carpets Edward Fields and Stanislav V'Soske began using the electric pistol to tuft the first area rugs, often rich in color and in high relief. Machine-tufted carpets became available, first in cotton, which was later displaced by nylon and the other "miracle fibers."

Early in the decade Evelyn Hill and Eszter Haraszty worked at Rancocas to give Knoll an extraordinary upholstery collection of wools mixed with nylon monofilaments in the colors of peacocks and persimmons. Haraszty also introduced prints of durable interest and two pivotal upholsteries: Transportation Cloth, tightly woven of crisp viscose yarns, which for a while sustained the false promise of miracle fibers, and Nylon Homespun by Suzanne Huguenin, which gave us a cosier hand with staying power. D. D. and Leslie Tillett introduced exotic hand-prints utilizing resists and drag boxes for free-flowing stripes and plaids. Alexander Girard developed whole ranges of exotic geometry for Herman Miller, both printed and woven, scintillating in dark-and-light contrasts or as vivid as Mexican folk art. This stage is particularly notable in his Caribbean collection. Boris Kroll popularized the iridescents we had learned to enjoy in the palettes of Dorothy Liebes and Jim Thompson.

From Astrid Sampe and Viola Grasten of the famous Nordiska Kompaniet studios in Stockholm came a series of printed linens and Jacquard domestics. We saw Vuokko's first fabrics for Marimekko—scintillating if simple prints in joyous colors. By the late 1950s Larsen had managed to weave on power looms fabrics we had, up to that time, considered hand-weaves. He introduced a new palette of light and dark naturals plus earth tones and started printing romantic patterns—often on cotton velvet.

Today's collectors are fortunate that many of these pioneering weaving efforts and designs were still available and can be preserved while still functionally enjoyed.

▣ ARTIST-INSPIRED TEXTILES

Fabrics literally became works of art in the 1950s when Fuller Fabrics created a line called Modern Master Print, based on the paintings of such popular artists as Joan Miró, Marc Chagall, Raoul Dufy, Pablo Picasso, and Fernand Léger. After the designs were shown to the artists, and approved, they were printed at the Fuller mill in Northhampton, Massachusetts. The cotton fabrics were not only used by homemakers for draperies and bedspreads but also by a few clothing designers, such as Claire McCardell, for casual wear.

Artist Fernand Léger designed two silk-screen-printed cotton designs in abstract style for the Italian Bossi textile firm. The colors were bright and bold, in his recognizable style of the 50s.

▣ AMERICAN TEXTILES

The postwar years saw the rise and importance of textiles in Modern designs. While established fabric houses such as Schumacher and Greeff gradually added Modern designs to their traditional lines, it was the independent designers who brought Modern to the attention of the general public.

In the late 1940s, an American graphic designer, Ray Komai, an admirer of African masks, created Masks for Laverne Originals in 1948. It was produced in fiberglass, and later as wallpaper. By using masks in circular and elliptical form, in a repeating pattern, his design fitted in with the Modern idiom.

George Nelson, known for his furniture and decorative pieces, also tried his hand at textile design. He opened a fabric division in 1952 at Herman Miller Manufacturing, and employed architect Alexander Girard to create Modern designs. Though expensive, they led the way to mass-produced and affordable fabrics.

Among the designers who brought Modern designs to consumers were Elenhank and Angelo Testa and Ben Rose. Their hand-screen printed designs were readily accepted by the decorator market.

As a fine arts major at the Art Institute of Chicago (1939–1943), Ben Rose (1916–   ) was inspired by influential painters of the day such as Picasso, Miró, and Klee, as well as by the architecture and spare interior design of architect Mies Van der Rohe.

His career began in 1946, when he presented architect and friend Henry Glass with a set of hand-printed place mats designed by him and his wife. Impressed, Glass asked him to create some print patterns for the first building he constructed in Chicago after World War II. At the time there were very few contemporary printed fabrics available. Encouraged, Rose and his wife, Frances, along with Helen Stern, formed a company and created print designs, showing them to residential showroom representatives in Chicago's Merchandise Mart.

By the end of 1946 he had won his first design award—the A.I.D. Honorable Mention for a printed fabric—with his Chinese Linear. In 1947 he designed sixty yards in a Hawaiian print for the first United Air Lines Stratocruiser flight from Chicago to Hawaii. The resulting publicity started him on his successful lifetime career.

Among his many firsts was his 1952 fabric for the first covered refrigerator door (1952); and a special group of linear prints designed for Packard Motors (1953). In the same year he received the Order of Leopold II of Belgium for promoting Belgian linen in the United States. In 1952–1953 the Walker Art Center in Minneapolis opened with a landmark textile exhibit. Along with the work of other top designers such as Alexander Girard and Angelo Testa were designs created by Ben Rose. Following the exhibit he opened his first Merchandise Mart show-room and is still there.

His designs can be seen in the collections of the Museum of Modern Art in New York, the Houston Contemporary Art Association, the Walker Art Center, the Art Institute of Chicago, the Museum Des Artes Decoratif in Montreal, the Rhode Island School of Design, and the permanent collection of Cooper Union in New York.

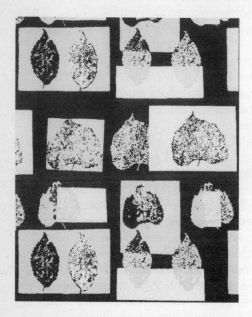

Textile, c. 1952. "Foliation," designed and manufactured by Ben Rose, first Ben Rose design using newly developed photo emulsion for design transfer to screen. *Courtesy of Ben Rose Designs.*

I'll never forget the first time we tried to sell our designs to the residential showroom people in Chicago's Merchandise Mart. We were politely shown the door with remarks like "We've had wild stuff like this before. It didn't sell then and it won't sell now." Fortunately we didn't pay any attention.

My wife and I set up a small print table (thirteen yards long) in a loft space for which we paid $75 a month. Most hand-screened printing is done with two printers, one on either side of the table. As I was the only printer, we had to make screens half the width of the table. I had to run around to the other side of the table to print the second half.

Henry Glass became our first client. He wanted simple abstract patterned drapery fabrics for his three-story art studio. Our plan was to set up a temporary factory to accommodate his 3,000-yard print order and to use the proceeds to set up a storefront gallery and studio where we could survive as fine artists. Due to material shortages after World War II, it took over a year to produce the order. In the meantime, Fran took samples of our patterns to several interior designers and we began to get orders that forced us to create a business we hadn't really planned on.

There was very little abstract design being screened on fabric in 1946, the year we began. At the time screen printing consisted of hand-cut stencils affixed to frames stretched with porous silk fabric. This resulted in hard-edged, simple patterns in two or three colors. About two years later, photographic emulsions were developed that allowed subtle textural effects, which greatly influenced the design process.

In the early days, before inexpensive design copyrights were available, our patterns were knocked off regularly. Copyrights were sold for over $200 and didn't protect you from copycats who made the most minor of changes. Today, copyrights cost $7.50 and are strongly protected.

I believe that creating a surface design is like producing a building material as functional in its visual expression as bricks, mortar, and stone are structurally. The printed designs represent a constant searching for the balance in line, mass, and scale as a textural unit and its relation to other textures in the space of the structure.

In the past ten years, with the proliferation of Jacquard looms, we have concentrated on upholstery fabrics. The Jacquard technology allows the designer to create woven designs unlimited in pattern, scale, and texture.

Recently the health care market (which is where most of our print patterns were sold) has enjoyed a resurgence in activity and is becoming an important area of business for us. We plan to reintroduce many of our designs from the 40s and 50s that are still contemporary—especially for pediatric areas.

Textile, c. 1946. "Little Horses," first Ben Rose print design, hand-cut film adhered to screen. *Courtesy of Ben Rose Designs.*

PRICES

Herman Miller Fabric. Cotton and linen blend with brilliant orange, green, and blue alternating triangles on off-white background creating optical honeycomb pattern; early Herman Miller label; 10 yards; 51 inches wide; never used; excellent condition; $550.

Herman Miller Fabric Shower, designed by Alexander Girard. Fiberglass and cotton blend of elongated icicles in taupe, aqua, blues, and various shades of green, creating a raindrop pattern; early Herman Miller label; 7 yards; 49 inches wide; never used; excellent condition; $450.

■ TEXTILES ■

PRICES

Roll of Fabric, c. 1955. Depicts whales in a stylized Northwest Coast design in colors of turquoise, yellow, orange, off-white, and black; approximately 10 yards; $175.

Bark Cloth Curtain Panels (pair), mid-twentieth century. Printed with overall design of a cityscape behind trees in brown, tan, beige, forest green, chartreuse, and salmon on white ground; marked "Manhattan" in original hand-print; 80 inches long × 48 inches wide; $175/set.

Textile, c. 1950s. Sheets of fiberglass lamp shade material, calligraphic swirls, black on white; $20/each. *Courtesy of Skank World, CA.*

Ray Eames Crosspatch, designed 1947, manufactured by Schiffer Prints. Screen-painted cotton textile; rare example of one of two designs submitted by Ray Eames for the Museum of Modern Art's exhibition "Printed Textiles for the Home," which ran from March 11 to June 15, 1947; 43 inches × 51 inches; $1,265.

Textile, c. 1950s. Bark cloth, cotton print, modern design, four panels; $229. *Courtesy of Alpha Antiques.*

▨ FLOOR COVERINGS ▨

PRICES

Wool Rya Rug, Scandinavian, c. 1955. Deep pile; coarse and fine tufts form a blurred weavelike pattern in shades of beige accented by sprinkles of rust; sewn label; 132 inches long × 98 inches wide; $75.

Hooked Rug, c. 1950. Aquatic forms in colors of mauve and ecru highlighted in black on beige field; 97¼ inches long × 58 inches wide; $350.

Reversible Flatweave Carpet, Scandinavian, mid-twentieth century. Repeating diamond and line pattern in coral and chartreuse with black divisions; 106 inches long × 68 inches wide; $45.

Westendeuchter Carpet, c. 1950. Charcoal-gray background; multicolored geometric shapes and stippled cream-colored brushstrokes compose design; 97 inches wide × 137 inches long; $1,000.

Woolen Rug, French, c. 1950. Taupe ground decorated with a geometric pattern of black intersecting lines with cream, red, green, and yellow triangles; 118½ inches long × 78 inches wide; $1,430.

Flatweave Area Carpet, mid-twentieth century. Brown ground with field of repeating geometric devices divided by narrow banding in colors of orange, yellow, and off-white; 136 inches long × 89½ inches wide; good condition; $100.

Walt Disney Rug, c. 1950s. Cotton; whimsical animated Disney characters in green, aqua, blue, and reds; 105 inches long × 69 inches wide; very good condition; $400.

Verner Panton Shag Rug, "Mira Romantica." Graduated square design; earth tones of brown and orange: 78 inches long × 55 inches wide; excellent condition; $100.

Spring Rain Fabric Design, after Salvador Dali, manufactured by Schiffer Prints, c. 1950. 47 inches long × 27 inches wide; $100.

Area Rug, 1950s. Fifteen squares of gray, brown, and tan on beige; border in brown and beige; 69 inches long × 49 inches wide; excellent condition; $220.

Kasimir Malevich Carpet, "Elisse Editions," Russian. Suprematis geometric composition in primary colors on off-white background; 100 percent wool; "handwoven in the Republic of Ireland" label; 115 inches long × 69 inches wide; excellent condition; $2,600.

Carpet, French, c. 1950s. Bauhaus-inspired geometric composition of intersecting black lines on elephant-gray background with brilliant red, yellow, and green geometric shapes; black and white stippling; 118 inches long × 78 inches wide; excellent condition; $2,500.

The Dinellis are acknowledged authorities on the subject of toys. Their monthly column on the subject appears in a variety of publications. As experts, they have appeared on Chicago radio and television stations to discuss appraising and investing in toys. As senior appraisers for the firm Noble House Ltd. of Libertyville, Illinois, they have appraised for clients such as Sears Roebuck and Company, Coca-Cola, and Mack Truck Corporation, to name a few.

Toymakers around the world reentered the toy market in the postwar years, when war machine manufacturing technology was transformed by those countries on the winning side of the war for the purpose of making toys. Scrap war materials and hand-crafting methods were used by less-fortunate countries. The dominance of certain countries in the post–World War II years was reflected in each nation's toys.

The most successful country to regain a market share was Japan. The Japanese manufactured lithographed tin toys from discarded metal such as soda and beer cans. The Made-in-Japan toys were handcrafted and cleverly designed. The Japanese began toymaking as a cottage indus-

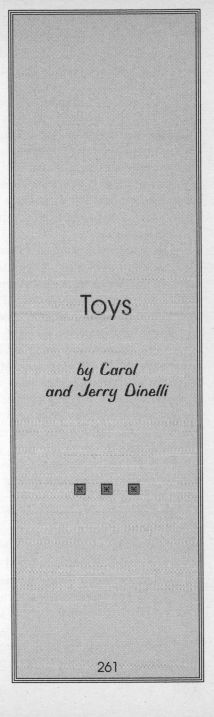

Toys

*by Carol
and Jerry Dinelli*

261

try. Toys were made in bombed-out factories and in small shops set up in homes. The finished products were then marketed throughout the world by the Japanese jobbers who put their own logos and names on the toys.

The superbly lithographed Japanese tin toys immediately flooded the world market and were sold inexpensively in every country by the millions. At this time the Japanese were responsible for the major design change from the clockwork toy to the battery-powered toy. Three important Japanese makers of battery-operated toys in the postwar era were Marusan, Yonezawa, and Normura. These included aircraft, space toys, cars, and trains. By then they had replaced their wind-up and friction-driven mechanisms with small electrical motors that ran on batteries.

The American companies were also busy. Toy manufacturers such as the Louis Marx Company returned to the production of toys at the war's end. Accustomed to the practice of not using metal during the war years, Marx, like other toy companies at the time, switched over to the easier-to-obtain plastic materials.

Wood and paper toys were still available since toy companies were disposing of existing inventories. Some of these "war" toys were sold well into the late 1950s. Wartime toys, such as soldiers, military vehicles, and other war paraphernalia, fell out of favor with the buying public, forcing toy companies to change their lines of toys to feature civilian models and figures.

Toy trains, as always, were still popular and rebounded after the war with some of the best toy trains ever manufactured.

Doll design experienced the most drastic change of all, with the innocent baby dolls giving way to the more realistic and mature-style dolls.

Toy trucks and construction machinery saw a major surge in popularity, almost in line with rebuilding efforts. Doepke model toys, Smith-Miller, Ertl, and Product Miniature offered an outstanding array of pressed-steel and the new die-cast toys.

Although Buck Rogers was a prewar conception of space travel and spawned many space toys, it was not until the 1940s and 1950s that manufacturers launched major toy lines created around space. Rocket ships, robots, and space explorers were conjured up so rapidly that many of them existed without names or identification. Battery-operated, wind-up, and friction-driven space toys flooded the market.

All in all, the 1940s and 1950s saw the production of peaceful, educational toys.

Keep in mind that toys in mint condition with original boxes bring top prices. As a result of this, many of the boxes are being reproduced through laser printing.

PRICES

Early Cutout of Paper Soldiers and Tanks. Actively sought after by collectors; price depends on condition; $200–$350.

Antiaircraft Jeep, 1950s. Made in Japan; metal and tin; five actions; 9½ inches long; mint condition and boxed; $160.

Toy Truck, manufactured by Smith-Miller, 1950s. One of the best lines of model trucks; expensive for its time period; commands high prices today depending on the particular toy; $250–$800.

Toys. Cut-out of paper soldiers and tanks; $250. *Courtesy of Noble House.*

Toys. Anti-aircraft jeep; $160. *Courtesy of Stanton Art Works.*

Toys, c. 1950s. Toy Truck; $800. *Courtesy of Noble House.*

Tin-Plated Lithographed Wind-up Donald Duck Duet, c. 1946. Small Donald playing drum; large Goofy dances; in its original box; 10½ inches; $2,640.

Japanese Tin-Plated Howdy Doody Clock-a-Doodle. When wound animated ringing clock displays Howdy swinging below clock; lithographed bird feeds while clock keeps time, ringing a bell every five seconds; in box; 9½ inches; $990.

Lux Metal and Hard Plastic Schmoo Wall Clock. From "Li'l Abner" comic strip; white clock shaped like Schmoo figure; with a blue "tail" pendulum; in box; 7¾ inches; $132.

Captain Marvel Wristwatch. Caped captain appears on watch's face in full colors; in box; 1½ inches; $495.

Li'l Abner Animated Wristwatch, manufactured by New Haven Clock Company, c. 1947. Li'l Abner salutes waving American flag; $440.

Chromed Superman Pocket Watch, manufactured by Bradley, c. 1959. Sweep red second hand; full-color Superman pictured flying through the air over a city on watch face; 2½ inches; $462.

Tin-Plated Wind-up Superman Rollover Airplane, c. 1940. Consists of a well-lithographed Superman chasing a red monoplane; 6¼ inches; $1,650.

Toys, c. 1950s. Japanese lithographed tin jeep, soldiers; $78. *Courtesy of Noble House.*

Toys, c. 1950s. Poppa Bear smoking, San Company, Japan, tin with cotton clothing; 9 inches tall; $120. *Courtesy of Stanton's Art Works.*

Charles Eames House of Cards, designed for Tigrett Enterprises, c. 1952. Early production of 54 beautifully illustrated cards in original box with original instructions; 5 inches high × 2 inches deep × 4 inches wide; very good condition; $225.

Charles Eames House of Cards (giant version), c. 1953. Largest of the three variations; 20 beautifully illustrated graphic cards in original box; 29 inches high × 10 inches deep × 30 inches wide; $950.

Charles Eames Memory Game, made in West Germany by Ravensburger, c. 1974. 110 beautifully illustrated cards in original box; 2 inches high × 8 inches deep × 8 inches wide; excellent condition; $160.

▦ PLASTIC TOYS ▦

THE BARBIE DOLL

Barbie could be called the doll that changed dollmaking history. Introduced at the New York Toy Fair in 1959, she was an original, molded of hard vinyl. Introduced as "Barbie Doll, Teen-Age Fashion Model," she had only a few items of clothing. She was the creation of Ruth Handler, who originally created the doll for her own little girl. It was Handler's husband, Elliot, and his partner, Harold "Matt" Matson, who already owned a small toy company, who decided to produce Barbie. She was launched by Mattel Toy Company. Since then over 600 million Barbies and Barbie line products have been sold.

Barbies number 1 and number 2 were always in fashion. Both had ponytails and curly bangs. The irises of their eyes were painted white, and the dark eyebrows resembled an inverted V. Barbie number 1 had holes in her feet to fit the prongs on her round stand and wore hoop earrings; Barbie number 2 had a new stand that made holes in the feet unnecessary. Instead, a stand with a tall wire back fit under her arms to hold her up. Her earrings were pearl studs.

Barbies 1 and 2 can sell in shops for between $1,000 and $2,500, depending on condition and the number of original accessories.

FRISBEE

The Frisbee could have happened only in the 1950s—the era of flying saucer fascination. It was originally named Morrison's Flyin' Saucer, after its inventor, Fred Morrison. He thought it looked very much like an alien aircraft. When the Wham-O Company bought the right to produce the toy its name was first changed to Pluto Platter, then in 1956 it was renamed the Frisbee after the baking company whose pie plates were the original inspiration for the design. If you are interested in collecting examples you have come in on the ground floor of this trend. There are no price standards yet established for this item. Look for examples that carry the early names and make an offer.

PEZ FLIP-TOP CANDY CONTAINERS

Pez candy was first made in Vienna, Austria, in the 1920s. It came in only one flavor—peppermint. The name Pez is taken from the German word for peppermint *(Pfferminz)*. However, the plastic dispensers are what collectors are interested in. The automatic flip-top holder made its way to America in 1952 along with fruit flavors. The colorful figure heads that seem to pop out of the top were made in a variety of forms—from Disney characters to the Muppets. They are still being made.

Because of the variety of head motifs, there is a crossover interest from many other collecting categories. Collectors of Disney and other toys look for dispensers to supplement their collections. The United States and Austria are not the only countries that manufacture these dispensers; they are also made in the former Yugoslavia and in Hong Kong.

Since Pez containers are not made from more than one piece of plastic, collectors look for examples with the greatest number of parts. For example, a dispenser could have a figure with a separate nose and hat parts. Such dispensers cost more to make and as a result fewer were produced.

Garage sales and flea markets are the best sources. Even in collectibles shops and shows prices range from $5 to $15 for a rarity.

PLASTIC MODEL KITS

On the road to rediscovery are the plastic model kits that were popular with the do-it-yourselfers in the 1950s. They were made in the 20s, 30s, and 40s of balsa wood as well as metals, and toymakers offered kits for everything from airplanes to ships and trains. Since they often utilized hundreds of small parts that were costly to produce, some kits were clearly intended for adult budgets rather than a child's allowance. In the 50s, manufacturers of hobby kits turned to plastic, realizing that both large and tiny parts could be mass-produced inexpensively through the use of injection molds and plastic. Among the most popular were World War II airplane model kits.

Many of the early plastic toys were made of untried formulas and the plastics soon warped and twisted out of shape. Shortly thereafter plastic formulas were perfected and the material became very stable, allowing for more detailed and refined toys.

The photo shows a plastic automobile dating from the 1950s and made by Ideal. It is complete with its spare tire and tools. Such take-apart toys are becoming more collectible as a new generation of collectors searches for the toys of its childhood. The value of this toy ranges from $125 to $250 depending on the particular model of the car and its condition.

The most valuable plastic kit toys are the never-assembled MIB (mint, in box) kits, preferably unopened. Flea markets are good sources for these examples. Car dealer samples were made to promote the new car models. Prices depend on the popularity of the car design, such as the first Thunderbird, which is very sought after and relatively expensive.

PLAYTIME TABLE AND KITCHEN ITEMS

The following information on plastic tables and kitchen items was furnished by Lorraine May Punchard, an authority and the author of several books on the subject.

> If you can't find any of Russel Wright's American Modern ceramicware, consider miniature toy reproductions of his designs. The toy set was manufactured by Ideal Toy Company in 1955. A full tea set of polystyrene includes a pink teapot, creamer and sugar bowl, three blue plates, three gray cups, and three mustard-colored saucers.

Toys, c. 1950s. Automobile, plastic; $125. *Courtesy of Noble House.*

Toys, c. 1950s. Cups and creamer, designed by Russel Wright, plastic, made by Ideal, part of American Modern pattern tea set of fourteen pieces; $75/full set. *Courtesy of Lorraine Punchard.*

Listed in this chapter are miscellaneous items—some with a brief history or description and prices—that may be of interest to collectors.

▦ ADVERTISING ▦ CHARACTER COLLECTIBLES

Whether they are toys, decorative objects, or jewelry, it seems that there has never been a time when advertising character collectibles were not around. The 40s and 50s were no exception. One of the most popular advertising symbols was Elsie the Borden Cow. Her path to fame climaxed at the 1939 New York World's Fair when she was part of the Borden World's Fair exhibit, with her own boudoir and Colonial-style four-poster bed. She made a film appearance in *Little Men,* and at the beginning of World War II she traveled cross-country selling war bonds. Many Elsie collectibles were made in the 1940s and 1950s.

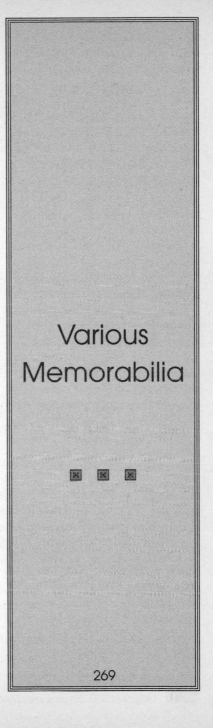

Various Memorabilia

▦ ▦ ▦

Ice Cream Dishes (set of eight), c. 1950s. Elsie the Cow motif; $125/set. *Courtesy of Stanton's Art Works.*

PRICES

Wooden Pull Toy, manufactured by Wood Commodities Corporation, c. 1944. Elsie as "The Cow that Jumped over the Moon"; boxed; $150.

Mug, c. 1940s. Color transfer print of Elsie; white china; $40.

Bank, manufactured by Caster Manufacturing Company, Chicago. Painted portrait of Elsie; white metal; 3½ inches high × 5 inches long × 7 inches wide; $90.

Reddy Kilowatt Figure, c. 1940s. Rubber; 3 inches high; $60.

Schmoo Bank, c. 1948. $30.

Red Goose, c. 1950. Plastic figural egg dispenser; 33 inches high; $100.

Smokey the Bear Doll, manufactured by Ideal, c. 1950s. Cloth; $85.

Speedy Alka Seltzer Figural Bank, c. 1950s. Painted rubber; $150.

Advertising Toy "Naugy," c. 1950s. Promotional item for Naugahyde, black and brown Naugahyde; $75. *Courtesy of Decades a Go-Go.*

▦ CATALIN RADIOS ▦

For some who collect old radios the fascination is purely nostalgic. They remember the plastic table models that were part of their family entertainment. For others the appeal is in the design and color. Bright colors and color combinations and Modern shapes spilled over into the design of small radios of the 1940s. Even the Catalin material they were made of was "modern." Catalin radios were first manufactured in the mid-1930s, and experts such as author and collector John Sideli are quick to point out that Catalin is not the same material as Bakelite. While both are of similar chemical makeup, the process used in their manufacturing is quite different. When the Catalin casting resins are poured into a lead form or mold, the hardened product is translucent and marbleized, unlike Bakelite. Dramatic color effects and combinations could be achieved with Catalin.

Many radios were made by companies now long forgotten: Addison, Cyarts, and Fada, to mention just a few of the near-twenty notable manufacturers. The designs are so exciting and Modern because they were conceived by avant-garde designers such as Norman Bel Geddes and Walter Dorwin Teague.

John Sideli's interest, collection, and sales at shows like New York's Triple Pier Show were the beginning of what is now an established collectible field. Major auction houses offer radios when they can get them, and the prices keep going up.

As in any collecting field there are rarities that command hundreds of dollars. Others are costly because of design or color combinations. Prices can range from a garage sale special of $25 to $5,000 when collectors get together and bid against each other.

Emerson Radio, Patriot Aristocrat #400, designed by Norman Bel Geddes, c. 1940. Issued to commemorate the twenty-fifth anniversary of the Emerson Radio and Phonograph Company; inspired by the American flag, with red body, white grille star handles, and blue dial; 7 inches high × 6 inches deep × 11 inches wide; very good working condition; $475.

Motorola Radio, #51 × 16, c. 1941. Very rare and collectible radio in red and black; 6 inches high × 6 inches deep × 10 inches wide; very good condition; $2,300.

Bendix Radio, #526C, designed by Frank Glover, c. 1946. Marbleized green top, sides, and knobs; black grille; sticker on bottom; 7 inches high × 6 inches deep × 11 inches wide; excellent condition; $625.

RCA Radio, #66X8, c. 1946. Marbleized oxblood red; label on bottom; 8 inches high × 7 inches deep × 15 inches wide; excellent condition; $950.

Deltrola Radio, c. 1950s. Chrome front; green Naugahyde body; brown plastic knobs and brown numbering; 8 inches high × 7 inches deep × 11 inches wide; very good condition; $210.

RCA Radio, #66X8, c. 1946. Marbleized black; original labels on back and bottom; 8 inches high × 7 inches deep × 15 inches wide; excellent condition; $210.

Radio, c. 1946. Fada Temple radio, 652, Catalin maroon with butterscotch; 6⅝ inches high x 11 inches wide; $440. *Courtesy of Skinner Inc., Boston/Bolton , MA.*

Fada Temple 625 Radio, c. 1946. Catalin maroon with butterscotch; 6⅝ inches high × 11 inches wide; $440.

Fada Bullet 1000 Table Radio, New York, c. 1945. Yellow cabinet with red trim; 6½ inches high × 10½ inches deep; $605.

Fada Table Radio, No. 263, New York. Cabinet veneered with various tropical woods; tambour door; paper label; 8 inches high × 6⅝ inches deep × 14½ inches wide; $165.

DECORATIVE ARTS AND MISCELLANY

Four-Panel "Citta di Carte" Trompe L'Oeil Screen, designed by Piero Fornasetti, c. 1958. Printed with a fantasy city of cards as castellated structures with turrets; recto with abstracted architectural components including a stairway; 79 inches high × 20 inches wide; $12,000.

Adjustable Tray Table, designed by George Nelson, manufactured by Herman Miller Furniture Company. Metal and wood; $250. *Courtesy of Decor Moderne*

Ice Bucket, Card Box, and Lighter, designed by Fornasetti, c. 1950s. Bucket with enamel decoration of bar items; box of metal and enamel has black background with stylized key design; ceramic lighter is decorated with jockey motif; ice bucket 9 inches wide × 11 inches high; box 12 inches × 4 inches; lighter 4 inches × 3 inches; all excellent condition; $210/set.

Plywood-and-Canvas Screen, designed by Charles and Ray Eames, manufactured by Herman Miller, c. 1946. Six identical plywood sections joined together by equally tall pieces of canvas sandwiched between the layers of wood; 67¾ inches high × 60 inches wide × ¼ inch deep; $2,420.

Coat Rack, French, c. 1950s. Twisted black metal frame; whimsical form with multicolored balls; 73 inches high × 30 inches in diameter; very good condition; $850.

Hand-Painted Ceramic Plate, designed by Desimone. Brightly colored stylized bird decoration; signed "Desimone, Italy, 7/64"; 10 inches in diameter; mint condition; $100.

Enameled Copper and Brass Cigarette Box, designed by Grerup, manufactured by J. Braun, c. 1950. Rectangular brass box with hinged lid set with an enameled copper plaque with abstract Cubist shapes in tones of red, brown, yellow, and blue; base stamped "J. Braun"; 6⅛ inches × 4 inches; $287.

Enameled Copper Bowl, designed by Grerup, c. 1955. Wide-mouthed footed vessel painted with juggler and a circus horse in the background; in shades of gray, lilac, yellow, turquoise, red, and brown; underside enameled in speckled brown and white; maker's mark; 6¾ inches in diameter; $287.

Brass-and-Copper Cigarette Box, designed by Otar, c. 1940. Triangular vessel composed of layers of copper plates; impressed factory mark; 4¾ inches high; $460.

Enameled Copper Bowl, designed by Grerup, c. 1955. Footed wide-mouthed vessel; decorated with a stylized depiction of Saint George and the dragon; in warm shades of yellow, blue, turquoise, and black with a dominance of red; underside enameled in speckled mint-green and white; has maker's mark; 6¾ inches high; $287.

Russel Wright Trolley, attribution, c. 1940s. Stylized birch frames, wheels and lower shelf, two glass shelves, glass rod handle, unmarked; 28 inches high x 34 inches deep x 17 inches wide; $350. *Courtesy of Toomey-Treadway Galleries, Oak Park, IL.*

Rolling Tea Cart with Reversible Tray, c. 1950s. Aluminum, Plexiglas, glass; $245. *Courtesy of Mark Bickford Antiques, Chicago, IL.*

Italian Ceramic Platter, manufactured by Raymor, c. 1950s. 12 inches x 12 inches; $50. *Courtesy of Decor Moderne.*

Porcelain Tray, designed by Fornasetti. Gold with two black-and-white pistols; signed "Fornasetti, Milano"; 5½ inches wide × 4½ inches high; mint condition; $120.

Covered Box, designed by Ermano Toso, c. 1959. Clear body with applied murrines of yellow and orange and a clear lid and finial with applied murrines; paper label says "Murano . . ."; 7 inches in diameter; mint condition; $115.

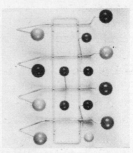

"Hang It All," designed by Charles and Ray Eames, c. 1940. Iron and wood, rare molecular design with white bend metal and multi-colored wood balls; 23 inches x 15 inches; $1,700. *Courtesy of Toomey-Treadway Galleries, Oak Park, IL.*

Enamel on Copper, designed by Richard Loving, c. 1959. Abstract figural motif of dancers in brilliant reds, purples, and blues; 19 inches wide × 10 inches high; excellent condition; $100.

Glass Mosaic, designed by Salvador, c. 1950. Brightly colored glass tiles in a figural Picasso style; 12 inches wide × 16 inches high; mint condition; $350.

Shelf Sitters (two pieces), designed by Fantoni, manufactured by Raymor. Caveman and cavewoman in yellows and greens; 6 inches wide × 8 inches diameter × 1 inch high and 7 inches wide × 3 inches diameter × 1 inch high, respectively; mint condition; $475/set.

Enamel Decorated Copper Bowl and Tray, c. 1950. Bowl designed by Claire Wyman, stylized animal interior decoration in shades of gray with red and white, exterior purple, signed, chips at foot, 6 inches in diameter; tray designed by Karl Grerup, polychrome cityscape on blue ground, artist's cipher, 10¼ inches long × 7¼ inches wide; $275/set.

Enamel Decorated Mahogany Boxes (two). One box designed by Ellamarie and Jackson Wooley of San Diego, orange and brown enamel abstract design, signed and numbered; the other designed by Earl Pardon of Saratoga Springs, cloisonné abstract design in shades of brown, green, and white, initialed; 2 inches high × 6 inches long and 4¾ inches long, respectively; $468/set.

Charger, designed by Ellamarie and Jackson Wooley, c. 1950s. Enamel on copper, abstract Cubist-style composition in brilliant blues, reds, greens, and purples; 9 inches in diameter; mint condition; $230.

Unusual Burled Wood Screen, in the manner of George Nakashima, c. 1965. Thick irregular slab mounted on a gnarled burled wood base; unsigned; 60 inches high × 50 inches wide; $920.

Decorative Tile, c. 1950s. Stylized fish design, blue and white, unmarked, thrift-shop find; $12. *Courtesy of the author.*

Porcelain Figurine, c. 1941. Depicts Rita Hayworth in *Blood and Sand* movie costume, marked ROYAL DUX; 14 inches high; $875. *Courtesy of Mark Bickford Antiques, Chicago, IL.*

Ceramic Ashtrays (two), designed by Dominio Stigl, manufactured by Gustavsberg, c. 1955. In two sizes; each square-form tray decorated in black and white with radiating concentric circles of triangles; molded Gustavsberg/Dominio/Stigl/numbered 15 and 13 and with manufacturer's anchor mark; 8 inches and 6 inches in diameter, respectively; $1,725/set.

Laminated Birch Four-Panel Folding Screens (pair), designed by Charles Eames, manufactured by Evans Products Company, c. 1946. Each composed of four U-form folded sections with canvas hinges; 68 inches high × 40 inches wide; $12,650/set.

Rosewood, Ebony, and Brass Jewelry Chest, designed by George Nelson, c. 1955. Rectangular case has eight drawers, some with interior fittings set with circular brass knobs raised on tapering brass legs; 13½ inches high × 20¼ inches long × 13 inches wide; $3,162.

▣ FLAMINGOS ▣

The symbol of the 1950s, the pink flamingo found its way onto postwar patios and into indoor decor. The first plastic lawn flamingos were designed in 1951 by Don Featherstone, an art student. His company, Union Products of Leominster, Massachusetts, continues to make them today. Obviously they were the inspiration for a whole category. Included are figurines in glass, ceramics, wood, metal, and plastic, not to mention jewelry. During the 1950s flamingo decor made it big. Look for the birds on mirrors, smoked glass-top coffee tables, paintings, and posters. The real thing is still alive and well in Florida and the Bahamas.

PRICES

Ceramic Figurine. Unmarked; 6 inches high; $15.

Plastic Pin. $8.

Lawn Decoration. Plastic with steel legs; 34 inches high; $50.

Carving. Painted wood; 15 inches high; $200.

Cocktail Swizzle Sticks. Glass with pink stem; flamingo head top; set of six; $25.

Souvenir Plate. Florida and Flamingos; 8 inches in diameter; $7.

Ashtray. 6 inches in diameter; $5.

▣ KITCHEN AND HOUSEHOLD DESIGNS ▣

One of the first companies in Italy to produce plastic items was Kartell S.p.A. The company, founded by Giulio Castelli in

1949, used bright colors for the small housewares designed by Gino Columbini. By the 1960s the company used name Italian designers to create its expanded line, which included furniture and decorative pieces.

Among the top-name designers working for them was Joe Colombo, who created a full-size dining chair molded from one piece.

Thermal Tumblers, c. 1950s. Plastic, exterior cane motif, pastel colors; $2/each. *Courtesy of Strange Cargo.*

Salt-and-Pepper Shakers, c. 1950s. Plastic in the shape and color of oranges, marked Florida and Japan; $5/set. *Courtesy of Strange Cargo.*

PRICES

Air-Clear Ionizer, manufactured by General Ozone Corporation, c. 1940s. Tortoise and amber marbleized Catalin; lightning bolt decoration on grille; original label; 6 inches high × 5 inches deep × 7 inches wide; excellent condition; $130.

Air Freshener, manufactured by Electro-Aire, c. 1940s. Brown and amber marbleized Catalin; perforated metal grille; original label on bottom; 5 inches high × 5 inches deep × 7 inches wide; $90.

Salad Bowl and Servers, mid-twentieth century. Square form of epoxy-resin composition; the ground within is decorated with metallic flakes accented overall with green disk shapes and various gray and black designs of fans, Buddhas, foo dogs, elephants, and so forth, accompanied by serving pieces of the same composition and design; 17¼ inches in diameter. $100.

Three Bakelite Desk Items, c. 1940. Butterscotch ink tray and two note boards; marked; $220.

Glossary

ABSTRACT   Emphasizing line, color, and nonrepresentational form.

ABSTRACT EXPRESSIONISM   Art movement popular from 1950 to 1955. A freedom of expression with nonrepresentational shapes, designs, and colors. Influenced by painting, two design styles were adapted for use in textiles. One resembled drips and blots, based on the drip paintings of Jackson Pollock. A second motif was based on paint splashes. It was also used in three-dimensional designs in metalwork and in the motifs of ceramics and glass.

AKARI   The Japanese word for *light* or *illumination.* Used by Isamu Noguchi as the name for his paper lantern-design lamp.

A.S.F.D.   American Society of Furniture Designers.

A.S.I.D.   American Society of Interior Designers.

ATOMIC IMAGERY   Designs based on atomic structures, popular in the 1950s. Designer George Nelson developed his "atom" clock with twelve painted wooden knobs projecting on radiating metal spokes. Nelson created the design in 1949 for the Howard Miller Clock Company. From that time until the end of the 50s, ball feet and colored knobs were adapted for various uses by designers around the world.

ATTENUATION   The stretching beyond an initial shape; examples include the elongated stems on Tulip goblets and the exaggerated high backs of Gio Ponti's Italian Superleggera chair. Sculptor Alberto Giacometti probably started the whole trend with his attenuation in sculptural figures such as *Femme Debout* (1949).

BARK CLOTH   Two-ply cotton woven to resemble the bark of a tree.

BAUHAUS   In 1919 the Bauhaus was founded in Weimar Germany as an art institute. Men who were later to internationally influence the Modern movement tested their ideas here. Among them were Mies van der Rohe, Lazlo and Lucia Moholy-Nagy, and Wassily Kandinsky. Over the years it changed location, eventually moving to Berlin in 1932. In 1937 it was established in Chicago under the leadership of Moholy-Nagy. From its beginnings the concept was to incorporate industrial design in all aspects of modern dwellings—from architecture to home furnishings.

BIOMORPHIC   Undulating forms, sometimes with rounded holes, suggesting amoeba or other organisms. Though considered part of Modern design in the postwar years, it can actually be traced to artist Jean Arp, who experimented with a variety of abstract shapes, including blobs that resembled living organisms, as early as 1915. By the mid-1930s biomorphism had become an accepted artistic term not only for paintings but also in reference to dimensional works of art. Biomorphic forms were used for furniture, glassware, and china by 1939. The style went out of fashion by the mid-1950s.

BOOMERANG   A flat, curved, wood missile used by aborigines in Australia. Popular form used in Modern organic designs. Based on the delta-wing jet aircraft.

BUBBLE GLASS   An innovation developed in the 1930s that typifies the Modern look in glass of the postwar forties. It was perfected in 1947 by Gunnel Nyman of Finland. He incorporated carefully controlled air pockets of the same size and in regulated patterns into his glasswork.

CAST PHENOLIC RESIN   A thermosetting material formed by pouring a liquid solution of phenolformaldehyde into open molds, where it hardens as it bakes at temperatures of 60 to 100 degrees C. Used most often in the 1930s and 1940s to make jewelry. It was a popular medium because it could be made in hundreds of colors, both opaque and translucent.

CATALIN   A trade name of cast phenolic resin, no longer used.

CHRISTIAN DIOR   French post–World War II designer who in 1947 changed the look of women's fashions with his New Look. Its lowered hemlines accentuated the female figure. It used new, modern terms such as "tulip," which described one of the most popular symbols for Modern designers from furniture to glassware.

CRANBROOK ACADEMY OF ART   Founded in the 1920s, it is famed for the work produced by its faculty and students during the 1930s and 1940s. Among them were the Finnish architect Eliel Saarinen (its first president), architect Charles Eames, and designers Florence Knoll and Benjamin Baldwin.

CRATER   The name used by studio potters Gertrud and Otto Natzler to describe their bubbled, pitted glazes that looked like volcanic lava.

ETHNIC REVIVALISM   Popular design movement of the 1940s that combined tribal and Modern images. Exemplified in the jewelry of William Spratling, who used pre-Columbian motifs.

FIBERGLASS   Glass fibers made by the Owens-Corning Fiberglas Corporation, trademarked under the name Fiberglas, and used mostly for producing fiberglass-reinforced plastic.

FREE-FORM   A flowing asymmetrical shape popularized by Modern design and used in all its aspects from furniture to textile motifs.

HANDKERCHIEF VASES   Refers to glass vases, in many colors and sizes, with rims that resemble the folds and scallops of a handkerchief. First made by Paolo Venini and copied by others.

INCISO   A technique developed by Paolo Venini that covered the surface of colored glass with a pattern of finely incised concentric lines. The result was a blurred matte texture.

LAMINATE   A plastic material made up of layers of resin-impregnated paper (or fiberglass, cloth, linen, or asbestos) bonded together under heat and pressure to form a single sheet.

LATTICINO GLASS   Centuries-old technique adapted by Modern Venetian glassblowers. An internal decoration of delicate filaments crossed in a diamond pattern.

LUCITE   Trade name for an acrylic manufactured by Du Pont.

LUREX   Trademark of the Dow Chemical Corporation for metallic fibers. Gold, copper, and silver Lurex yarns were used by designers of the 1950s.

MIX-AND-MATCH   After World War II, designers in Sweden and the United States for the first time used radical (for the time) color combinations—orange with pink, blue with green, and new color glazes for ceramics. The term "mix-and-match" spilled over into the way people used the new colors. Potteries deliberately offered table services that mixed colors: a chartreuse cup with a seafoam blue saucer is one example. Italy followed suit with decorative glass that either mixed unlikely colors or offered a series of pieces in new color combinations.

Mobile   Abstract sculpture form developed in the 1950s by Alexander Calder, an American sculptor. Movable parts were suspended by wires and moved by circulating air. Calder adapted the form to textiles and jewelry.

Modernism   Refers to the various forms, shapes, styles, and uses of materials popular from approximately 1935 to 1965.

Modern Historicism   The borrowing of designs from the past, combining them with Modern motifs and materials.

Modular Units   Originally designed by Charles Eames and Eero Saarinen in 1940 as an entry in the Museum of Modern Art's first major competition, where it won first prize. At the time the concept was called "unit furniture." For the first time a variety of case pieces could be used in various combinations or by themselves. Designs were not produced in the early 40s because of the war. Postwar modular storage units used basic steel frames with plywoods and other materials.

Lazlo Moholy-Nagy   Designer and teacher. One of the most important influences from the beginnings of the Modern movement in the 1930s. He immigrated to the United States from England and established the Institute of Design in Chicago based on the Bauhaus concepts of structuring space through the use of line, color, and light.

Organic   Pertaining to or derived from living organisms. As interpreted by Modern designers, it meant incorporating the shapes of living organisms into functional designs.

Pebble Cloth   One of the many popular textured fabrics, with a granitelike surface.

Plywood   Pieces of laminated wood glued together. It is made from veneers that are laminated with the grain of one sheet perpendicular to the grain of the facing sheet. Not all laminated wood is plywood. One of the most popular woods used in the production of plywood was birchwood, because of its malleable quality.

Postwar Modernism   Design emphasis on long, flowing peaks, curves, and arcs. Streamlining and biomorphism are associated with the style. Also important were light weight and simplicity of design. Mass-production made even the most important designers' work available to many.

EMILIO PUCCI (1914–) Italian-born designer whose Modern print silk scarves and shirts, using vivid and unusual mix-and-match colors, were a fashion status symbol in the 1950s.

ROCKET IMAGERY Space symbols used in designs on textiles, wallpaper, and glass. The flying saucer was part of this design motif, brought on by the variety of so-called saucer sightings in the United States during the mid-50s. Everything from lamp shades to toys featured the saucer look.

RYA RUGS The textured, long-pile textiles that had been a tradition in Scandinavia were reinvented in the 1950s as the perfect floor covering to go with Modern furnishings. They influenced Italian designers, who created long-pile rugs in boldly colored abstract designs.

STABILE An abstract sculpture consisting of immobile units made of sheet metal, wire, and other materials attached to fixed supports. Used by sculptor Alexander Calder.

STREAMLINED A branch of Modernism popular in the 40s that combined the principles of aerodynamic engineering with the functional geometry of the International style, which began in Europe. The earliest examples were the fronts of trains and automobiles, formed into elongated, rounded shapes.

Glossary of
Glass Terms

AIR BUBBLES Used for decorative purposes, most often in Scandinavian glass.

ANNEALING The process of placing a glass piece in a chamber of the furnace in order for the glass to cool after forming, thus reducing brittleness in the glass and making it stronger.

APPLIED DECORATION A type of relief ornamentation made by adding glass threads, blobs, prunts, and other motifs to the piece's surface.

BLOW PIPE A long and hollow iron rod approximately 5½ feet long. The thick end is used to gather a blob of molten glass, the other has a mouthpiece used for the blowing process that shapes the hot glass into the desired size or form.

CASED GLASS A glass piece consisting of two or more fused layers of different colors, often decorated by cutting them so that the inner layers show through. It is also referred to as case glass.

COLD PAINTING The use of lacquer or oil-based pigments to create a color design on the glass without subsequent firing.

ENAMEL A glass composition applied by fusion at a fairly low temperature. It is often used in powdered form to decorate the surface of metalwork, glass, or pottery.

ENGRAVING The use of several types of tools to decorate the glass surface. Wheels are used in wheel engraving and diamond- or sharp-pointed tools are used to produce linear patterns, dotted-stipple engraving, and diamond-point engraving.

ETCHING A decorative technique that incises the surface or makes it shiny, matte, or frosted by exposing the piece to hydrofluoric acid.

FIRE POLISH A finish given to the surface of glass that has lost some its surface smoothness from having been worked on. This is done by putting the piece back into the furnace in what is called the glory hole, which is an opening made expressly for this purpose.

FLASHING The process of coating a glass piece with a thin layer of either colored or clear glass to achieve a particular effect.

FLUX A chemical substance, such as potash, lead, or soda, that is used to lower the melting point of the main silica constituent of the glass material.

FREE-BLOWING   The forming of objects on the blow pipe by blowing and manipulating hot, ductile glass.

GRAAL TECHNIQUE   A type of glass originating in the Orrefors glasshouse in Sweden. Etched or cut designs in a colored layer of glass are placed over the original piece. The piece is then reheated and covered with a flashing of colorless glass.

LEAD CRYSTAL   Clear and colorless glass fluxed by the use of lead oxide.

MARVERED LAMPWORK   Glass made by manipulating tubes and rods in the flame of a lamp or burner. A marver is a metal slab on which the glass is gathered and rolled into the desired shape or smoothness.

METAL   Glass that is in a molten state.

MIXED MEDIA   A combination of substances, such as metals, used in glass decoration.

MOLD-BLOWN   Glass that is blown into a mold to create both the pattern and the shape.

OVERLAY   An ornamental veneer of either colored or clear glass that is placed over the original piece. Similar to cased glass.

PATE DE VERRE   A technique that melts down already-powdered glass into a mold.

PRUNT   A decorative pad of glass applied to the wall of a vessel and usually drawn out into a thornlike projection or stamped with a die to create a pattern of raised dots.

SANDBLASTED   A decorative technique of exposing glass to a blast of sand in order to create a matte or frosted surface.

SLUMPING   A "warm" technique done in the kiln, where temperatures do not reach those needed in the furnace for glassblowing. It was developed in the 1970s.

STIPPLING   A decorative technique in which the glass surface is tapped gently with a pointed instrument to create a design and tonal effects with tiny dots.

Resources

SHOWS

Baby Boombazaar—May and Memorial Day weekend. Show promoters: Carol Perry and Sharon Ogan. 40s, 50s, 60s, 70s collectibles from Disneyana to jewelry. P.O. Box 8822, Madeira Beach, FL 33738 (held in Lakeland, FL)—(813) 398-2427.

National Hammered Aluminum Show, Schnecksville, PA, late October.

Modernism, Promoter: Sanford Smith. The Armory, Park Ave. and 67th Street, New York City.

Miami Modernism—January 7–9. Show Promoter: Jacques Caussin, Caussin Productions. James L. Knight Center, 400 East S.E. Second Ave., Miami, FL. Caussin Productions located at 12150 East Outer Drive, Detroit, MI 48224—(313) 886-3443, fax (313) 886-1067.

Annual Los Angeles Modernism Show, Santa Monica Civic Auditorium, Main Street and Pico Boulevard, Santa Monica, CA. Memorial Day weekend. Promoters: Caskey Lees and Olney. P.O. Box 1637, Topanga, CA 90290—(310) 455-2886.

Modern Productions, Promoter: Cynthia Barta. 33339 Lansmere Road, Shaker Heights, OH 44122—(216) 751-5922.

Modern Times, October and April at the Glendale Civic Auditorium in Los Angeles. Promoter: Tauni Brustin. 1325 Abbot Kinney, Venice, CA 90291—(310) 392-6676.

Modern Show, November. Winnetka Women's Club, 485 Maple Ave., Winnetka, IL 60093—(708) 446 1830.

Annual Toy Dish Collectors Convention and Auction. Minneapolis, MN. Contact F. J. Steffen, 9705 Mill Creek Drive, Eden Prairie, MN 55347—(612) 944-1041.

MUSEUM COLLECTIONS

Art Institute of Chicago, Michigan Avenue at Adams Street, Chicago, IL

Brooklyn Museum, 200 Eastern Parkway, Brooklyn, NY

Cooper-Hewitt Museum, 2 East 91st Street, New York, NY

Note: There are small collections in various categories in museums around the United States. Check locally.

Cranbrook Academy of Art Museum, 500 Lone Pine Road, Bloomfield Hills, MI

The Detroit Institute of Arts, 5200 Woodward Avenue, Detroit, MI

Emerson Museum of Art, 401 Harrison Street, Community Plaza, Syracuse, NY

The Haeger Potteries, Seven Maiden Lane, Dundee, IL 60118-2397

Houston Contemporary Arts Museum, 5216 Montrose Boulevard, Houston, TX

77006 Association, Houston, TX

Los Angles County Museum of Art, 5905 Wilshire Boulevard, Los Angeles, CA 90036

Metropolitan Museum of Art, Fifth Avenue at 82nd Street, New York, NY 10028

Museum of Modern Art, 11 West 53rd Street, New York, NY 10019

Museum of the City of New York, Fifth Avenue at 103rd Street, New York, NY

The Newark Museum, 40 Washington Street, Newark, NJ

MUSEUMS OUTSIDE THE UNITED STATES

Le Musée des Arts Decoratifs de Montreal, Canada

Design Museum, London, England

Victoria and Albert Museum, London, England

The new Twentieth Century Gallery at the Victoria and Albert Museum in London spans the history of consumer design from 1900 to 1992. Over 600 objects are drawn from the museum's permanent collection and range from lighting to tableware, accessories, furniture, clothing, and radios. American designers' work in the gallery includes furniture by Charles and Ray Eames and textile designs by Ruth Reeves.

Sources

STUDIOS

Higgins Glass Studio, Frances and Michael Higgins, 33 East Quincy Street, Riverside, IL 60546—(708) 447-2787

SHOPS AND DEALERS

Decades A Go Go, Dan Rubin, 1514 East 7th Avenue, Ybor City, FL 33605—(813) 248-2849

Metropolis, Wade Herman, Ybor City, FL 33605—(813) 823-2939

Private Estate Liquidators, Inc., Jimmy Lamena, 445 East Palmetto Park Road, Boca Raton, FL 33432—(407) 338-9999

Decor Moderne, Yvon Belisle, 2101 N.E. 14th Avenue, Wilton Manors, FL 33305—(305) 563-0154

Moderne Antique, 1812 Maryland Avenue, Baltimore, MD 21201—(405) 685-8999

Catalina Productions, Sheila Steinberg, 200 East 65th Street, New York, NY 10021—(212) 832-8228

Modern Times, Martha Torno and Tom Clark, 1536 North Milwaukee Avenue, Chicago, IL 60622—(312) 772-8871

Uniquities, Francine Cohen—(201) 763-1778

H G Limited, Harry Greenberger—(718) 549-4712

A Alpha Antiques, Susan Dods, Somerset, NJ—(908) 220-8880

H G Limited, 20th-Century Decorative Arts, Harry Greenberger—(718) 549-4712

Dan Ripley, Italian Glass, 1502 W. McCarty Street, Indianapolis, IN 46221—(317) 264-5034

Partners in Time, 66 Jobs Lane, Southampton, NY 11968—(516) 287-1143

Boomerang, Mid-Century Design, David Pinson, in association with John Toomey Gallery, 818 North Boulevard, Oak Park, IL 60301

Skank World, Linda Gershon, 7205 Beverly Boulevard, Los Angeles, CA 90036—(213) 939-7858

South Beach Furniture, Leonard Riforgiato, Design and Decor Building, 180 N.E. 39th Street, Miami, FL 33137, P. O. Box 370687, Miami, FL 33137—(305)576-4240, fax(305) 576-1527

Noble House, Carol and Jerry Dinelli (toy appraisers), 124 East Cook Street, Libertyville, IL 60048—(708) 367-8588

Mark Bickford Antiques, 2929 Western Avenue, Chicago, IL

Stantons Art Works, Inc., 2929 North Western Avenue, Chicago, IL 60618

Gillian Hine Antiques, 2929 North Western Avenue, Chicago, IL 60618

Antiques and Collectibles, Eric Fiveash, 2347 Wilton Drive, Fort Lauderdale, FL—(305) 981-7581

Fifty/50, Mark Isaacson, 793 Broadway, New York, NY 10003—(212) 777-3208

Lost City Arts, James Elkind, 275 Lafayette Street, New York, NY 10012—(212) 941-8025

POSTERS

Miscellaneous Man Mail-order, George Theofiles, New Freedom, PA—(717) 235-4766, fax (717) 235-2853

Poster Graphics Inc., Peter Langlykke and Robert Perrin, 376 South County Road, Palm Beach, FL 33480—(407) 833-8448

Illustration House, original illustration art and auctions, 96 Spring Street, 7th Floor, New York, NY 10012-3923—(212) 966-9425

SILVER

Cecil Skillin, 111 Caribbean, Naples, FL 33963-2795

Imagination Unlimited, 4302 Alton Road, Suite 820, Miami Beach, FL 33140

Matchmaker of Iowa, P.O. Box 43, Waterloo, IA 50704

Mrs. Kay's, P.O. Box 291245M, Los Angeles, CA 90029

Replacements, Ltd., 1089 Knox Road, P.O. Box 26029, Greensboro, NC 27420

Tere Hagan, Box 25487, Tempe, AZ 85285

BOOKS AND MAGAZINES

Book Castle, Inc. (books, posters, back-issue magazines), 200 North San Fernando Boulevard, Burbank, CA 91502—(818) 845-1563

ALUMINUM

The Aluminist newsletter, Dannie Woodard, Editor, P.O. Box 1346, Weatherford, TX 76086
Harvey Hesse, 7800 N.W. 74th Avenue, Tamarac, FL 33321—(305) 721-3030

AUCTION GALLERIES

Butterfield and Butterfield, 220 San Bruno Avenue, San Francisco, CA 94103—(415) 861-7500
Christie's New York, 502 Park Avenue, New York, NY 10022—(212) 546-1000
Christie's East, 219 East 67th Street, New York, NY 10021—(212) 606-0400
William Doyle Galleries, 175 East 87th Street, New York, NY 10128—(212) 427-2730
Du Mouchelle Art Galleries, 409 East Jefferson, Detroit, MI 48226—(313) 963-6255
Leslie Hindman, Inc., 215 West Ohio Street, Chicago, IL 60610
Illustration House (original illustration art, movie, posters, etc.), 96 Spring Street, 7th floor, New York, NY 10012-3923—(212) 966-9444
Skinner, Inc., Bolton Gallery, 357 Main Street, Bolton, MA 01740—(508) 779-6241
Sotheby's, 1334 York Avenue, New York, NY 10021—(212) 606-7000
John Toomey Gallery, 818 North Boulevard, Oak Park, IL 60301—(708) 383-5234, fax (708) 383-4828
Don Treadway Auction Gallery, 2128 Madison Road, Cincinnati, OH 45208—(513) 321-6742

RENTALS

Modern Props, Michael Ladish, 4063 Redwood Avenue, Los Angeles, CA 90066—(310) 306-1400

TEXTILES, DESIGN STUDIO DISPLAYS

Jack Denst Designs, (old patterns can be viewed and ordered through decorators) 7355 South Exchange, Chicago, IL 60649—(312) 721-5515, fax (312) 721-5515

Jack Lenor Larsen Design Studio, 232 East 59th Street, New York, NY 10022—(212) 674-3993

Ben Rose Designs, Space 11-123 Merchandise Mart, 222 Merchandise Mart Plaza, Chicago, IL 60654—(312) 467-6253

Bibliography

CERAMICS

Ann Kerr. *The Collector's Encyclopedia of Russel Wright Designs*. Paducah Collector Books, 1990.

Jack Chipman. *The Collector's Encyclopedia of California Pottery*. Collector Books, a Division of Schroeder Publishing, Inc., 1992.

A Century of Ceramics in the United States 1878–1978. Dutton, New York, 1979.

FURNITURE

Ed. Robert Harling. *Modern Furniture and Decoration*. Condé-Nast Publications, Viking Press, 1971.

Habegger, Jerryll, and Joseph H. Osman. *Source Book of Modern Furniture*. Van Nostrand Reinhold, 1992.

Bent Wood and Metal Furniture: 1850–1946. New York: The American Federation of Arts, 1987.

New Furniture, an International Review from 1950 to the Present. Nerlag Gert Hatjie, Stuttgart, 1982.

Carol Hogben. *Modern Chairs: 1918–1970*. The Whitechapel Art Gallery, London, 1970.

Cara Greenborg. *Mid-Century Modern: Furniture of the 1950s*. Harmony Books, New York, 1984.

GLASS

Geoffrey Beard. *International Modern Glass*. Barrie and Jenkins, London, 1976.

Venini and the Murano Renaissance: Italian Glass of the 40s and 50s. Fifty/50, New York, 1984.

Franzoi Umberto. *Art Glass by Archimede Seguso*. Arsenale Editrice, Venezia, 1991.

The Venetians: Modern Glass 1919–1990. Murial Karasik Gallery, New York, 1989.

JEWELRY

Jewels of Fantasy. Catalog of the Victoria and Albert Museum exhibit. Harry N. Abrams, Inc., New York, 1992.

Schiffer, Nancy. *Fun Jewelry.* Schiffer Publishing Ltd., 1991.

Baker, Lillian. *Plastic Jewelry.* Collector Books, 1992.

Burkholz, Matthew, and Linda Kaplan. *Copper Art Jewelry.* Schiffer Publishing, 1992.

METALS

Woodard, Dannie. *Hammered Aluminum-Hand Wrought Collectibles.* Book Two. Aluminum Collector's Books, P.O. Box 1346, Weatherford, Texas, 76086, 1993.

POSTERS

Kisch, John, and Edward Mapp. *A Separate Cinema. Fifty Years Of Black Cast Posters.* Farrar, Straus and Giroux, New York, 1992.

Rebello, Stephen, and Richard Allen. *Reel Art: Great Posters From The Golden Age of the Silver Screen.* Abbeville Press, N.Y.P.O. Box 1346, Weatherford, Texas, 1994.

RADIOS

Johnson, David. *Antique Radio Restoration Guide.* Chilton Book Company, Wallace-Homestead Book Company, Radnor, Pennsylvania, 1992.

Sideli, John. *Classic Plastic Radios of the 1930s and 1940s.* E.P. Dutton, New York, 1990.

TEXTILES AND WALLPAPER

Larsen, Jack Lenor. *30 Years of Creative Textiles.* Jack Lenor Larsen, New York, 1981.

Hinchcliffe, F.. *Fifties Furnishing Fabric*. Victoria and Albert Museum, London, 1989.

Bosker, Gideon, John Gramstad, and Michele Mancini. *Fabulous Fabrics of the 50s*. John Gramstad, Chronicle Books, 1992.

TOYS

Tempest, Jack. *Post-War Tin Toys*. Wallace-Homestead Book Company, Radnor, Pennsylvania, 1991.

Punchard, Lorraine May. *Playtime Kitchen Items and Table Accessories*. Lorraine May Punchard Publisher, 1993. (8201 Pleasant Ave., South, Bloomington, MN 55420.)

———Child's Play. Lorraine May Punchard Publisher, 1982. (8201 Pleasant Avenue, South, Bloomington, MN 55420.

MISCELLANEOUS

Zeisel, Eva. *Designer for Industry*. Catalog of the Musee des Arts Decoratifs de Montreal, Le Chateau Dufresne, Inc., 1984.

Jackson, Lesley. *The New Look Design in the Fifties*. Thames and Hudson, 1991.

Hanks, David A. *Frank Lloyd Wright (Preserving an Architectural Heritage): Decorative Designs from the Domino's Pizza Collection*. E.P. Dutton, New York, 1939.

Machine Age in America 1918–41, Wilson, Pilgrim & Taschgian, 1986.

Design 1935–1965: What Modern Was. Catalog of the Musée des Arts Decoratifs de Montreal. Harry N. Abrams, Inc., New York, 1991.

"Frank Lloyd Wright: His Contribution to the Beauty of American Life." *House Beautiful,* 98, no. 11. (November 1955).

House Beautiful, 95, no. 11. (November 1953). Issue devoted to Alfred Browning Parker and his Pace Setter House.

Index

118, 121–122, 124, 125, 129, 133, 136–137
Italian, 148, 150
Scandinavian, 141, 143
Takaezu, Toshiko, 52
Taxco, Margot de, 192, 204
Teague, Walter Dorwin, 13, 15
Tea set, ceramic, 57
Testa, Angelo, 250
Textiles
American, 252–258
artist-inspired textiles, 252
designers
Alexander Girard, 251, 253, 257
Angelo Testa, 250
Astrid Sampe, 252
Ben Rose, 250, 253–256
Doris Kroll, 251–252
D.D. Tillett, 251
Donald Brothers, 251
Dorothy Liebes, 250
Edward Fields, 251
Eszter Haraszty, 251
Jim Thompson, 251
Leslie Tillett, 251
Marianne Strengell, 250
Ray Komai, 252–253
Toni Prestini, 250
Viola Grasten, 252
design studio displays, 302
floor coverings, 258–259
general information, 249–252
Thompson, Jim, 251
Tiles, ceramic, 76
Tillett, D.D and Leslie, 251
Toso, Ermanno, 164
Towle Manufacturing Company, 243

Toys
Barbie Doll, 265
Frisbee, 266
general information, 261–263
Japanese made, 261–262
Pez candy containers, 266
plastic model kits, 266–267
price listing, 263–265
table and kitchen items, 267–268
Travel posters, 231–232
Trays
aluminum, 41
glass, 157
silver, 245
Tulip look, characteristics of, 16
Tupperware, value of, 27–28
TWA pattern, flatware, 95–96
2720 pattern, flatware, 86

U
Union Products, 277
Urns
ceramic
American studio potters, 55, 58, 59–60
Scandinavian, 73–74
Spanish, 75–76

V
Van Koert, John, 243
Vases
aluminum, 42
ceramic
American studio potters, 55, 58, 59–60
British, 68
Cuban ceramics, 77